India's Agrarian Structure, Economic Policies and Sustainable Development

VIJAY SHANKAR VYAS, *Professor Emeritus,* Institute of Development Studies, Jaipur is currently a member of the Economic Advisory Council to the Prime Minister and also a member of the Central Board of Directors of Reserve Bank of India (RBI) and National Bank for Agriculture and Rural Development (NABARD).

Prof. Vyas, Ph.D in Economics from Bombay University, taught in Bombay University, Sardar Patel University and Institute of Management, Ahmedabad. He was a visiting scholar at the Boston University, U.S.A.

Prof. Vyas served as Director, Agro-Economic Research Centre for Western India, Director, Indian Institute of Management (IIM), Ahmedabad; and Director, Institute of Development Studies (IDS, Jaipur).

He has served as Chairman/Member of various Boards, Committees and Commissions at the International, National and State Levels. He served as a member of the Board of Trustees of the International Food Policy Research Institute (Washington, U.S.A), member of the Governing Board of the Institute of Development Studies of Sussex University (U.K), member of the National Commission on Integrated Water Planning, member of the Scientific Advisory Committee to the Cabinet, and Member Agricultural Prices Commission of the Government of India.

Prof. Vyas has written extensively on key issues of agricultural policies and rural development, and has been honoured by academic community in India and abroad.

He is an elected Honorary Life Member of the International Association of Agricultural Economists and is also a Fellow of the National Academy of Agricultural Sciences in India.

India's Agrarian Structure, Economic Policies and Sustainable Development

Variations on a Theme

V.S. Vyas

Academic Foundation
NEW DELHI
www.academicfoundation.com

First Published in 2003 by
ACADEMIC FOUNDATION
4772-73 / 23 Bharat Ram Road,
(23 Ansari Road), Darya Ganj,
New Delhi - 110 002. INDIA.

Phones : 23245001, 02, 03, 04.
Fax : +91-11-23245005
e-mail : academic@vsnl.com
www : academicfoundation.com

India's Agrarian Structure, Economic Policies and Sustainable Development: Variations on a Theme
by V.S. Vyas

ISBN 81-7188-323-0

Laser-Typeset at AF's DTP Division.
Printed at Print Perfect, Mayapuri Industrial Area, New Delhi.

Contents...

SECTION – III

Food Security and Poverty

SECTION – IV

Economic Reforms in Agriculture

SECTION – V

Future Scenario

Acknowledgements

I wish to record my gratitude to the people who made me think about issues in agricultural and rural development in coherent and logical ways, and particularly with a human angle. My guru, Prof. M.L. Dantwala is no more with us. This book is a humble tribute to that great teacher. I would also like to mention the names of those stalwarts who gave me the opportunity to observe and study the process of rural development and, occasionally, to participate in that process. For this I owe a huge debt of gratitude to H.M. Patel, Sartaz Aziz, Nurul Islam, David Hopper and Don Antiporta. I have greatly benefited from the wisdom, insights and sagacious advice of two remarkable persons Dr. M.S. Swaminathan and Dr. Abe Weisblat.

This book owes its existence principally to four persons: my wife Laxmi and my sons Vikram and Rajiv, who always made me feel guilty for not bringing out my researches and observations in the form of a book. And, to the undaunted and ever-supportive Uma Kapila, Senior Editor, Academic Foundation.

VSV

Foreword

– M.S. Swaminathan

What you and I hear are different
You hear the sound of closing doors,
But I of doors that open

(Persian Poem)

This book bears testimony to Prof. V.S. Vyas's approach to the major national and global challenges facing Indian agriculture. He has outlined opportunities for enhancing India's agricultural competitiveness and has not been overwhelmed by difficulties. The book contains a message of hope in relation to India's agricultural future. It outlines policy initiatives which can help to improve the productivity, profitability and sustainability of our major farming systems.

His intimate knowledge of the agricultural progress and problems of Asian countries in general and India in particular, makes the book, "Agrarian Structure, Economic Policies and Sustainable Development" an authoritative source of information and analysis relevant to the formulation of strategies and policies for launching an ever-green revolution movement in Asia.

The five sections of the book deal with topics which are mutually inter-related and reinforcing. It is characteristic of Prof. Vyas's vision that he examines issues in a holistic manner. Thus, the book deals with the inter-relationships between poverty and sustainable development, productivity and profitability, production technology and post-harvest technology and on-farm and non-farm employment in rural areas. The book covers all major developments in the evolution of agricultural technologies and policies since our independence in 1947. I would like first to briefly give a synoptic view of our progress in achieving the goal of "food for all".

The great Bengal famine of 1943 provided the backdrop to India's independence. Mahatma Gandhi said at Naokhali in 1946, "to the hungry, God is Bread; the God of bread should prevail in every home and hut of the country". Jawaharlal Nehru aptly remarked soon after our independence in 1947, "everything else can wait, but not agriculture". This pronouncement got reflected in several public policy and investment decisions, particularly in the areas of irrigation, fertilizer production, land reforms and community development.

Some major initiatives started from the beginning of planned development in 1950-51 are the following:

Steps were taken to improve our capability in science and technology as applied to agriculture. Several new research institutes, as for example those dealing with rice and potato, were set up. The first Agricultural University was established at Pant Nagar in 1958. Several All India Coordinated Research Projects were initiated. Second, steps were taken to produce and supply inputs like seeds and fertilizers and to expand the area under irrigation. Large multi-purpose projects like the Bhakra Nangal project were initiated. Credit and extension services were improved. Third, several public policy measures like land reform, including the imposition of ceilings on land holdings and the redistribution of ceiling-surplus land, and the promotion of cooperatives and Panchayati Raj Institutions (PRIs) were initiated. Finally, an Intensive Agricultural District Programme (IADP) was initiated in the early sixties in order to maximise production and productivity in irrigated areas by providing a package of inputs like seeds, fertilizer and pesticide.

Thanks to advances in preventive and curative medicine, population also started growing at a fast rate since 1950. Advances in food production did not keep pace with the growth in food requirements caused by both increased population and higher purchasing power. The result was increasing dependence on food imports particularly under the PL 480 programme of the United States. Several leading foreign experts concluded in the early nineteen sixties that India is a hopeless case from the point of view of achieving a proper balance between the rates of growth in population and food production. It was under such an atmosphere of gloom and doom that Indira Gandhi released a special stamp titled "the Wheat Revolution" in July 1968.

How did this transformation take place? Prof. Vyas had described with great clarity these issues in Sections II and III of this book. The IADP or the Package Programme, as it was popularly known, had one important missing ingredient in the package, namely genetic strains which can respond positively to the rest of the package like irrigation water and fertilizer. It was this missing ingredient which was provided under the High-Yielding Varieties Programme of 1966 comprising semi-dwarf varieties of wheat and rice and hybrids of maize, jowar and bajra. In 1968, Indira Gandhi wanted a buffer stock of 10 million tonnes built up speedily since she saw clearly the link between food security and national sovereignty. This buffer stock was built by the early nineteen seventies.

Because of our policy of ensuring minimum support price to basic food crops through the Food Corporation of India, as well as State Food Corporations, the production of wheat and rice increased steadily and in 2001-2002, the Government of

India had food stocks exceeding 60 million tonnes. This enabled the Government to initiate several Food for Work programmes to insulate the poor from hunger. Inspite of our agricultural progress and food safety net programmes, we now have as many children, women and men suffering from poverty induced hunger as the entire population of India in 1947. This tragedy is self-inflicted, since there is no political, scientific, economic or managerial excuses for it today. Prof. Vyas has summarised in Chapter IV the various issues and options relating to building sustainable food security systems in South Asia. It is the South Asian region which has the maximum number of under nourished children, women and men in the world today.

In my view, the political will, backed by appropriate political and administrative action to eradicate chronic and hidden hunger caused by protein-energy and micronutrient under-nutrition is yet to emerge. If the following five steps are taken, we can still achieve a hunger-free India by August 15, 2007, which marks the 60th anniversary of our independence.

First, we should bring about convergence and synergy among all on-going food safety net programmes, on the basis of a life cycle approach to nutrition. Such a programme for "nutrition security at all stages in one's life" should begin with pregnant women and infants and extend upto old and infirm persons. The programmes are all there already, but what is missing is the political will to break down the administrative walls preventing convergence and synergy in delivery through Gram Sabhas.

Second, we should foster the establishment of Community Food and Feed Banks in all the hunger hot spots of the country, which will help to both diversify the food basket by including local grains like millets and pulses, and ensure delivery to the hungry at a low transaction cost.

Third, an integrated approach to rural on-farm and non-farm employment should be promoted as China has so effectively done. The micro-credit supported self-help group revolution, if carefully developed on the basis of market-driven enterprises, can help to provide the income needed for food security at the household level to the assetless population, i.e., those who have no land or livestock or productive skill.

Fourth, as shown by Prof. Vyas, the causes of hunger are diverse and the cures are also diverse. Hence, rigidly structured national programmes alone will not lead us to the desired goal. There is need for location and culture specific responses. For this purpose, it will be prudent to set up a National Food Security Trust, with an initial allocation of 10 million tonnes of food grains. The Trust could make small allocations of 50 to 200 tonnes of grains to Gram Sabhas/Nagarpalikas as well as credible NGOs in the hunger hot spots of the country to undertake "food for social capital development" programmes designed to ensure food for everyone without destroying human dignity.

Finally, there is no time to relax on the production front. There is an urgent need to strengthen the ongoing process of farming systems intensification, diversification and value addition. In a predominantly agricultural country like ours, an ever-green farm revolution based on higher productivity in perpetuity is the best safety net against hunger and poverty.

I would like to highlight a few areas in the fields of conservation, commercialisation and consumption among the topics covered in the book. The need for an action - reaction analysis with reference to all development activities has been stressed by many experts. B.F. Skinner, for example, once stated, "Every new source from which man has increased his power on earth has been used to diminish the prospects of his successors. All his progress is being made at the expense of damage to the environment which he cannot repair and cannot foresee". Integrated natural resources management rooted in the principles of ecology, economics, gender and social equity and employment generation is the need of the hour.

In the past, land use decisions were taken by farming families largely based on the home needs of the family and of the immediate neighbourhood. With the modernization of agriculture, farmers produce food grains and other commodities not only for themselves but more importantly for the market. When this transition takes place, opportunities for producer-oriented and remunerative marketing become essential for sustaining and stimulating farmers' interest in modern technology. Our agriculture is usually referred to as a "gamble in the monsoon". Increasingly it is becoming a gamble in the market.

In domestic trade, both cost and quality influence consumer demand. In international trade in addition to competitive cost and desirable quality, stability of supply becomes extremely important. If appropriate technologies and remunerative marketing opportunities co-exist, impressive production gains can be achieved, as our experience during the last 20 year shows. Under commercial agriculture, the old distinction between "food and cash crops" vanishes and all crops become "cash crops". This is where government policies in the area of infrastructure development for improved post-harvest technology, marketing and transport as well as steps for ensuring fair returns to producers and reasonable prices to consumers become very important. Most developing nations have to simultaneously improve production by small farmers and consumption by the rural and urban poor and hence attention to policy formulation becomes crucial to success, particularly in the context of globalisation of trade.

In the area of consumption also we face two contrasting challenges. On the one hand, the rural and urban poor suffer from under nutrition and malnutrition due to inadequate purchasing power. On the other hand, the food habits of the more affluent sections of the population are fast changing with greater emphasis on fruits, vegetables and animal products. We also witness the paradox of abundant grain reserves co-existing with millions of people suffering from under nutrition in our country. As early as 1861 Col. Baird Smith remarked that "Indian famines are not famines of food but of work. Where there is work, there is money and where there is money there is food". If a famine of food was the major obsession in the immediate past, a famine of jobs or livelihood opportunities is currently the cause of endemic hunger. Imaginative Food for Work programmes will help to mitigate the situation.

Prof. Vyas has dealt with, in an authoritative manner, the implications of the ongoing Doha-round negotiations of the World Trade Agreement on Agriculture (AoA) to the future of our agriculture as well as food security. I note he has supported my view that in the revised AoA, there should be a "livelihood box" which will permit nations where over 50 per cent of population depend upon agriculture for their livelihoods, to impose quantitative restrictions on imports, where there is clear evidence that such imports will erode job/livelihood opportunities in rural areas.

It is obvious that the farm sector alone cannot absorb all the surplus landless labour in the rural areas. We have to give a new orientation to the concept of land reform and widen this concept to include all forms of asset reform. For example, one of the greatest assets in rural areas could be the intelligent and effective use of emerging technologies such as biotechnology, and information and communication technologies. Unless steps are taken immediately to train rural women and men particularly belonging to landless labour families in relevant technologies, the poor will again be bypassed by the new technological opportunities. In fact, rural development should be defined as the conversion of all unskilled persons into skilled ones. It is only in this way that productivity can be enhanced and quality of life improved. Instead of just measuring "yield gap", we should turn our attention now to the study and removal of the constraints responsible for "knowledge gap" in rural professions.

The volume ends with Prof. Vyas's Presidential Address to the 4th Conference of Asian Society of Agricultural Economists. This book is a must for all those interested in the future of Indian agriculture. An understanding of the issues discussed in the five sections is essential for fostering sustained progress in agricultural production and productivity as well as sustainable food and livelihood security. We owe Prof. Vyas a deep debt of gratitude for the trouble he has taken to share his ideas and analysis with a wider audience. Our thanks also go to Dr. Uma Kapila and the Academic Foundation for bringing out this important publication.

15th August, 2003. M.S. Swaminathan

1

Introduction

OVER the years, I have tried to understand the main features of our agriculture and, to some extent of other developing countries, and the way they are impacting the economy of those directly dependent on it for their livelihood. At another level I have tried to probe, how the policy interventions, technological changes and institutional developments are moderating or aggravating these effects. The third aspect which has engaged my attention is the nature of inter sectoral relations in a developing economy like ours. The Essays in this book address these major issues from different angles. Most of these essays were written as public lectures during the last few years.

The essays in this book are divided into five sections. The first section focuses on the relationship between poverty and sustainable development. The second section outlines the main features of Indian agriculture, its sources of growth, the changes taking place within the sector and the problems that are being faced. The third section discusses the issues of poverty and food security not only in India but also in other developing countries of the region. It spells out the role of the state, markets and civil society in resolving the problems of poverty and food security. The fourth section analyses economic reforms in the context of India and discusses the possible directions for these reforms. In the last section we speculate on the directions which Asian agriculture is likely to take in the coming few years and the implications of these changes for the sector, as well as for the economy of the region.

The starting point of an economic analysis of Indian agriculture ought to be the recognition of the fact that Indian agriculture is essentially small-farm agriculture. Nearly 40 per cent of the arable land is cultivated in holdings of less than 2 hectares. While the remainder of the holdings can be identified as semi-medium and medium holdings, barring a thin crust of 'large' holdings. There are demographic, institutional, market-induced and technical factors which suggest that this feature of our agriculture is likely to become progressively more prominent. In other words, the proportion of small holdings is likely to increase before an 'exodus' from agriculture starts. It should be recognised that the existing size distribution of holdings in itself is not a major handicap. Most other Asian countries (including China) have a much larger proportion of their land in small holdings, and most of these countries have a better record in agricultural production and productivity compared to India. Why then has Indian Agriculture been plagued with the problems of low value production, low productivity, declining contribution from 'modern' inputs and wasteful use of natural resources of land and water ?

More often than not, the inadequacies in the supportive institutions and the impact of economic policies are ignored while discussing the inefficiencies in Indian agriculture, and blame is put on the small-farm dominated agrarian structure. The debate on sustainability is an example. It is widely believed that the poor, generally small, producers, have a greater responsibility in damaging the natural resources of land and water, not due to any inherent perversity but because of the circumstances facing them. They have larger families; because of their small production base, they over-exploit the resources, and they heavily discount their future income. In the Elmhurst Memorial Lecture, included in this volume, I have tried to contest all the three propositions, and establish that *ceteris paribus* the poor have to take greater care of their limited resources. With proper technical assistance, institutional support and societal arrangements to cope with uncertainty, the poor are in a better position to conserve their meager resources.

It is important to underline the fact that with the small-farm dominated agrarian structure, the performance of Indian agriculture in the sixties, seventies and eighties was quite satisfactory. This could be ascribed to some growth augmenting measures which did not discriminate against the small-farm sector, an important measure among these being the rapid spread of flow irrigation coupled with substantial public investment in rural areas. This process was halted in the nineties, with immense harm to agriculture and to the economy. The second driving force, especially from the mid-sixties to the mid-eighties was a technology centered around improved seeds, fertilizers and water management. In principle, it was size – neutral technology but, in practice it required command over non-land resources, and hence on credit. Here too, reforms in the credit agencies made possible the phenomenal coverage of agricultural producers by credit agencies, especially after the Bank Nationalisation in 1969. Most importantly, policy measures, particularly the price policy, supported the extension of the new technology, while restraining a rise in the real prices of the foodgrains. Even the land reforms of the fifties and the sixties, though they were truncated and ill administered, made some salutary contributions for example bringing into existence one dominant type of land tenure system, approximating to *ryotwari* system, halting the expansion of large holdings, providing security of tenure in several parts of the country and, facilitating convergence of management and ownership of land on even larger areas. These are no mean achievements.

The unfinished agenda of the Pre-reform period, mainly comprising the neglect of dry areas, weak extension efforts, weakness of the self-help institutions especially cooperatives and neglect of the environmental considerations, has not been attended. On the other hand, the declining trend in public investment and a 'high subsidy – high prices' regime has further aggravated the situation. This has left a large majority of agricultural producers ill prepared to cope with the changes in the domestic as well as international economic environment. I have documented these changes and their implications in the essays in this volume. These are basically demand – induced changes, although the changing nature of technology, institutions, and economic environment are also making profound impact.

It should be recognised, however, that reforms initiated since the early nineties have also resulted in some positive outcomes. The stranglehold of bureaucracy has been loosened, by instituting reforms in industry and trade the policy bias against agriculture has been softened, by doing away with zoning and 'cordoning' the country is emerging as a large unified market for agricultural produce. I have given details of these measures and their impact on Indian agriculture in the essays in the section on Agriculture and Economic Reforms.

While recognising the satisfactory rate of growth in agricultural production, at least till recently, one has also to admit that the impact of this growth on poverty alleviation was not particularly noteworthy. India and other developing countries, can learn important lessons from our past experience. Apart from the lacunae in the design and implementation of the Poverty Alleviation Programmes in this country, the most serious among these being a top-down approach and the neglect of the social sector (education, health and nutrition), a glaring weakness has been the nature of linkages. Due to the weak cash nexus, as far as the economy of the large majority of the agricultural producers is concerned, the demand for non-agricultural goods from this section was subdued. The demand generated by relatively more affluent medium and large farmers was for goods and services which were not necessarily labour intensive. As a result, the diversion of labour from agriculture to the industrial sector, even during the phase of high rate of growth in agriculture, was insubstantial.

In addition to this handicap, i.e. the low cash income of a large majority of the rural population, two more policy failures contributed to the inadequate creation of non-farm employment opportunities: (i) low investment in infrastructure creation in rural areas, and (ii) our industrial policy. The latter was mainly guided by the considerations of import substitution, and had a bias towards heavy, capital intensive industry. In the context of these major handicaps, there has been some correction in recent years in our industrial policy. However, on the other two counts, namely low value added agriculture on the small farms and neglect of rural infrastructure, progress is slow and tardy.

Directly related to the problem of poverty is the problem of Food Security. I have emphasised the development of the concept of Food Security from a rather simplistic notion of food self-sufficiency to a multi-dimensional concept incorporating availability, stability, entitlement and nutritional enhancement. Although refinement of the concept is going on, and there is a large degree of agreement on the four essential attributes of food security at the household level, intra household food security is still a largely unexplored area.

What is missing in the current discussion is the examination of the respective, and most of the time complementary, roles of the State, Markets and Civil Society. This gap in the understanding is even wider when it comes to the role of the Civil Society. In this discussion, I maintain that there is a need for paradigm shift. Concepts of sharing, restraint on wants and social obligations have to be incorporated in a discussion on Food Security. These elements may sound outlandish to a narrowly trained economist, but we have to remind ourselves that in traditional societies like ours these values are held in high esteem. In any case, a notion of sustainable development cannot be built unless these values are recognised as achievable objectives, and suitable strategies designed accordingly. For the latter, the role of the Civil Society institutions will emerge as the critical factor.

An examination of the record on Food Security in India and in the neighbouring countries suggests that some progress has been achieved in reaching this objective. For example, domestic availability of food has increased without lowering the productivity as reflected in the increase in yield per hectare; hunger in the sense of starvation has been largely eliminated; countries have developed the capacity to cope with year to year fluctuations in food production; real prices of foodgrains have, by and large, been contained; some progress has been made in reaching food to the needy by Public Distribution System and by food-for-work programmes. However, on every count, it is clear that a large number of people are food-insecure, and their number expands vastly in the lean seasons. We are far behind the Millennium Goals, and have hardly made any progress in enhancing nutritional status of the people, particularly women and children.

From the array of statistics and analyses, three lessons emerge as critical if the objective is to ensure Food Security to every citizen in the country. One, employment generation, year round as well as seasonal, is important. Equally important is the containment of the real prices of the foodgrains. Finally, some form of Public Distribution of food for vulnerable sections of the population is essential.

One of the principal criteria to judge the efficacy of economic policies is their impact on ensuring Food Security. The other major criterion is, of course, their impact on enhancing productivity, especially of small farms. Finally, one has to adjudge the mutually supportive role of the macro policies and the sectoral policies in the perspective of sustainable growth. I have addressed, admittedly in a partial way, some of these considerations in the series of essays on Economic Policies. While pursuing agricultural policies we have to take into account economic environment within the country and at the international level. The essays in this volume address India's response to globalisation and liberalisation of the domestic economy. In both cases, it is important to recognise the initial conditions while spelling out the direction of change we are contemplating.

On the international plane, a significant development has been our membership of the World Trade Organization. All member countries of WTO have signed, (apart from other agreements), one of the most important agreements – the Agreement on Agriculture. There are three basic stipulations of this agreement: liberalising market access, elimination of subsidies on domestic production and liberalising foreign trade. Although the international trade regime in agriculture has not proved to be as favourable to developing countries as was promised, this organization has imparted some discipline to agricultural trade. In any event, we are not handicapped on the WTO stipulated criteria on market access and on domestic subsidies, and have had little difficulty in adjusting to a liberal foreign trade regime.

India, like other developing countries, is handicapped on two grounds. Most importantly the record of some of the developed countries in eliminating their domestic subsidies to provide a level playing field is, to say the least, discouraging. The other source of worry is the attempt to include several non-trade issues which are detrimental to the interests of the developing countries. Our approach in this situation should be two-fold: try to change the 'rules of the game' by forging alliances with other countries, and strengthen our domestic economic base. Although the emphasis has to be on the latter, it is important to forge alliances with countries that have similar views on variety of issues as, even among the developed countries themselves, interests may conflict. For, there are probably as many disputes between U.S.A. and EEC as between the developed and the developing countries. The principal agricultural exporting countries, the Cairns Group, are in conflict with both — and on several grounds. And the position of these Groups change from issue to issue. Developing countries are not faced with one monolithic and powerful country or group of countries which has taken an adversarial position on all trade issues. This is a favourable feature in the current circumstances.

How far a country like India would be able to take advantage of the situation will depend on our own preparedness and negotiating skills. It is important in the first place to be clear about what areas we wish to fight and where we are prepared to yield. The area where we should put all efforts to 'win friends' is in the inclusion of a 'livelihood box' as a concession to the countries where the agricultural workforce accounts for more than 50 per cent of the total workforce. This demand will be consistent with the importance of 'rural development' recognised by WTO. Another version of this demand could be to include the products grown in the poor areas by poor people as 'special' products. This demand will find a sympathetic response from a large number of developing countries. An area where we should be prepared to give way is in lowering the upper limits of tariff, (a few reach up to 300 per cent), to a more reasonable level, especially so, because we do not use these upper bindings to protect our domestic products.

More attention should be given to domestic reforms in agriculture. There is a full agenda to attend to. However, there are two areas where we should 'hasten slowly'. I have argued that our insistence on food self-sufficiency as well as the current provisions on ceiling on land holdings should not be changed till certain conditions are fulfilled. So long as a large proportion of our workforce is engaged in foodgrain production, and a large part of poor peoples' budget is devoted to acquiring food, the case for meeting our foodgrains demand from domestic supply is very strong. It is more so if we look into our past record. We have been able to raise productivity, and bring down the real prices of food, while pursuing the policy of food self sufficiency.

Similarly, in the case of ceiling on land holdings, it has to be appreciated that any removal of ceiling will result in large scale dislocation of the small and marginal farmers. The non farm sector, at present, is not resilient enough to provide gainful employment to people so displaced. More importantly, the agrarian structure of our neighbouring countries in East and South East Asia which is characterised by small holdings, has not inhibited the growth of productivity in agriculture of these countries. I have maintained that there are no economies of scale in primary production. There are scale economies in processing and marketing. The experience of several countries in Asia and several regions in our own country has shown that through certain organizational innovations it is possible to avail ourselves of these economies even while primary production is carried out on small holdings.

A reform in land legislation which is urgently needed is the unfreezing of the lease market by making tenancy a legal transaction. This could enable farmers who are operating non-viable holdings to add on leased land and make their holdings viable, without the small land owners losing the safety valve provided by the ownership of land. This provides a ladder for the small farmers to progress, with minimum dislocations. As it is, concealed tenancy is widespread, but due to its 'illegal' nature, full benefits are not availed of by either the land owner or the tenant.

A process of liberalisation in agriculture has already been introduced. Measures such as removal of zonal restrictions, amendments in Essential Commodities Act, privatisation of several services, including extension services, reforms in external trade policies, etc. are already afoot. There is still an unfinished agenda in all these regards. The process of liberalisation, or rather debureaucratisation has to be accelerated. Fortunately, there is a consensus on speeding up these reforms. The hurdles placed in reaching the objectives – competitive politics and bureaucratic hangover are now well recognised.

This, unfortunately, is not the case when it comes to several reforms in agricultural price and trade policy. There is no agreement even among the scholars. As reflected in the following essays, I have taken a position on all these key policy issues. I have set two guiding principles while analysing policies and recommending changes. One, we cannot ignore the initial conditions. Any reform measure has to take cognisance of the prevailing structures, institutions and practices, and arrive at some judgement on the resilience of the system to change. Two, important changes in the organization and functioning of the system have to be viewed in a medium to long term perspective. I have examined and suggested reforms in the agricultural price policy, input policy, public distribution of food, external trade in agricultural commodities, etc., following these two ground rules.

In the mid-sixties, we had evolved an agricultural prices and food distribution system which served us well till the beginning of the nineties. Since then, the objective conditions have changed, and several distortions have crept into the system. The original scheme envisaged a minimum support price to enable the producers to recoup their variable costs even if the market prices plunged down, a procurement price at which governmental agencies could procure grains for the buffer stock and for distribution to the vulnerable sections through 'fair price' shops at issue prices which would be below the market prices of foodgrains. Institutional underpinning was provided by establishing the Agricultural Prices Commission to give advice on prices, and the Food Corporation of India to operationalise the scheme. To counter-balance the restraint on output prices, input prices, particularly of fertilizers, were subsidised to encourage their use as productivity enhancing measure. In other words a 'cheap-input cheap-output' price policy was put in place.

The policies were evolved in a situation of scarcity, and in an inward looking regime. Both the conditions have changed but the policies have not been amended accordingly. In these essays, and elsewhere I have argued that the scope of Minimum Support Prices should be limited and major attention should be given to crop insurance and forward trading. Procurement operations should be followed in a 'business-like' manner. In the public distribution of foodgrains, the states and the lower units of government should be given major responsibility. I have also pleaded for diversification, taking into account the emerging demand, from cereals to high value and more 'dynamic' crops, for domestic markets as well as for exports. These are all debatable issues. I have tried to relate the proposed changes in the context of the emerging scenario in demand and supply of agricultural products in our country as much as the changes in the economic environment in our trading partners.

This volume ends with my Presidential Address to the 4th Conference of Asian Society of Agricultural Economists where I dwelt on the medium term prospects for Asian agriculture. A review of agricultural development and economic growth in Asia for the last two decades or so suggests a remarkable similarity among the countries within the three sub-regions of Asia, South Asia, South East Asia and East Asia. A more meaningful division would be on the basis of the relative importance of agriculture in GDP, in the workforce and in the share of agricultural products in consumer expenditure. Identifying the countries where the share of agriculture is high on all the three counts, I have speculated on the future of Agriculture in this group of countries in the next ten years or so. My prognosis is based on the likely developments in three critical areas: demand for agricultural products, supply of agricultural products and the emerging economic environment. The emphasis is on food crops, partly because they account for a substantial area, and presumably a large part of the workforce in the poor developing countries of Asia, partly also because data on food crops are readily available.

Of the dynamic factors impinging on the demand for food, namely population, income and tastes and habits, the changes in the last named are difficult to measure. As regards the remaining two variables, available evidence suggests that the rate of growth in population will decelerate and income elasticity for food will go down. Even with the projected high

GDP in these countries, rate of growth in demand for food will be much slower than in the previous decade. I have maintained that the inclusion of demand for foodgrains as feed will change the picture to some extent as the demand for animal husbandry products will rise faster than the demand for cereals, and hence the rise in the demand for feed. However, the overall impact in most of the countries of Asia, including ours, is not likely to be overwhelming.

On the other hand, the supply side scenario is not at all encouraging. One comes to this conclusion mainly because of the following reasons: the production base of agriculture i.e. soil and water, is weakening; linkages between agricultural growth and non-agricultural growth are not strong enough; there is a growing incongruence between agrarian structure and supply systems; the research shelf seems to be bare; there is confusion about the role of the state. With these handicaps, liberalising trends in domestic policies and a move towards greater integration with the world economy are not likely to yield desirable results. In fact they may exacerbate the difficulties faced by agricultural producers in the poor countries.

The challenge which poor countries of this region face today, and to which they will have to respond in the coming years, revolves round the three major goals of agricultural policies: to preserve the ecological balance, especially stopping degradation of land and water resources; improving the incomes and living standards of rural producers; ensuring food and nutritional security for the population. The extent of success in achieving these objectives will define the country's progress towards sustainable development.

— V.S. Vyas

August 2003

2

Agrarian Structure, Environmental Concerns and Rural Poverty

POVERTY eradication and sustainable development are now being recognised as important dimensions of development. Public pronouncements at the national level as well as the policy documents issued by international agencies reflect these over-riding concerns; so also the work of scholars and the stand taken by social activists. Various factors have helped in highlighting these two issues.

The "lost decade of the eighties" had brought to the fore the plight of the poor, particularly in the countries of Africa and Latin America. The development of means of communication has heightened the awareness of the poor towards their miserable plight. When juxtaposed with the immense possibilities of improving their economic well-being, this awareness has further sharpened. With the spread of democratic institutions, the importance of the poor as a constituency has enhanced; and one finds a large number of spokesperson for poverty alleviation. Concern for environmental degradation, particularly for unsustainable

---

(Elmhirst Memorial Lecture, XXI International Conference of Agricultural Economists, Tokyo, Japan in 1991).

The author is grateful to his colleagues at IDS and elsewhere who substantially contributed to the content and logic of this presentation. In particular, the contributions of Deepak Gianchandani, Anil Gupta, Vidya Sagar and Davendra Tyagi are gratefully acknowledged.

agriculture has become urgent with the alarming speed of deforestation and desertification, spread of soil erosion, ingress of salinity, water shortages, increase in pests and crop diseases and other symptoms of environmental degradation.

While there is seldom any dissent on the importance of both these issues, there is a discernible lack of clarity on the nature of inter-relationship between rural poverty and environmental constraints which inhibit sustainable agriculture, and a good deal of confusion on how to tackle them simultaneously.

This paper is a modest effort to discuss some aspects of poverty eradication and (economically and environmentally) sustainable agriculture, and the critical role which agrarian structure plays in reaching these objectives. The next section deals with the nature and extent of rural poverty in the developing countries, the impact on poverty during last few years and the approaches to poverty eradication. In section three environmental aspects of sustainable agriculture is outlined, pressure on natural resources, particularly land is highlighted and the question of poverty and over-exploitation of resources examined. The fourth section underscores the economic aspects of sustainable agriculture and elicits the importance of structural change in agriculture as reflected in the access to land, an issue which has been generally side-tracked in the discussion on sustainable agriculture. The last section points out the scope for conflict as well as convergence between the twin goals of poverty eradication and sustainable agriculture through the mediation of structural change in agriculture which ensures more equitable access to land to the poor households.

For empirical support to various premises I have relied heavily on the experience of the developing countries of South Asia, particularly India. This reliance is partly because I am more familiar with this part of the world and partly because the largest number of the poor inhabit the countries of this region. I may point out one more limitation of my presentation. The time-horizon I have selected for the prognosis is medium term, i.e., the decade of the nineties. I am aware that we are on the threshold of some momentous changes in technology, e.g., advances in biotechnology and, may be also in social organization. However, these changes will take time to unfold fully and make their impact felt.

II

EXTENT AND NATURE OF RURAL POVERTY

Over the years an awareness of the poverty problem has resulted in a deepened interest of the policy makers and researchers alike in the concepts and measurement of poverty. So much so, that in the words of a researcher, it has become an "industry". The cause of poverty alleviation in recent years suffered as the definitions of poverty adopted were either too wide or too narrow. With too broad a definition poverty alleviation could hardly be distinguished from socio-economic development as such, with too narrow definition the purpose of poverty alleviation, i.e., enabling the poor households to lead a decent human life, is defeated. Thus a UN Report, true to its tradition, defined minimum subsistence to include physiological, legal and social necessities. It did, however, suggest that these were roughly hierarchical: each employing a higher quality of, or additional, goods and services than the *preceding* one[1]. At the other extreme is the narrow, single index, definition of poverty using per capita income or per capita consumption.

1. U.N. *Social Policy and the Distribution of Income in the Nation*, New York, 1969.

Definition of poverty currently in vogue is one which translates a calorie norm into monetary value and adds expenditure on other non-food items generally consumed by the households in that income bracket which satisfies the minimum calorie intake[2]. The latter i.e., expenditure on non-food items, is generally arrived at on the basis of budget studies. A serious lacuna in this definition is the total reliance on *private income*. It is important to remember that in one of the pioneering efforts in measurement of poverty, that by a group of experts set up by the Planning Commission of India in the sixties, it was explicitly mentioned that while defining poverty in terms of minimum household income, the group had assumed that *public services* like elementary education and health were available to all[3]. In later discussions this vital aspect, i.e., provision of and access to public goods, was ignored. In any event an income-based poverty line can only serve as a first approximation. For a poverty alleviation strategy, access to public goods, like elementary health and education needs to be taken into account. A partial correction to the income/calorie based definition is provided by the recent efforts of UNDP to construct a Human Development Index (HDI) for different countries[4].

The poor households subsist at various levels of deprivations and their poverty could be transitory or chronic. We are here

---

2. It seems that in this respect the concept of poverty is going in circles. In the early part of this century the English social commentators, notably B.S. Rowntree, defined primary poverty as "minimum necessary expenditure for maintenance of merely physical health". See, B.S. Rowntree, *Poverty: A Study of Town Life*, Macmillan, London, 1901, quoted by Wold Scott, *Concept and Measurement of Poverty*, UNRISD, Geneva, 1981, p.5. Note this concept was not much different from the current definition of absolute poverty.

3. See, Sagar Sushma, *Poverty Measurement - Some Issues*, Jaipur, 1988, p. 2.

4. The methodology and justification for HDI is provided in the *Human Development Report*, New York, 1990, p. 10-16.

concerned with the chronically poor, although it should be understood that transient poverty, say due to a natural calamity, can soon degenerate into chronic poverty in the absence of some devices – household, social or public – to absorb adverse shocks. The chronic poor are those who lack the skills, assets and stamina. The intensity of poverty of different sections of the poor households could be measured by the "Sen Index of Poverty"[5]. Less sophisticated but equally remarkable is Lipton's categorisation of poor into the poor and the ultra poor on the basis of whether the household is able to meet its calorie needs[6]. These distinctions are important to evaluate the effects of various poverty alleviation measures.

The Extent of Poverty

For international comparisons, frequent use is made of the World Bank's country specific statistics on income levels and income distribution. The World Bank also makes use of global norms to arrive at approximate figures of the poor. Thus, according to the World Development Report 1990 (WDR, 1990), in 1985 an estimated 1.1 billion people in developing world lived in poverty. Of these nearly 633 million were absolutely poor. These estimates were based on an income of $375 per person per year for the poor and $275 per person per year for absolutely poor (amount being in constant 1985 PPP prices). The World Bank's estimates are not universally accepted[7], but they are more comprehensive in their coverage than other global estimates.

---

5. See, Sen. A.K., "Poverty Inequality and Unemployment" *Economic and Political Weekly* (EPW), Special Number, August 1973, for the logic and methodology of the "Sen Index".
6. See, Lipton. M., *Poverty, Under-nutrition and Hunger*, World Bank Staff Working Paper No. 597, World Bank, Washington D.C., 1983.
7. See, Saith Ashwini, "Development Strategy and the Rural Poor" in *The Journal of Peasant Studies*, p. 172-176.

The geographical distribution of the world's poor as estimated by the World Bank suggests that one-third of the developing world's total population was living under poverty, of which 18 per cent were extremely poor. Major concentration of poverty was in South Asia which accounted for nearly half of the developing world's poor, and nearly half of extremely poor. Sub-Saharan Africa reported an equally high proportion of the poor in relation to the region's overall population, and Latin America and Caribbean region was not far behind.

The Recent Developments

In recent years, on the basis of some welfare indicators like life expectancy, infant mortality and literacy, one finds that there has been a distinct improvement in the living standards in practically all developing regions. Per capita income in developing countries has increased by nearly 3 per cent per year, more people have access to health services, drinking water and better sanitary facilities. Daily calories supply has improved significantly[8]. The improvement has not been uniform over the regions or among countries in any particular region. Also the "average" figures at the country level mask severe deprivation suffered by various groups of people. Yet the fact remains that a remarkable improvement in the living standards of the people in the developing world has taken place according to these welfare measures.

The same, however, cannot be said about the performance on the basis of income or expenditure based poverty criterion. The East Asian countries continued their commendable progress towards poverty eradication, the Philippines being the main exception, and some of the poor countries in south Asia, for example, India did improve their performance. There was a stagnation in Sub-Saharan Africa and a retrogression in

8. Human Development Report 1990, op.cit., p. 27.

countries of Latin America, mainly because of the burden of external debt and the falling commodity prices. Putting these two facts together, better performance on the basis of some of the welfare norms and persistence of poverty in terms of entitlement for goods and services, it is clear that rigours of poverty have softened even in the countries where widespread[9] poverty prevails.

Characteristics of the Poor

A large number of studies the world over have brought out the main characteristics of the poor. While the situations differ from country to country, certain common features stand out. Most of the poor in the developing world are concentrated in rural areas, and a large number of them depend directly or indirectly on agriculture, they own or control few physical productive assets.

They face a fragmented and exploitative market for their main asset, i.e., labour; women are more discriminated against in this market. Those among the poor households who have a land base, have marginal holdings and or are tenant-at-will. They are generally over represented in the marginal regions. Their capacity to take risk is, probably weak. They have larger dependence on common property resources.

The poor are handicapped by social disabilities as much as by economic constraints. They are powerless and marginal, inspite of their large numbers in several countries, both as producers as well as consumers. They have a larger number of dependents, though not necessarily large sized households. Mostly they do not possess saleable skills, are malnourished and physically weak. In other words, not only do they not have adequate claim on current production, the future prospects

9. See, Jodha, N.S., "Poverty Debate in India: A Minority View", EPW, Special Number, November 1988.

are also not very encouraging[10].

Approach to Poverty Alleviation

Basically two approaches have been adopted to resolve the poverty problem. These are not exclusive, yet the emphasis on one or the other is quite clear. In one approach a large measure of reliance is placed on the "trickle down" effect of rapid growth while the other relies more on public intervention.

There cannot be any doubt about the fact that without growth poverty eradication will not be a practical proposition. However, a heavy reliance on "trickle down" or "spread effect" of growth raises several questions and is not supported by the historical experience. Historically "trickle down" has benefitted the poor when atleast one of the following two conditions had been present: (a) the rate of growth of the economy had been very high, say, 8 to 10 per cent per annum, or (b) the poor had some asset base. Neither of the two conditions can be taken for granted.

There are not many examples of countries recording consistently high rate of growth in recent times. Experience suggests that even if a spurt in growth rate is achieved it becomes difficult to maintain the tempo without incurring inflationary pressures or running into balance of payment difficulties, usually both[11]. I will come back to the transient nature of such growth swings in inequitous societies a little later.

Similarly, if the asset base of the poor is absent or depleted

---

10. In a yet unpublished document, Subodh C. Mathur, has presented a review of literature bearing on the characteristics, economic environment and the behaviour of the rural poor in India. Above paragraphs draw heavily on this review.

11. See, Saith Ashwini, op.cit, for a discussion of the failure of different types of models of economic/industrial growth to sustain "trickle down" effect.

– and the assets could comprise not only physical assets, like land, but also assets such as skills and physical stamina – the poor households will not be able to respond to the growth stimuli. That is why even those who put much faith in "trickle-down" also worry about the *composition* of growth rather than growth *per se*. For example, a plea for labour intensive pattern of growth is advocated in order to ensure a larger participation of the poor in the growth process.

The interventionist policies by themselves can not be counted upon to eradicate mass poverty in the developing countries. This is not only because of the faulty project designs and wrong implementation strategies of the poverty alleviation projects, on which much has been written, but also due to the diversion of scarce resources which could enhance the asset base of the poor households to these projects.

The case of India's Integrated Rural Development Programme may be used to illustrate these points. In the scale of operations and clarity of objectives it could be considered as an exemplary programme. Yet its cost-effectiveness can be seriously questioned. Even with a massive investment of resources and political support at all levels the impact on eradication of poverty has not been commensurate. A careful researcher has estimated that over a period of 10 years this programme has helped nearly 9.3 per cent of the poor households in rural areas to cross the poverty line. Even this small impact was selective in terms of the households and the areas. For example, the households who were nearer to poverty line received more benefits and the programme fared better in developed regions compared to backward and remote regions[12].

---

12. Hirway Indira, "Poverty Alleviation Programme in India: Past Experience and Future Direction" in *Poverty Eradication in India*, Proceedings and papers of a Workshop. The Hague, 1990 (mimeograph).

Over a period of time there have been some improvements in the performance. Bureaucracy has become more sensitive, local institutions are getting involved, some forms of participatory management are being experimented with. However, participatory management which is the king-pin in the delivery of these programmes has to go beyond tokenism.

A pre-requisite to genuine people's participation is an institutional underpinning. With gross inequities in the ownership of assets, particularly with a large section being assetless, it is doubtful whether participatory institutions capable of delivering economic goods and services in an equitable manner would emerge.

The experiences of India and other countries suggest that trickle down effect of growth depends on the recipients having access to assets, possession of skills or physical stamina. The public programmes of poverty eradication have also helped the category of the poor households so endowed. It will be instructive in this context to review the quality of the main productive asset in the rural areas of the developing countries, i.e., land, and then look into the question of access to this resource by the poor. The next section addresses the first question and in the following section the issues pertaining to agrarian structure are examined.

III

THE LAND RESOURCES

In the context of poverty eradication there are questions on environmental sustainability as well as economic sustainability of the present mode of agriculture. Let me briefly comment on these two aspects. Current anxiety about the sustainability of the present mode of agriculture[13], from the environmental angle can be ascribed to two related factors: the growing pressure of population on land resources and deteriorating quality of earth resources (land, water, air) atleast partly due to intensification of agriculture.

For the poor countries raising agricultural productivity without endangering its sustainability poses a serious challenge. In the past, the "open frontiers" provided an outlet for the poor. Most of the developed countries of today could circumvent the initial crowding of the people on land by using spaces available within the countries or because migration to other land-abundant countries was easy. This is no longer true for the developing countries whose surplus rural labour cannot find any outlet in the countries where the lands are still abundant and labour relatively scarce. The poor in the developing countries have to find solution to the poverty problem within their own country. In this situation the main source of livelihood in the rural areas, namely, agriculture, plays a pivotal role.

The possibility of raising agricultural production has now to be examined only in the context of intensive, and not extensive, agriculture. This is true globally, and with a few exceptions for a large number of countries. According to FAO estimates, the amount of arable land in developing countries will increase by less than 10 per cent, to 850 m. hectares, by the year 2000. Amount of land per inhabitant in the developing world will fall from 0.85 hectares at the beginning of the 1980s

---

13. I find the definition of sustainable definition adopted by FAO council in 1988, quite satisfactory. The definition is as follows: "The management and conservation of the natural resource base, and the orientation of technological and institutional change in such a manner as to ensure the attainment and continued satisfaction of human needs for present and future generations". Quoted in *Issues and Perspectives in Sustainable Agriculture and Rural Development*, FAO, 1991, p.3, see the same publication for further analysis and delineation of issues.

to 0.6 hectares by 2000. New land which will be brought under cultivation will be of poor quality[14]. In any case, by 2025 no high quality land will be available for arable purpose. Already the area under severe risk of erosion and salinity is increasing, as the lands on slopes of hills, fringes of forests and borders of deserts are brought under the plough.

Another way the arable area can be extended is through irrigation. Among several possible benefits, such as increase in productivity, lowering of risks etc. a major benefit of irrigation is the multi-season cropping. Particularly in areas where concentration of rainfall to a few months makes crop production in non-rainy seasons very risky if not an impossible enterprise, perennial irrigation contributes substantially to increase in arable areas. In several parts of the developing world, especially Asia and Africa, land base was significantly augmented with the introduction of irrigation. The amount of irrigated lands have trebled since 1950. But almost all easy sites for irrigation development have already been exhausted. Now, the cost of new irrigation development is becoming prohibitive. Also ecological damage done by surface as well as ground water irrigation to the soils and environment, coupled with increasing threat of water borne diseases, is making the irrigation option much less attractive. As it is, nearly 10 per cent of the irrigated hectares have already become saline. Another 25 per cent show early signs of salinity.

In brief, there is very little scope for extensive farming either by extension of cultivated areas on fallow lands or by an extension of irrigation. Whatever solutions to poverty and

---

14. In fact the new land often prove not to be of much help. An estimated 20 per cent of new ranches in Amazon failed within a few years. The loss of existing agricultural land through erosion is estimated at 6-7 million hectares per year; additional 1.5 million hectares are lost from water logging, salanization and alkanisation see, *World Resources*, 1990-91, A Report of the World Resources Institute, New York, 1990, p.6.

environment degradation we seek, should be in the context of fixed, rather shrinking, land surface and water resources. This would require greater ingenuity and greater care to conserve the land and water resources. Eminent scientists such as M.S. Swaminathan have been warning us for more than two decades against the ecological disasters if proper methods of conservation are not adopted[15].

The Poor and Environmental Degradation

It is sometimes presumed that the poor are responsible for the depletion of natural resources, not because of any perversity, but because of the compulsions of poverty. How far are these fears genuine? There is a great dearth of usable data to establish any proposition very firmly. However, few tentative conclusions can be advanced. In the first place, in the resource rich regions there is no evidence to suggest that lands cultivated by the poor, in this case the holdings of the small and marginal farmers, are in any way inferior to the holdings of the large or medium farmers. At the same time, in ecologically degraded tracts or the resource poor regions there is a relatively larger concentration of the poor holdings. The latter fact by itself does not suggest that poor are "responsible" for environmental degradation in these areas.

The poor could be charged with over-exploitation and consequent degradation of natural resources on two possible counts. Because of faster rate of growth of population and because of their larger dependence on the natural resources (say, for fuel and fodder) coupled with high subjective discount rate, they may be responsible for fast depletion of some of the resources (mainly forests) and degradation of other resources (such as soils).

---

15. Swaminathan, M.S., Presidential Address to the Agricultural Science Section of Indian Science Congress, January 1968, Varanasi.

Of these the argument based on higher population growth is more serious and has a wider currency. If this is true, the expanding numbers in poor households would have been pushing cultivation to the fragile, or marginal lands with serious consequences[16].

But this view has been seriously challenged by some scholars in India and other South Asian countries. In a recent publication, results of case studies from four countries Pakistan, India, Bangladesh and Nepal and from Bihar state of India, were reported. The authors brought out the complexity of the economic and demographic relationships. Some of their major findings summarised in an overview by the editor Garry Roger, may be noted: "(i) there is no evidence in the studies that the poor have relatively high fertility, and there is a hint that their fertility may be lower than middle income groups at least. Moreover, because child survival rates are lower among the poor the achieved family size appears to be particularly low among the poorer groups; and more explicitly (ii) there is powerful association between household size and wealth ... poor households are small"[17]. The effect of poverty on the exploitation of resources is not because of the large size of the households of the poor but, as the authors of the study quoted above have put it, due to "pre-existing patterns of inequality and exploitation".

The poor are also blamed for "over-exploiting" the resources, as they depend heavily on natural resources and also heavily discount the future value of the income streams. This is particularly true of the exhaustible resources, such as

---

16. The earlier studies in India as summarised by Lipton, Visaria and few others did suggest that "as a general rule poverty and large household size within a locality go together", quoted in Subodh C. Mathur, op.cit., p. 8-9.

17. *Population Growth and Poverty in Rural South Asia*, (ed. Garry Rogers, New Delhi, 1989) p. 18-19.

forest products. However, one should not over-estimate the damage caused to the natural resources by petty pilferages by the poor. These pale into insignificance when compared to the depletion of natural resources by the rich due to their wasteful living style[18]. More demand on land and natural resources is made by the life style of the rich than by the need-based exploitation by the poor. We will not be able to talk about preservation of environment unless we seriously question, and suggest alternatives to, present style of living.

The fact that the poor depend heavily on natural resources gives them greater motivation to conserve these resources, provided their interests are not overlooked. No plans of environmental protection can succeed unless these involve the poor as participants *and* beneficiaries, be it regeneration of forests or control of water pollution or soil erosion. Unless the poor cooperate the rot cannot be stopped. And in order to ensure their cooperation some tangible benefits should accrue to them. The arguments that environmental protection measures generate positive externalities do not persuade poor households to sacrifice their immediate income for the sake of medium to long-term gains of the community. A cardinal principle of sustainability is to ensure protection, if not an enhancement, of the incomes of the small and marginal farmers and others whose livelihoods depend on these resources.

The poor household are as much interested in conserving natural resources as any other section of the society[19]. The

---

18. World Commission on Environment and Development, *Our Common Future*, 1989, Table 1.2, p. 33.

19. In a Newsletter, *Honey Bee* Edited by Prof. Anil Gupta at IIM, Ahmedabad, India, on behalf of an international network for documentation and experimentation of local innovations, numerous examples of eco-friendly innovations are quoted. Also see for a logical base for small peasants environmental concern, Gupta Anil, "Survival Under Stress in South Asia: A Socio-Ecological Perspective on Farmer Risk Adjustment and Innovations" in *Capitalism, Nature, Socialism*, October 1990.

agricultural and forestry practices improvised over generations bear testimony to the ingenuity of the poor to eke out a living from shrinking and depleted resources. In any effort to preserve environment the poor must be stake-holders.

It is important in this connection to recognise the role of collective efforts to conserve resources. With their subsistence orientation, the poor cannot be disciplined to conserve resources with reliance on the instruments of pricing and subsidies. They can be disciplined mainly by community efforts. In the past many of the conservation practices depended on community efforts e.g., preservation and rejuvenation of village commons. With the disintegration of the relevant social institutions these practices are also being gradually abandoned.

The relationship between the people and their environment was based on a robust system which ensured that the basic needs of the households dependent on natural resources were met and the households in turn preserved and safeguarded the environment. This balance was disturbed with rapacious claims on these resources by the rich and the powerful, by pressure of population of the households which could not find enough alternative sources of earning livelihood and by the erosion of institutional safeguards to protect the environment. Underlying all these causes was the deterioration of agrarian structure, basically a deteriorating relationship to land.

IV

AGRARIAN STRUCTURE

The countries, and regions within the large countries, where least impact has been made on the eradication of poverty often suffer from an inequitous agrarian structure, or marginalised and depleted resources, or both. Inequitous agrarian structure is characterised by unequal access to land for the rural households depending on agriculture either as owners or as lease holders and a large army of landless labourers depending on wage labour in agriculture. Extreme forms of such inequitous structures exist in parts of Latin America. In a number of South Asian countries also large landowners co-exist with numerous small owners, owner-cum-tenants, pure tenants and landless labourers. The rigours of small ownership holdings are softened if there is an active lease market, or when non-farm employment opportunities are present and expanding. In the absence of either of these two conditions a strong correlation exists between the inequality in ownership of land and the extent of poverty, as in South Asia, Southern Africa and large parts of Latin America[20].

In the absence of a buoyant non-farm sector which, as I will discuss later, itself is predicated in the countries we are referring to upon a dynamic agriculture, two important factors could contribute to the relaxation of limitations imposed by an inequitous agrarian structure: functioning of the land and labour markets and technology. Unfortunately, in countries with large concentration of poverty, i.e., in the countries of South Asia, these factors reinforce the inequities.

Land and Labour Markets

In a situation of grossly unequal access to land the functioning of labour and land markets do not provide the poor with an alternative of non-farm work or of augmenting their holdings with leased-in land. The labour market is fragmented not only on the basis of skills compounded by difficulties in transport and communication but also because of the differences in gender, castes, tribes and other social characteristics. All these impose restrictions on the mobility

20. *World Development Report*, op.cit., p. 31-32.

of labour. The macro policies of the governments, especially those pertaining to pricing and subsidies inhibit whatever limited opportunities may arise to expand non-farm employment. An abundant supply of rural labour with limited, and more or less fixed demand in agriculture and related activities, results in low wage rates, except during the time-bound seasonal operations.

In any case, as is now well documented, the employment elasticity of labour in agriculture is quite low. Even in the intensively cultivated areas it will not at the margin exceed .5, compared to addition to the workforce in the farm sector which exceeds 2 per cent per year or more in the countries of South Asia[21]. Further, most of the additional employment even in the good agricultural years gets translated into fuller employment for underemployed family labour rather than additional work for wage-labour. The dependence of labour on the landlords in other markets, e.g., for credit, compounds the handicaps, lead to what are known as semi-feudal conditions[22].

Following Marshallian formulation many commentators of the rural scene have concluded that the organization of production on leased-in lands, especially when these are under share-cropping arrangements, may not be as efficient as on the owner-operated holdings. These findings have recently been questioned[23]. There is a large body of empirical evidence, and plausible logic to explain it, which suggests that even in the circumstances of overcrowded agriculture, crop-sharing

21. See, Asian Development Bank *Rural Asia Challenge and Opportunity*, New York, 1978, Chapter 3, p. 49-61.

22. Bhaduri, A. "Study in Agricultural Backwardness under Semi-Feudalism" *Economic Journal*, March 1973.

23. Otsuka, Keijiro and Hayami, Yujiro "Theories of Share Tenancy: A Critical Survey" *Economic Development and Cultural Change*, 1988.

provides for the landless rural labourer and marginal farmers a better alternative to limited opportunities for wage labour. That is why, despite the numerous lacunae in lease contracts, the poor households do take recourse to share cropping. For example, in India the area under cultivated holdings is larger than the area under owned holdings in the lower size-groups of land holdings. The difference is obviously accounted for by land leased-in by the small and marginal land owners.

However, this option of augmenting land is not available to many poor households when the large holdings are cultivated extensively, or in some cases left uncultivated. Another situation, where poors' access to land is circumscribed arises when because of capital intensive technology or other socio-economic considerations an "inverse" tenancy system prevails i.e., medium and large farmers leasing-in land rather than the small farmers having an access to it[24]. The imperfections in the lease market get compounded because of misplaced policy interventions (e.g., an insistence on owner operation in many land legislation), which have only resulted in 'concealed' tenancy and made the terms of lease more onerous for small tenants.

Finally, I may touch upon one other alternative which, in the past and atleast in some countries, was favoured as a panacea for increasing incomes of small farmers, i.e., joint or collective farming. For quite some time, this solution had an ideological appeal. However, even in those days perceptive writers had unravelled all the inconsistencies in the logic on which a case for joint-farming was based[25]. The subsequent

---

24. I had drawn attention to this phenomenon of 'reverse tenancy' in the early years of Green Revolution in India, see, Vyas V.S., "Tenancy in Dynamic Setting" *Economic and Political Weekly*, Review of Agriculture, June 1970.

25. For a critical review of the issues in collectivisation in South Asian Agriculture, see, Deshpande S.H., *Some Problem of Cooperative Farming*, Bombay, 1977.

historical developments, first in China and now in Eastern Europe and Soviet Union, have clearly demonstrated, if such an evidence was at all necessary, that technological and social correlates of agriculture militate against the principle of collectivism at the production stage.

Technological Developments

Technological development in agriculture in the developing countries in recent years were mostly aimed at yield augmentation to ensure food security at the national level. The major vehicle for yield augmentation was high yielding varieties (HYV) of seeds, mainly of wheat and rice and to some extent maize, which with the complement of assured water-supply and chemical fertilizers and pesticides promised a remarkable increase in yield per hectare. In theory this technology was divisible and neutral to scale. But in practice it favoured medium to large farmers who could take recourse to their own saving, or had easy access to financial institutions to obtain credit, to purchase inputs. It is true that over a period of time state interventions in the credit market did ease the conditions of access for small farmers in a number of countries. Thus, those who had small holdings in the well-watered areas could take advantage of the advances of HYV technology, though only after a time-lag. The implicit bias of technological development was clearly in favour of the resource-rich farmers in the resource-rich regions. In regions with uncertain or inadequate water supply, i.e., in the large rain-fed tracts, no yield augmenting technology of the type of HYV technology was available. There the access to land and poverty were more clearly, and inversely correlated.

V

POVERTY, AGRARIAN STRUCTURE AND SUSTAINABILITY

Let me at this stage pose the basic question: can one bypass a defective agrarian structure and lift the poor households in rural areas from the mire of poverty? The relationship between poverty and access to land could be subjected to several qualifications. Population pressure, quality of land, nature of technology and development of non-farm activities make this relationship rather complex[26]. However, if we take into account the medium to large countries, where a large proportion of rural work force is dependent on agriculture, the links between the agrarian structure and the extent of poverty are fairly general. Contemporary history hardly provides an example of a relatively *swift and sustainable* transformation taking place in the context of an inegalitarian agrarian structure in such societies.

The underlying logic is not difficult to follow. Under special circumstances a section of the farm sector can develop, irrespective of the overall stagnation in agriculture, and can forge strong linkages with the non-farm sector, for example, with the modernisation of agriculture on large holdings or export-oriented developments on these holdings. Thus, a farm sub-sector catering to a sizable urban demand or export markets can co-exist with a largely stagnant rural sector. In such cases, really speaking two-worlds, of the poor and the non-poor, exist without close interaction. Such cases, although rare, are not unknown. Even in these cases sustainable development is questionable in the absence of some mechanism which ensures

---

26. See the concluding chapter by Mellor John, W. and Desai Gunwant, M. "Agricultural Change and Rural Poverty: A Synthesis" in *Agricultural Change and Rural Poverty*, (ed. Mellor and Desai), Delhi, 1986.

an expanding rural demand. And expansion in the rural demand especially if the sector is dominated by a large number of poor households would require a more dynamic small farm sector or a substantial rise in real wages. An inequitous agrarian structure mitigates against both these developments. Even if the overall growth rate is high, in the absence of an equitous agrarian structure the sustainability of such a growth is always doubtful. Brazil in Latin America and the Philippines in Asia provide good examples of the need for equitous agrarian structure as a precondition for sustainable growth.

However, reverse is not automatically proven. But – and this we can say now without revisiting the now famous size productivity debate – there is enough evidence to suggest that size by itself is not a constraint in raising productivity. A more important question is whether this type of a small-farm dominated system would be environmentally sound? And whether and how would it make agriculture sustainable? By itself a small farm dominated and economically viable agriculture is no guarantee for sustainable agriculture. But it could pave the way for the same. By generating surplus it enables the poor households to invest in skills and diversifying enterprises thus relieving pressure from land. Even then the tasks of facilitating skill formation by education and training, and diversifying enterprises with the provision of infrastructure and development of markets, falls on public investment policies. More than investment policies, the policies on science and technology are of critical importance.

Even in the past, technological developments have yielded several land augmenting measures. From perennial irrigation to non-photo-sensitive and short maturing varieties, a number of technological interventions could be identified which have increased the usable land surface. Also, the small farmers, especially those who were potentially viable, could be made viable by generating and extending a technology which will enable them to have higher value of products from their limited land base. In other words where quality of land could, to some extent atleast, substitute for the quantity. This could mean high value crops but it could also mean a different enterprise mix. The crops grown by the small farmers and the resource base available to them generally do not attract attention of the mainstream scientific establishments to improve their economic prospect.

A small farm dominated agriculture will by definition be in nature an intensive agriculture. With the present-day technology this would mean high yielding varieties of seeds, chemical fertilizers and chemical pesticides. These are not the ingredients for sustainable agriculture. If there is a threat to sustainability it comes largely from these sources. The only way to cope up with this problem is to harness technology to solve the problems of soil nutrients, pests and diseases in a way that does least harm to environment. There are several promising leads in different regions. But today these efforts do not constitute the mainstream technological research. It is only by according priority to these efforts and providing them with resources that a credibility will be built and the technology generation in these directions could be given a fillip.

The other constraints which have to be faced by the small farmers are their limited access to cash resources and hence inability to use high capital intensive techniques. Coupled to that is their inability to take risks. Both these aspects take us from the field of technology to that of macro policies.

The critical role of macro policies in rural poverty alleviation is now fully appreciated. The role of pricing, subsidies, exchange rates, trade policies are well documented. What is largely missing in this discussion are (i) how poor can benefit from the free markets and (ii) how they can be insured from the attendant risks. The poor face two difficulties vis-a-vis markets. In the first place, they find it difficult to 'enter'. This may not be as much a handicap in the markets for agricultural products, because of the competitive structure of these markets. However, it may not be so in case of the labour and lease market as noted above. These markets are fragmented and extra-economic consideration do play their part. The second major handicap is the return to small farmers, again, in the lease and the labour markets. Because of uneven bargaining power it is not easy for them to secure a 'fair' wage or 'fair' share from gross produce (in case of leased-in land).

The role of macro policies, pricing, trade, subsidies, will become more important, once technologically feasible solutions are available. They will fine-tune the basic thrusts provided by institutional change and technology. This has been amply demonstrated by the experience of High Yielding Varieties Programme in some countries such as India, where the institution of price and credit policy helped once a superior technology was available for extension[27].

The role of state in this respect is important. The state policies should facilitate an easy entry and ensure fair returns. The other aspect is the regulatory aspect. However, in both these cases more than the state efforts the organizations of poor can play a critical role. The implementation of the legislative provisions for minimum wages or the stipulated tenant's share in case of leased-in land illustrate the regulatory role of the state as much as the critical part played by peasants movements.

---

27. See, Vyas, V.S., "India's Rural Development Strategies: Lessons in Agricultural Growth and Poverty Alleviation" in *China's Rural Development Miracle with International Comparisons* (ed. John W. Longworth), St. Lucia, 1989.

If we are not yet fully equipped to use the market institutions in favour of the poor we are at a very rudimentary stage in our understanding of the risks faced by them, their coping strategies and the institutions and macro policies which can help them either to minimise the incidence of risk or to equip them to face the risk or compensate them in the event of an adverse outcome. Here again there is a role for researchers, for social activists and the state to devise appropriate "safety-nets".

The task of poverty alleviation is as important as the move for sustainable agriculture. In fact, properly conceived poverty alleviation could be a step in the direction of environmentally safe world. For poverty alleviation, an access to assets is important. The earlier we realise the interdependence among agrarian structure, environmental sustenance and poverty eradication in the over-populated developing countries more realistic would be our approach to attain sustainable agricultural development.

3

Indian Agriculture

An Overview

INTRODUCTION

AGRICULTURE still plays a key role in the economy of India. Nearly one-third of the gross domestic product is accounted by agricultural sector. About two-third of the work force is engaged in agriculture. Over the last decade there has been a decline in the contribution of agriculture to GDP but hardly any significant change in the proportion of work force depending on agriculture. Food and agricultural product occupy a major share in the consumers' budget. Agricultural inputs account for an important part of the raw material base of Indian industries. Agricultural exports contribute significantly to the total exports of the country. Although today the old adage, "Indian budget is a gamble in monsoon", may not be exactly true because of the declining weight of the sector in the economy, the fact remains that performance of agriculture influences the course of the economy in a profound way.

Importance of agriculture is not likely to diminish for quite some time to come. There are three important reasons which justify continuous emphasis on agricultural growth in the

(Lecture delivered at the 10th World Congress on Agriculture Credit, New Delhi in 1991).

country's development strategy. These are, concern for food security, for fuller employment and, for availability of the wage-goods. Indian economy has to reach a much higher plane before food security concerns could be de-linked from domestic production of foodgrains. The same is true about the labour disposition. At least in the near future agriculture will remain an important source of livelihood of the rural households and, as a corollary, an important instrument for alleviating rural poverty.

The third major contribution of agricultural growth is in terms of the provision of the wage goods which determine to a significant extent the general price level. Increase in agricultural production, especially foodgrains production, contributes to the containment of inflation, reverse may happen if foodgrains production stagnates. These considerations juxtaposed with India's comparative advantage in several agricultural products in the international markets and hence their potential in contributing to foreign exchange earnings suggest that agricultural growth should be accelerated. Estimates of a desirable rate of growth in agricultural production vary, but there is a unanimity of view among the scholars that the current rate of growth in agricultural output, at 2.8 per cent per annum should be further lifted.

II

PERFORMANCE OF AGRICULTURAL SECTOR

On the basis of several important criteria it can be concluded that pace of agricultural development during the recent years was quite satisfactory. The overall rate of growth in agriculture was 2.8 per cent per year during the last decade, which was higher than the growth in population at 2.4 per cent per annum. The imports of foodgrains to meet domestic food requirements are no longer a drain on the country's economy. India is now in a position to export not only the so-called "commercial crops" e.g. tea, coffee, cotton, tobacco etc., but also substantial quantities of staple foodgrains i.e. wheat and rice. Within a period of a decade a net importing country is emerging as an exporting nation.

There are other dimensions of agricultural development which make the performance of the sector all the more welcome. Agricultural development now encompasses even those parts of the country which were, earlier, stagnating. Rapid agricultural growth in the eastern region where a veritable revolution in rice production is taking place is an outstanding example.

Production policies were supported by complimentary measures in the area of price policy and trade policy. As a result while agricultural production increased and with that incomes of the producers increased too, the real price of food which is of crucial interest to the poorer sections in urban as well as in rural areas, actually declined. Real prices of rice came down by 2.2 per cent per year and that of wheat 3.3 per cent per year. This has contributed in a significant manner to the food security for the poor.

The performance of agricultural sector is all the more impressive once we realise that additions to the output have been realised by increases in yield per hectare rather than by an expansion of cultivated area, latter has remained more or less stable. It can be well appreciated that to obtain increases in production by intensive agriculture is much more difficult than raising additional output with the expansion of culturable area. The former requires not only a better access to non-land inputs but also much more careful use of these inputs.

Another, and equally remarkable, feature of Indian agricultural growth is that it is taking place in an agrarian structure where there are relatively few "large" farmers. The agricultural development in this country is shouldered mainly by the small and medium farmers. Further, the bulk of agricultural producers are handicapped not only by the small size of land holdings but are also disadvantaged because of the widespread illiteracy, lack of infrastructure and neglect by an urban biased bureaucracy. There are very few examples in recent history where a large number of the small and medium farmers raised themselves virtually by their "shoe strings", and in the process turned a shortage economy to a surplus economy. However, this has not been accomplished without its cost. A number of original weaknesses in the sector persist and quite a few new hurdles have been introduced. It is also important now to understand whether the same policies and processes can continue to yield results without major improvements in the system.

Atleast four weaknesses plague Indian agriculture which need prior attention. Preponderance of low-value agriculture, low cost benefit ratio, inefficient use of natural resources and the deterioration in the self-help institutions. These can be identified as major factors inhibiting sustainable agricultural growth. To these is added the policy induced distortion caused by huge subsidies, to fertilizer, irrigation, electricity, credit and other agricultural inputs. Today agricultural subsidy bill accounts for nearly 80 per cent of the public expenditure on agriculture. Anomaly of this situation becomes apparent when we realise that the amount of subsidies on agricultural inputs is larger than the amount spent on agricultural development programmes.

The other distributing factor is the declining trend in capital formation. Over a period of time public capital formation is diminishing. In real terms (at 1980-81 prices), public investment in agriculture has come down perceptibly (from Rs. 17960 million in 1980-81 to Rs. 10650 million in 1992-

93). Private capital formation could not fill the gap. There is a strongly held view among Indian scholars that private investment in agriculture is complimentary to public investment. Actually the latter acts as an engine of growth. Importance of investment in agriculture can be very well appreciated in an agriculture where major reliance is to be placed on non-land factors of production.

III

NEW CHALLENGES

Since the beginning of the 1990s, Indian economy has entered in a new phase, of deregulation, liberalization, privatization and globalization. These policy changes have important implications for agriculture. There are three important directions in which reforms in agricultural sector have been initiated. In the first place, restriction on the movement of foodgrains from one region to other has been removed. An all-India market in agriculture products has emerged. Secondly, agricultural trade policy is liberalized, and exports are being encouraged. Indian agriculture is slowly but progressively getting integrated with global economy. Thirdly, far-reaching reforms have been introduced in the credit delivery system. At the same time important productive and supportive measures e.g., rural poverty alleviation programmes, agricultural price support policies, etc., have continued.

Indian agriculture has responded to these measures in a positive manner. Agricultural production has increased satisfactorily, and export performance, with a growth in agricultural exports by more than 15 per cent per annum, has met the expectations. However, there are persistent weaknesses in the sector which need to be attended to meet the emerging challenges.

There are several important areas which warrant immediate attention. In the first place, the pace of agricultural growth will have to be accelerated significantly to meet with the future requirements. On the basis of a careful study jointly conducted by the International Food Policy Research Institute (IFPRI) and the Indian Agricultural Research Institute (IARI), demand for cereals for the year 2020 has been estimated at about 293 million tonnes as against present supply of around 180 million tonnes. The IFPRI-IARI estimates are based on realistic, rather conservative assumptions. These projections assume an income growth of 5 per cent per year, a gradual decline in population growth with an average annual growth between 1995 and 2000 of just over 1.8 per cent, rate of urbanization is assumed at the recent historical trend, and inequality in distribution of expenditure across income groups the same as in 1987-88. The study concludes that unless a substantial step-up takes place in cereal production the gap between the demand and supply will continue to widen.

The situation is further complicated as the demand for non-cereal food, i.e., sugar, meat, dairy products, eggs, fruits and vegetables is likely to increase much faster, as the consumption pattern both in the rural and the urban areas is fast changing with higher weight being assigned to non-cereal food. For example, per capita sugar consumption has almost doubled from 1975 to 1990 (from 6.2 kg. to 12.5 kg.) per capita egg consumption has gone up from 16 to 26. Vegetable and fruit consumption is increasing at the rate of 5 per cent per year. These trends in the consumption of non-cereal food items are likely to continue in coming years. Non-cereal food products will also have a claim on the fixed and limited land surface; they will also claim other agricultural inputs that go in the cereal production. In fact, for producing the same amount of calories the non-cereal food products require higher levels of input use compared to cereals.

The increasing demands for agricultural products has to be viewed in the context of a situation which suggests that we might have reached a plateau in agricultural production. The accelerated pace in agricultural production witnessed during the "green revolution" period is petering out. An important development in the past years was that the supply of the foodgrains and other agricultural products was enhanced at lower costs in the real terms because of improved technologies. (However, no such trend was observed in coarse cereals as the technological change in the production of these crops had been limited). Momentum of decline in the real cost of production has been halted in the recent years. The total factor productivity (TFP) growth, or the growth in the amount of output generated by a unit of inputs, seems to be declining. A question is seriously debated whether Indian agriculture has become a high cost agriculture.

The agrarian structure in the country has not changed much. Over a period of time there is a slight tilt in favour of the small holdings. Therefore, in the ensuing period a substantial contribution to agricultural growth will have to come from the small and medium holdings. There is enough evidence to suggest that given an easy access to productive inputs the small farmers also produce as efficiently, in fact, more efficiently than the large farmers. However, the critical factor is the access to resources, and among these resources availability of timely credit on fair terms is of critical importance. The institutions of input delivery, particularly those for credit delivery, are not yet attuned to serve the small farmers.

There is the related problem of employment in the rural areas. It is quite clear that in foreseeable future we cannot expect a substantial withdrawal of labour force from farm to non-farm sectors. A very large number of existing households owning or cultivating small holdings will continue to be attached to the land for their livelihood as well as for employment. To improve their living as well as to enable them to cross the poverty line, which is one of the important objectives of our national economic policy, creation of such conditions that the income from these holdings improves satisfactorily should be given a priority. In order to achieve this objective, one approach is to improve TFP on these farms. But that will not suffice. In an exercise, in which I had also participated. (I am referring to the study titled "Agriculture Towards 2000 A.D.") it became clear that merely by improving yields of the existing crops a majority of the small, non-viable, agricultural households cannot be brought above the poverty line. For that it is necessary to introduce high value crops on these farms. Such a change in cropping pattern or enterprize-mix would entail even greater reliance on the modern inputs and, therefore, on credit.

Finally, a development which is as worrisome as the decline in TFP is the neglect and or misuse of the natural resources i.e., land, water and forests. As a matter of fact both these developments are inter-related. Degradation of natural resources leads to decline in TFP. And rejuvenation of natural resources could augment agricultural production and serve other objectives, such as employment generation. Soil conservation practices is one such example which strengthens production base and provide gainful employment. In the absence of knowledge of natural resource conservation (or in the absence of the practice of such knowledge), there is excessive exploitation of these resources which weakens the base of agricultural production. On the other hand, proper usages of some resources, say, water, would enable not only substantial economies in the input use, it would at the same time contribute to improved production. Introduction of many of these technologies pre-supposes organization of people around the watersheds or other micro farming systems. In some cases these technologies may require higher investment of capital, for example, the use of sprinklers or drip irrigation to conserve water. Agricultural growth in coming years will be more knowledge intensive and, in some areas, more capital intensive. We have to be prepared for these challenges.

IV

NEW DIRECTIONS

It is clear that if the present trends continue and corrective steps are not taken the gains which we have accumulated during the last 25 years or so will be dissipated. Certainly, we will not be able to avail of the new opportunities which are opening up. On the other hand, with proper attention to the critical areas I have pointed out we may emerge as one of the leading agricultural exporters in the world in next 20 to 25 years without jeopardising other objectives, of food security or poverty alleviation. The IFPRI-IARI projections have shown that depending on the achievements on the productivity front we may end up, by the year 2020, with a deficit of nearly 23 million tonnes in the cereals if the present trends continue, or a surplus of about 20 million tonnes if we are able to raise the productivity. Key to the increase in productivity is the generation of proper technologies and their extension on farms.

Such technological change has implications in terms of greater public investment in agriculture, including investment in human resources in agriculture. It is clear that we cannot continue the present regime of indiscriminate and growing subsidies if funds have to be diverted to capital formation in agriculture and for human resource development in the rural areas. In time to come role of private sector investment in rural infrastructure will become important but by no account the private investment will be able to substitute public capital formation in agriculture much less to finance investment in education, health and nutrition of the rural people. If large parts of the public funds continue to be diverted to subsidies there is little hope of reviving public investment in agriculture and rural areas and thus providing a lasting solution to our agricultural problems. The choice before the policy makers is difficult but clear.

Agricultural policies have in the recent years corrected the distortions in the inter-sectoral prices, and also provided a safety cushion to agricultural producers. This was done without jeopardising the interest of the poor consumers, mainly because price policies paid a complimentary role to R&D policies. Former was not assigned the driver's seat. The policy makers will have to continuously maintain the fine balance between the producers prices and the paying capacity of the bulk of the consumers in the country. This suggest that as in the past, more attention will have to be paid to the non-price factors, i.e. technological and organizational factors, for increasing agricultural production.

An equally important aspect of our agricultural growth is to ensure wellbeing of the millions of producers who constitute this sector. Eventually, a large number of small and marginal farmers will have to leave agriculture and go for non-agricultural occupations, as has happened in practically all developing countries. However, let this shift in occupation be through the "pull" factors rather than "push" factors. People with higher incomes, better access to resources and information may go in for non-farm occupations in the villages and in the nearby towns. Cultivators with smaller holdings may be provided opportunities to expand their holdings by activising the land and lease markets. The alternative of pushing people out of the land, especially those who are least prepared for such shift will not only be inhuman, it will also be counterproductive.

There are distinct possibilities of improving the incomes of a sizeable section of the small farmers who can be termed as "potentially viable". Technological research and input and output delivery systems should be addressed to assist this group, rather than to bye-pass them and concentrate on those who do not need any special considerations from the state to obtain income augmenting resources or to seize opportunities for profit making.

It should be remembered that the small holding size has not been an unsurroundable difficulty in several of our neighboring countries whose agricultural performance has been better than ours. If different components of Indian agricultural system i.e., research, extension, input delivery, marketing and above all credit, can adapt to the multitude of the small farmers, as has been the case in a number of the east and south east asian countries, we can confidently look forward to a situation where not only agricultural growth will be rapid, it will also be more equitable. The small farmer lead agricultural will also benefit non-farm activities in the rural areas with its more powerful "spread effect". One of the important programmes to encourage such pattern of growth is the Small Farmers Agro-Business Consortium (SFAC) programme which addresses the basic question of introducing high value agriculture on small farms.

Efforts are being made in a number of regions and by a variety of governmental and non-governmental agencies, including the banks, to organise producers in the country-side in small, homogeneous, self-help groups. More than the economic benefits which the farmers as recipient groups can obtain through such organizations, the spirit of self-reliance that these inculcates is of lasting value.

In one or the other way basic weaknesses of the agrarian structure and its supporting systems are being attended to in this country and measures are being undertaken to impart buoyancy to this sector. What is happening in India, rather in different parts of India, could be of interest to other developing countries who can avoid our mistakes and profit from several of our positive initiatives.

4

Mainsprings of Agricultural Growth in India

RAPID and sustained agricultural development in this country can take place only when all agricultural workers – cultivators and wage-paid labourers – can contribute to the production programmes. Since a vast majority of the cultivators are small and marginal farmers, the nature of technology, institutional change, and supportive systems have to be adopted to small farm agriculture.

Let us briefly review the performance of the Indian agriculture during the last 25 years, speculate on the magnitude of future demands, examine the strategies followed so far to augment production, look at the contribution of different groups of cultivators to the total production, and finally, suggest the need for broadening the production base of agriculture in this country.

I

PERFORMANCE OF THE INDIAN AGRICULTURE

The agricultural sector's performance can be assessed in various ways. One way, for example, can be to compare the

---

(Dr. Panse Memorial Lecture delivered at the Indian Institute of Agricultural Statistics, New Delhi in 1977).

domestic supplies with the demands made on agricultural production. Another way can be to examine the extent of actual utilization of the production potential in the sector. Return on scarce factors, say, land or capital, can also be used as a critical indicator. As the performance of the agriculture cannot be viewed in isolation, the impetus that the sector provides to economic activities in other sectors is, again, an important consideration.

It is not my intention to evaluate the performance of the agricultural sector on all these counts. The purpose is to clarify that a unidimensional measure, such as rate of growth, is not adequate to explain the various implications of the sector's growth. At the same time, the rate of growth in aggregate production can be taken as the starting point for an evaluation of the performance of the sector, and other measures can be subsequently introduced to complete the picture.

From 1949-50 to 1973-74, i.e. roughly for the period beginning with the Independence and spanning the first four Five-Year Plans, agricultural production increased at an annual rate of 2.7 per cent. This rate of growth, when juxtaposed with the increased demand from various sources i.e., demand for food, agricultural raw materials, and agricultural exports, was inadequate. For example, roughly during the same period (from 1952 to 1972) the demand for foodgrains increased at the rate of 3 per cent per annum while the foodgrains production increased at the rate of 2.4 per cent per annum. Demand and supply got adjusted at the market place, partly by the augmentation of foodgrains supplies by imports, and partly by a rise in prices which affected the consumption of these essential commodities among economically vulnerable sections.

A more disturbing feature of the agricultural scene was the deceleration in the growth of production, especially during the last decade or so. This was highlighted by the compound rate of growth of agricultural production in successive Five-Year Plans (Table 1).

TABLE – 1

All India Compound Rates of Growth of Agricultural Production, Area and Yield+*

(per cent per annum)

Period	*Agricultural production*	*Area under crops*	*Yield*
First Plan (1951-52 to 1955-56)	4.1	2.6	1.4
Second Plan (1956-57 to 1960-61)	3.1	1.3	1.8
Third Plan ** (1961-62 to 1964-65)	3.3	0.6	2.7
Fourth Plan (1969-70 to 1973-74)	2.2	0.8	1.0
1949-50 to 1973-74	2.7	1.1	1.3

* 1. Growth Rates in Agriculture, New Delhi, DES.
2. Fourth Five Year Plan, 1969-74.

** The Year 1965-66 has been excluded for purpose of calculating the growth rates due to its being an abnormal year.

+ Plan-wise growth rates have been calculated on the basis of triennial averages with the base and last year of each Plan as mid years except in the case of Third and Fourth Plans when instead of triennial periods the years 1964-65 and 1973-74 respectively were taken as end periods.

It is true that trend in production for a short period is heavily influenced by the performance in the terminal years and can be seriously distorted by large increases or decreases during one or few years within the reference period. Yet it is obvious that over the period of the four Five-Year Plans, the momentum in agricultural growth could not be sustained. In fact the reverse happened to be true. Much of the deceleration in growth was the result of declining contribution of area under crops, which the increase in yields failed to compensate.

The second disquieting feature was the extent of instability in agricultural production which, it seems, instead of declining was becoming more acute. This was clearly evident from the performance in the foodgrains sector. The National Commission on Agriculture (NCA) on the basis of a simple exercise, i.e. fitting trend lines to peak and trough points on the production (adjusted) of foodgrains from 1950-51 to 1960-61 and from 1960-61 to 1973-74, concluded that foodgrains production in the second period was more unstable than in the first period (NCA 1976).

Three facts emerge from this review of the performance of the agricultural sector in the last 25 years:

1. The overall rate of growth in agricultural production was slow in relation to the growing needs.
2. The rate of growth decelerated during the later part of the period.
3. The last half of the period was characterized by higher instability.

The decelerating trend in agricultural production has led to stagnation in agricultural incomes, even though the terms of trade have marginally shifted in favour of agriculture. This as will be noted below has a serious repercussion on the national economy. The main brunt, of course, is borne by the poor among the rural households.

There seems to be a direct relationship between the mean level of agricultural incomes and the extent of poverty in rural areas (Bhatty 1974). In an exercise based on NSS data, I had earlier concluded that in the 1950's, when agricultural growth was rather satisfactory, the poverty problem had eased, even though insubstantially (Vyas 1972). On the other hand, a number of studies on rural poverty concluded that in the 1960's, when agricultural production was sharply fluctuating around a more or less static trend, no dent could be made on the problem of rural poverty (Bardhan 1974, Minhas 1974). A few studies on agricultural wage determination showed that the wage incomes, on which the majority of rural poor depended, was closely correlated to the demand from and productivity of agricultural sector (Bardhan 1977).

Moreover, the labour market in agriculture behaved in a manner that the incidence of decelerating income was largely shifted to agricultural labour. Only in the areas of high agricultural growth, the real wages of agricultural labourers showed some improvement (Lal 1976).

An equally important consequence of a slow growth of incomes in agriculture, is tenuous links which persist between agricultural and non-agricultural sectors. These sectors can play mutually reinforcing roles if interrelationships are strong. Such relationships can be examined from several points of view. More important among these are: (a) production linkages, (b) consumption linkages, (c) saving, investment linkages, (d) employment linkages, and (e) linkages with the foreign sector. In a recent study, with which I had the privilege of being associated, I am referring to the Second Asian Agricultural Survey (AAS-II in brief), some of these relationships existing in the Asian economies were examined in detail.

I will briefly comment on the first two of these linkages, i.e., production linkages and consumption linkages. Adequate data are not available to meaningfully discuss saving, investment linkages and employment linkages. The importance of the linkages with the foreign sector in relation to total agricultural output, though crucial, is not overwhelming.

Linkages induced by input demand and those induced by output supply were examined by the AAS-II in four different ways:

1. A measure of the strength of the direct backward linkage caused by changes in the level of production within a sector, known as the "coefficient of backward linkage," and denoted symbolically as (U).
2. A corresponding measure of the strength of direct forward linkages between one sector and the rest of the economy, known as the "coefficient of forward linkage," and denoted as (W).
3. Another measure of the economy-wide impact of increased production within a sector, known as the "total linkage coefficient," which accounts both for direct linkages and for the indirect linkages induced via feedbacks and spillovers to other sectors not directly linked with the sector in which production initially increased; this index is denoted by (Y).
4. An index which measures the total of direct and spillover inducements to a particular sector (say agriculture) caused by changes in the levels of production in all of the other (non-agricultural) sectors. This measure is known as the "coefficient of total linkage receipt" and is denoted by (Z) (AAS-II, P. 112).

Let me summarize the results of the study (Table 2). The table clearly brings out the weak inter-sectoral production linkages though agricultural processing activity is an exception.

The same holds true for consumption linkages. Given the low levels of incomes, it is not surprising that the rural poor in our country, spend a large part of their incomes on foodgrains and a very small part on non-food goods and services. The most disturbing factor emerging from the data is that this expenditure pattern has not improved over time (Table 3).

TABLE – 2

Relative Strength of Intersectoral Linkage Co-efficients (Based Upon Standardized Average Rankings Within Broad Sectoral Categories)

India (1973-74)	*Coefficient and Relative Strength*			
	U	*W*	*Y*	*Z*
Foodcrops[a]	W	M	W	MS
Industrial Crops, Animal Husbandary[b]	W	M	W	MS
Agricultural Processing				
1. Foods[c]	S	MW	S	MW
2. Industrial Crops, Animal Products[d]	S	MW	MS	MW

a includes foodgrains, other agriculture.
b includes animal husbandry, plantations.
c includes sugar and gur, vegetable oil, other food products.
d includes Tea and Coffee, Cotton Textiles, Jute Textiles, Leather Products, Rubber Products.

Notes: U = Coefficient of Direct Backward Linkage
W = Coefficient of Direct Forward Linkage
Y = Total Linkage Coefficient
Z = Coefficient of Total Linkage Receipt Inside of Table
S = Strong
MS = Medium strong
M = Medium
W = Weak

TABLE – 3

Percentage Distribution of Average Total Consumption Expenditures for Food Items, Non-Food Items, Services etc. in Rural Areas

	Time Early	*Mid*	*Period Late*	*Early*
	1960s	*1960s*	*1960s*	*1970s*
Food Items	-	74.0	-	73.6
Non-Food Items[a] Services, etc.[b]	-	26.0	-	26.4

a Non-food items include liquor, tobacco, fuel, electricity, clothing, shelter, household furniture and equipment.
b Services include health, education, recreation and transportation.

The reasons for the lack of interactions are also not far to seek.

The high yielding varieties programme, which did affect agricultural incomes in a measurable way, could not cover more than 27.6 per cent of the total cropped area under principal cereals, i.e., less than one-fifth of the gross cropped area in the country. In certain other crops, returns did improve either due to increase in productivity or due to a favourable price situation. But for none of the principal crops was the impact on incomes comparable to, say, that registered in areas growing high yielding varieties of wheat. As incomes of the farm labourers as well as the wage component of the incomes of the small and marginal farmers depended on the prosperity of agriculture more than on any other factor, agricultural incomes remained depressed in large parts of the country. Even in the areas affected by the new varieties programme or by other income augmenting measures, the share of additional incomes going to wages remained relatively low. The net result was that, in real terms, the agricultural incomes over a large part of the country and the wage incomes over practically the whole of the country did not rise significantly. Thus the basic element ensuring larger interaction between different sectors, viz., a strong cash nexus, was missing and in its absence agricultural non-agricultural interaction remained by and large, passive.

II

FUTURE DEMANDS ON AGRICULTURE

If the progress during the last two decades can be considered as not very satisfactory, prospects for coming years are all the more daunting. Nature and magnitude of pressures on agriculture will make the tasks before the sector more difficult. The more important tasks in the future will be to:

1. Increase domestic supply of foodgrains to meet the rising demands.
2. Provide adequate jobs for a growing work force in rural areas.
3. Enlarge contribution of agriculture in earning and/or saving foreign exchange.

In the study (AAS-II) that I referred to earlier, we tried to assess the production potential which various economies of the region including India could possibly reach by 1985. A Model of Agricultural Demand Supply, and Employment and Trade Systems, better known by its acronym ADSETS, was prepared. A series of variants were run for each country of the region to test the sensitivity of projections to different assumptions about key economic variables.

I will briefly report on the results obtained from two of these variants.

Variant A, the "High" growth situation, presents feasible increases in cropped area and yields within a period of 10 years or so. These are not merely the extrapolation of past trends, but imply, "substantial efforts to apply available knowledge, mobilizing resources, overcome institutional obstacles and appropriately adjust domestic policies". These projections will fructify if the production conditions, by past criteria, turn out to be "exceptionally good".

The second variant, Variant B, the "Low" growth situation, postulates the "average" conditions while projecting supplies, and more or less approximate to the extrapolation of the past trends.

Both these projections pertain to the period 1975-85. For India, Variant A suggests a rate of growth of 3.9 per cent per annum, and Variant B a rate of growth of 2.8 per cent per annum in agricultural production. It is easy to relate these two projections to the demands which are likely to be placed in coming few years on agricultural sector.

Let us underline the implications of these growth rates in agriculture for the Gross Domestic Product. ADSETS calculated elasticity of GDP for agricultural production at 1.32. Thus, a growth rate of 3.9 per cent per annum in agricultural production will mean a growth of 5.1 per cent in GDP, while the lower variant growth of 2.8 per cent per annum will mean growth of GDP at the rate of 3.7 per cent per annum. With a projected population growth of 2.3 per cent per annum, the high and low variants will mean all the difference between a continuing precarious existence and the prospects of slightly more comfortable living for the masses.

The implications of these growth rates come out more sharply in the three related concerns to which I made a reference earlier. Coming to the demand for foodgrain in the first instance, with 2.3 per cent per annum rate of growth in population the estimated requirements for foodgrains due to population growth alone will be 128 million tonnes by 1985. But this will mean perpetuation of low level of cereal intake, which in the absence of other sources of energy means a low caloric diet. If the diets of the projected population has to reach the nutritionally satisfactory levels, the foodgrain requirements will be 140 million tonnes. With the achievement of high agricultural growth situation, namely, Variant A, domestic production will only be marginally below domestic requirements, i.e., a deficit of 2.9 million tonnes, at the end of the period (1985). However, if the current trends in supplies continue, i.e., the rate of growth is around 2.8 per cent per annum, the gap between the requirement and availability will be 12.5 million tonnes.

The agricultural growth does not relate merely to the demand for foodgrains. It has significant repercussions on the employment situation as well. The ILO has estimated that India's labour force will grow from 1975 to 1985 at the rate of 2.2 per cent. This mean's that 47 million new entrants will be available in the labour market during that period. I have shown elsewhere that a very large bulk of these, nearly two-thirds, have to be absorbed in agriculture itself (Vyas 1970). We do not have reliable studies of labour absorption in agriculture under different technologies. However, in other developing countries of this region, it has been found that employment-output elasticity in agriculture is roughly 0.5 (AAS-II). (Incidentally, it should be noted that in these economies agriculture is more labour intensive than in India.) Thus, even with the high growth situation, additional labour force in the country-side will be barely absorbed in productive occupations; with low growth situation slightly more than half of the additional labour force will be gainfully employed in agriculture. When the "residuals" are translated into actual number of people for whom additional jobs have to be provided in the non-agricultural sectors and are related to the past performance in employment creation in these sectors, grimness of the situation becomes obvious.

The projected foreign exchange needs of the Indian economy suggest that the past growth rates in exports have to be considerably increased to earn adequate foreign exchange. As in the past, in coming years also agriculture will play a crucial role in foreign exchange earning (or savings). With high agricultural growth situation, agricultural exports, which are at present 1.08 times cereal imports, can rise to 1.27 times cereal imports. If the postulated rate of growth is not achieved and instead of high growth situation the low growth situation prevails, agricultural exports will barely be able to finance 30 per cent of the necessary cereal imports. This obviously is not a tenable situation.

There are of course pitfalls of such aggregative models. But the lessons that ADSETS has thrown up should not be lost. It is clear that the minimum rate of growth in agricultural production for the next decade, which will be consistent with a desirable rate of growth in per capita incomes, domestic food supply, employment, and exports, will be 3.9 per cent per annum. An achievement lower than the one indicated by this figure will exacerbate existing difficulties to unmanageable proportions.

To achieve a rate of growth postulated in high variant, though not impossible, is certainly not an easy task. It is true that in the early fifties we achieved a rate of growth approximating to this figure but then the bulk of increases came from the expansion in cropped area. Once the possibility of area expansion (barring that from multiple cropping) is discounted and the major reliance is placed on the growth in productivity, it will be clear that the rate of growth in productivity will have to be more than doubled. Be that as it may, while there is room for manoeuvring in setting targets for different sectors, the target for agricultural production in the coming years is more or less given. The rate of growth in agriculture has to be postulated at around 4.0 per cent per annum and other planning exercises have to begin by taking this as a base.

III

STRATEGIES ATTEMPTED SO FAR

Can we raise a significantly large production from the same land surface? This is the most pertinent issue. Many eminent Indian and foreign scholars have looked at the sector's performance and have pointed out important lacuna in agricultural planning and implementation of agricultural programmes. Much can be learnt from these analyses. However, a puzzling factor in the Indian situation is that virtually every measure one could suggest for revitalizing agriculture, has been tried out on a small or a large scale at one point of time or another.

Within the socio-political framework where not only market forces favour the rich but even the action of the state benefits those with wherewithals, the best one can hope for is that the effect of growth will trickle down to other sections of the society. With this "percolation effect" syndrome it is difficult to find a new initiative or a radically different thrust, either in technology or in institutional change or in the organisation of supportive services.

Whatever has been done so far, in aggregative terms, is not insubstantial. An extensive infrastructure for supporting agricultural production has already come into existence. We have, for example, a very large and competent research establishment. The country has an extension system whose size is unmatched by any similar system in the world. Supportive services in marketing and credit are being progressively streamlined and extended. Several land reform measures, which purport to affect relationship in land in a revolutionary way, have been enacted. Nor can one find much fault with the prices and investment policies. By and large, the agricultural producer has been fairly treated in regard to the product prices once the paying capacity of the consumer is also taken into consideration. Similarly, in spite of certain lack of emphasis for brief periods, e.g., during few years covered by the Second Five-Year Plan, the state's concern for agricultural growth as reflected in agriculture's share in the total public outlay has remained quite substantial. Differences of opinion can exist on the extent of support needed for an action or a programme, but it will be difficult, more so after Dantwala's persuasive writings on this subject (Dantwala 1976), to establish that in aggregative measures – legislative, fiscal, or organizational – agriculture as an economic activity has been neglected.

Inspite of the contrary impression in certain sections, the fact is that in all plan periods, the package of technological change, public outlay, institutional reforms, and organizational innovations – all aimed at imparting vigour to this sector – continuously found an important place. The First Five-Year Plan not only boosted irrigation but also introduced a series of land reform measures to eliminate functionless intermediaries. During the Second Five-Year Plan agricultural programmes coincided with the reorganization of the cooperative movement and a radical land reform measure like "land-to-the-tiller". The Third Five-Year Plan period can be remembered as much for the Intensive Agricultural District Programme experiment as for ushering in the Panchayati Raj. During the Fourth Five-Year Plan not only wheat revolution was ushered in through the High Yielding Varieties Programme, but several states in the country enacted more stringent ceiling legislation. The emphasis on one or the other programme during a particular year or two could have been influenced by fluctuations in agricultural production – periods of euphoria and alarm have alternated quite frequently in the policy making circles – but if one were to look into successive quinquenniums, it can be concluded that all the major elements of an agricultural strategy exist in our plans right from their inception. It is futile, therefore, to search for an answer in terms of neglect of the sector as a whole or indifference towards major variables, such as technology or institutional change. This is the situation as far as planning is concerned.

At the same time, inclusion of all desirable elements in the plans does not necessarily imply the same seriousness in their execution. The most glaring lacuna in implementation is the lack of coordination among various measures. Different programmes are implemented more or less in a parallel fashion. For example, at no stage was a conscious effort made to bring the supportive systems of credit and marketing in line with the institutional reform, or to relate the public outlay with the desired direction in supportive systems, or to adapt the research systems to the emerging socio-economic realities.

It is also true that even while pursuing a programme policy makers and administrators in most instances stopped short of taking hard decisions, and thus several measures remained as mere symbolic gestures. One can cite several such measures to illustrate the lack of courage in executing them. Any effort to vitalize agriculture must resolve the problems of synchronization and administration.

IV

CONTRIBUTION OF DIFFERENT GROUPS OF CULTIVATORS

Mere streamlining of the existing measures, or shifting relative emphasis among different programmes, or allocating larger resources for different activities will not provide the answer. This is so because while engaged in all these manipulations we are still neglecting the mainsprings of agricultural growth. To my mind, the mainspring of agricultural growth consists of the whole multitude of men and women who form this sector, and only a few among them, today, are partners in the growth process.

This realization dawned on me when I started looking at the share of different groups of farmers in total agricultural production. The exercise was confined to foodgrains production and was admittedly based on a crude methodology. The method employed was to take the area under foodgrains in each size group of holdings in 15 states which accounted for 97 per cent of the total area under foodgrains in 1970-71. The average yield for the foodgrains for the state as a whole was applied to the foodgrains area in each size groups of holding. A computer programme was devised to identify the minimum number of farmers who could supply different proportions of the total output. The exercise had two limitations. It assumed that (a) the composition of different grains in different size groups was the same and (b) the yields on different holdings were the same. For a more realistic understanding, both these assumptions will have to be relaxed. But in this exercise, since the effort was to arrive at a broad order of magnitudes, the above listed assumptions, hopefully, did not vitiate the results.

TABLE – 4

*Share in Total Foodgrains Production Accounted by Cumulative Percentages of Holdings**

Cumulative percentage of total foodgrains production	*Cumulative percentage of holdings*
25	0.72
50	7.40
75	24.30
90	49.90

* Relates to production in fifteen states accounting for 97 per cent of the total foodgrains production of the country in 1970-71.

N.B. : See text for methodology.

It is evident from Table 4 that out of 68 million holdings in the country less than one per cent of holdings account for 25 per cent of the foodgrains production. About 90 per cent of total foodgrains production comes from less than 50 per cent of the holdings. The remaining 50 per cent of the holdings in the country are by and large redundant from the production point of view. Naturally they do not attract serious attention when various agencies, which provide support to agricultural growth, search for a clientele. In other words, these producers are marginal to the production system.

It can well be argued that if the bulk of the production is accounted for by a relatively small number of larger farmers, what is wrong in concentrating efforts on them? This line of argument is not tenable on two grounds. First, it assumes that there is enough "slack" on the large farms and that there is no "slack" on the marginal farms. There is no evidence to support this claim. On the other hand, the available evidence suggests that in terms of quality of land, extent of irrigation and, of course, availability of labour small farms have an edge, which with necessary complementary inputs may be easy to exploit. The factors which they lack are in the nature of "working capital". But more importantly, concentrated attention on the large farms will not generate adequate purchasing power among the left-out sections, and this lack of purchasing power itself will act as a bind on the expansion of the market for additional production.

There is another reason why it has become more urgent than ever before to bring the small and marginal cultivators on to the centre of the stage. Over a period of time due to various factors – market induced, institutional, but more importantly, demographic, the proportion of small and marginal farmers is increasing and Indian agriculture is progressively acquiring not only a small farmer but also a small farm complexion. The results of two NSS surveys, one pertaining to 1961-62 (17th round) and the other pertaining to 1970-71 (26th round), corroborate this statement.

In brief, the comparison between the two surveys revealed the following:

(i) The number as well as proportion of households in

the marginal holding group have significantly increased.

(ii) Acreage under marginal holdings has slightly declined.

(iii) The number of small land owners has increased, but their importance in terms of proportion of total number of land owners has marginally declined.

(iv) Area under small holdings has increased both in acreage as well as in proportion to the total owned area in the country.

(v) In numbers, total area and per household area, medium sized holdings displayed trends more or less similar to small sized holdings.

(vi) The number as well as proportion of big and large holdings have declined.

(vii) Acreage under big and large holdings has declined both in absolute terms and as proportion of total acreage (Vyas 1977).

Given the present social and political milieu, it may be possible to stop the erosion of holdings of the small and marginal farmers, but it will not be possible to stop the division of large holdings and their further expansion is out of question. It is imperative, therefore, to adjust existing institutions, technologies, and supportive agencies to the needs of a small farm agriculture. And this has to be done without sacrificing the growth target of 4 per cent increase in agricultural production per year, which, as suggested earlier, is the irreducible minimum for ensuring adequate food supplies, employment, and export surplus from agriculture.

V

BROADENING THE PRODUCTION BASE

There is a wide spread feeling that an emphasis on small farms may be justified on egalitarian grounds but cannot be defended on grounds of production efficiency. In fact, measures to assist small farmers are cited as perfect examples of trade-off between growth and justice. In countries like ours, where a precarious balance exists between demand and supply of agricultural commodities, policy makers are naturally cautious on such matters. They are even more cautious when the need to accelerate the growth rates of agricultural production is emphasised.

It is true that with the constraints imposed by imperfections in factor and product markets, absence of appropriate technology, and lack of supportive systems attuned to small farms' requirements, the small farmers cannot contribute to production efforts in a meaningful way. But none of these constraints is insurmountable. Many of these constraints can be relaxed through appropriate social interventions.

An important question which needs to be answered at the outset is how small a viable small farm can be. The institutional and market induced constrains broadly define the minimum size of a viable holding. However, the available technology and supply institutions do play an important part. With the present technology, cultivators with tiny holdings cannot obtain their subsistence from cultivation alone. In their case, there is a need to ensure fuller wage-paid employment. For the planned development in a country like ours, programmes for land reform, fuller employment and enhancing production capability on small farms are not mutually exclusive. There is, however, a large number of farms which are today considered to be non-viable, say, holdings between one to five acres. They constitute one-third of the total number of holdings. These holdings can be brought into the mainstream of production. Even in their case, supplementary occupations, like dairying, poultry, or piggery, may be necessary. This means that a small farm oriented growth strategy should examine the problems of complementarity much more carefully. Physical and social scientists will have to address themselves to the task of evolving agricultural-cum-supplementary occupation systems for different micro environments.

In crop production also the picture is not as discouraging as it looks at the first sight. In many of the South-East Asian countries, a man with a one-hectare holding can make a decent living from its produce, and a man with a two-hectare holding has surpluses for reinvestment. I do not, however, like to leave the impression that in these countries all the problems connected with small farms have been solved. The situation is far from it. But we can certainly learn some lessons from these countries about a small farm agriculture.

In the Indian context, one can list some basic handicaps which prevent small farmers from contributing to the production in a meaningful way. The principal handicaps are as follows:

1. The small farmers and the small industrial entrepreneurs face input and output prices which do not truly reflect their relative scarcities. State should correct these distortions through taxes, subsidies, and interest rate policies. Since these price distortions are not specific to agriculture but pervade the whole economy, the scope of state intervention will have to be much wider and will have to include a reassessment and corrections in the tariffs and other protection devices.

2. Because of the small farmers' inability to bear risk,

there is a sub-optimal use of production factors on small farms. Strategies which reduce risk and uncertainty will help small farmers in mobilizing and more efficiently utilizing resources on farms. Appropriate technology and input and output price policies will form important elements of such a strategy. Certain organizational forms which can help in socialization of risks also fall in this category.

3. The monopolistic control over some of the scarce inputs and easier access to useful information give an edge to the large farmers vis-a-vis the small farmers. Financial institutions and the extension machinery – as they function today – instead of restoring the balance, tilt the scales in favour of haves. Correction of such distortions in input markets, particularly the credit, and output markets and dissemination of right type of information among small farmers is another priority area.

4. In several parts of the country, landlords continue to perform the "trinity" role by controlling employment, credit, and product markets. Small farmers' dependence on large farmers in all these markets creates semi-feudal conditions. Under these conditions it is perhaps a "rational" decision on the part of the large farmers to restrain productive efforts on the small farms. These relationships have been overthrown or at least considerably weakened in areas where a neutral technology with the promise of measurable gains in productivity is available, as it happened in case of HYV wheat areas. But when the main thrusts of technology are towards only small though steady gains – and this seems to be present direction – it becomes difficult to break the semi-feudal stranglehold. State

intervention in such situations should start with the recognition of the interdependence of these markets. The emphasis, however, should be on provision of adequate supplementary employment which, more than anything else, will enhance the small farmers' bargaining power.

5. Should the public agencies like credit or marketing agencies decide to work with the small farmers, the sheer large number of such farmers acts against them. A consolidation of decision making units in one form or another is necessary to facilitate public programmes for small farmers. The need for the organization of the disadvantaged section is felt on other grounds also. Problems of development cannot be divorced from the problem of sharing power. Only by organizing themselves, the have-nots can prevent diversion of goods and services which are their due. But the experience so far suggests that universalistic institutions like panchayats or cooperatives have failed to emerge as spokesman for the small farmers. Nor have the trade union type of organizations made much headway. New forms of organizations have to be devised to take advantage of group action without stifling individual initiative.

All these are obviously difficult tasks. But then hardly any soft options are left.

Development in agriculture, as development in other fields, is not accomplished by inputs or organization; it is accomplished by the individual decision makers. The mainsprings or agricultural growth are the men and women toiling in the fields. The material inputs, technologies, and organizations are there to support them. Social scientists and physical scientists together with policy makers and administrators can play a significant role in devising and implementing a system which brings the bulk of workers in the agricultural sector into the mainstream instead of keeping them at the margin as at present.

5

Changing Contours of Indian Agriculture

THE move towards "open frontiers" implicit in the policies of liberalisation and globalization will undoubtedly affect the product mix and the input composition in agriculture sector in a significant way. Naturally the impact will vary from region to region, and will differ from one section of agricultural producers to other. Various implications of new economic policies for agriculture have been examined by the scholars and policy makers (Gulati and Sharma 1990; Alagh 1994; Krishnaswami 1995; Vyas 1996; Desai 1997). However, important developments taking place within agriculture sector have gone largely unnoticed. Significant changes are taking place in the rate of growth and composition of agriculture sector, in the structure of agricultural holdings and access to land, in the use of land and water, in input structure, in the quantum and the terms of credit, in cropping pattern and, in the domestic and international markets. In all these respects Indian agriculture has undergone substantial transformation during last few years.

In this paper we will discuss some of these changes, look into the causative factors and indicate the implications for the

(Lecture delivered in the Golden Jubilee Lecture Series of the National Council of Applied Economic Research, New Delhi in 2000).

sector as well as for the economy. Period covered is the last 25 years or so, roughly from the early 1970s to the mid 1990s. Our main focus is on the domestic aspects of agricultural development i.e. developments within the sector and within the economy.[1] The changes observed in five important aspects of agricultural structure and growth are discussed and explanation for the particular developments are provided. The aspects covered are: growth and composition of agricultural sector; changes in agrarian structure and access to land; changes in the production base; changes in input structure; and, extent and nature of crop diversification. In the last concluding section we underline the major trends and indicate directions for future development.

I

Growth of Agriculture Sector

The decade of 1980s witnessed a faster rate of growth in agricultural output compared to the decade of the 1970s. Compound Annual Rate of Growth in the 1980s was 3.7 per cent, it was 2.0 per cent in the 1970s (CMIE, 1996). Rate of growth in agriculture has slackened in the last few years.

With economic growth importance of agriculture declines in terms of its contribution to GDP. In India too share of agriculture in GDP has progressively declined. At constant (1981-82) prices it was close to 45 per cent in 1970-71 and came down to 26 per cent in 1995-96 (Table 1). There was a sharper fall in more recent years in the share of agriculture in GDP, from nearly 31 per cent (in constant prices) in 1990-91 to 26 per cent in 1995-96. Share of agriculture in GDP

---

1. I have examined the developments in the external trade in agriculture in my presidential address to the XIIth Conference of the Indian Society of Agricultural Marketing, under the title *Agricultural Trade Policy and Export Strategy*, (Vyas, 1998).

however, does not reflect adequately the role agricultural growth has played, and will continue to play, in Indian economy. The work of several scholars (Haggblade, *et al* 1991, Hazell and Haggblade 1990, Bhalla *et al* 1990) have shown that agricultural growth has strong "spill over" effect on the economy.

TABLE – 1

Share of Agriculture, Forestry & Fishing in GDP (at 1980-81 prices)

Years	*Agriculture GDP (Rs. Crores)*	*Share in GDP (Per cent)*	*Share of Crop and Livestock Income in Agriculture GDP (Per cent)*	*Share of Fishery in Agriculture Sector (Per cent)*	*Share of Forestry in Agriculture Sector (Per cent)*
1970-71	40214	44.47	89.35	1.74	8.91
1980-81	46649	38.10	91.03	1.97	6.99
1990-91	65653	30.93	92.90	2.73	4.73
1995-96	71907	26.04	93.06	3.07	3.87

Source: CMIE, *Income Statistics*, November 1998.

The contribution of agriculture to the growth of the non-agricultural sector, and *vice versa*, is determined by the strength of their linkages. In an earlier exercise my colleagues and I estimated the strength of linkages of agriculture in the Asian economies including India. These linkages were defined in terms of Forward Linkages, Backward Linkages, Demand Linkages, Employment Linkages etc. (Asian Development Bank, ADB, 1977). Importance of various linkages varies over of time. For example, contribution of agriculture to economic growth in terms of capital transfer may decline, but the sector's contribution through backward linkages, i.e. due to higher share of non agricultural inputs in the input structure, gets progressively strengthened. (Gandhi, 1996). The ADB study quoted above also found that the overall linkages were weak in the relatively poorer countries of Asia, (e.g., India) and relatively stronger in the richer countries of the continent (e.g., South Korea). Similar finding were obtained in the recent studies on agricultural growth in India i.e., the multiplier effect of agricultural growth is higher in the developed states, e.g. Punjab, Haryana etc. (Hazell and Haggblade 1990). This is mainly because of well developed infrastructure in these states which facilitates 'spill-over' effects. Implication of this finding is far reaching: as the infrastructure development takes place in other regions of the country, the linkages between agriculture and non-agriculture sectors will be further strengthened.

Most important impact of agricultural growth in our country is in terms of poverty alleviation. In his celebrated study Ahluwalia drew attention to this linkage in the late seventies (Ahluwalia, 1978). In a more recent and a more rigorous exercise Datt and Ravallion (1997) have shown the importance of agricultural growth to the poor, due to (a) containment of the real prices of foodgrains on which the poor spend a large portion of their income and, (b) contribution to employment growth, as agriculture is more labour intensive occupation. They also find that eventual impact of agricultural growth on poverty is even more significant than the initial impact.

Indian economy will not be as dependent on agriculture as in the past – when Indian Budget was characterised as "a gamble in the monsoon" – yet for a foreseeable future agricultural growth will be of critical importance to the overall growth of the economy, and more so for the poorer sections of society.

Composition of Agricultural Sector

An important aspect of the change in Indian Agriculture is the growing importance of the non-crop sectors, commonly known as sub-sectors or ancilliary sectors. For example, the share of livestock products in gross value of agricultural product (i.e. crop production *plus* livestock raising) is progressively increasing. In 1970-71, it was less than 16 per cent, by 1995-96 it has increased to 26 per cent. Same is true of the share of fisheries in agricultural GDP, which has increased from 1.7 per cent to 3.1 per cent during 1970-71 to 1995-96. This, unfortunately, is not true of forestry, where the share of the sub-sector has actually declined from 9 per cent in 1970-71 to 4 per cent in 1995-96 (See Table 1 and 2). These changes in the composition of agricultural sector, i.e., growing importance of the sub-sectors, have significant implications for income and employment of the households depending on agriculture.

TABLE – 2

Share of Income from Livestock in Total Value of Agricultural Output

Year	*Value of Output (Rs. in Crores)*		*Total*	*Income from Livestock as % of*
	Agriculture	*Livestock*		*Total Agricultural Income*
1970-71	17306	3197	20503	15.59
1980-81	46278	10597	56875	18.63
1990-91	128657	42041	170698	24.63
1995-96	217840	76580	294420	26.01

Source: CMIE, *India's Agricultural Sector*, July 1996.
CMIE, *Monthly Review of Indian Economy*, April 1998.

The main engine of growth for the sub-sectors such as livestock, poultry and fishery, was the increase in income and consequent changes in the dietary pattern.[2] The state policies

2. Dietary changes in India are much slower than in other neighbouring countries. For example, share of animal products in the dietary composition in India increased slowly from 5 per cent of the total calorie intake in 1980 to 7 per cent in 1990 (FAO, *Production Year Book*, 1994). However, because of the large population on the one hand and small, initial, share of the subsectors on the other, even marginal change in dietary pattern makes a large impact on these activities.

aimed at encouraging these activities also helped. Other important contributing factor was the role of the producers organisations, which imparted collective strength to the small producers and contributed positively to the growth of these sub-sectors. This is particularly true of the dairying and poultry. In fishery sector also the cooperatives and the unions of small artisan fishermen played an important role. These sub-sectors also attracted private enterprises, including some multi-national companies.

Relative decline in the importance of forestry has serious implications for the public revenue, on the income of the households dependent on forestry and, more importantly, on the ecology of the affected regions. The declining importance of forestry in the agriculture GDP was mainly due to the stagnation in the area under forests. It was also due to the failure of public policies. The main policy thrust in this sector was to encourage fuelwood and fodder raising on the private land and using forest lands for growing trees for industrial and timber needs. Both components of policy did not succeed (Saxena, 1997). The individual producers as much as the state were losers due to shortfall in both the segments of forestry.

Livestock sector has registered an impressive growth rate of nearly 7 per cent (6.69) per year from 1980-81 to 1990-91. Milk accounts for two third of the total produce of the livestock sector. India is the second largest producer of milk in the world. Its cost of production compares favourably with the cost of production of other important milk producing countries, with the exception of New Zealand. Even though there is progressive commercialisation of livestock industry, it has remained, basically, small scale, supplementary activity to crop production. The small farmers seem to have benefitted from the growth of livestock sector as much as the large farmers.

Fishery, on the other hand provides more or less full time employment to nearly 4 million (3.84 m.) fisherman (in 1991). The share of fishery in agricultural GDP has almost doubled, from 1.97 per cent in 1980-81 to 3.7 per cent in 1995-96. Momentum has accelerated in more recent years. Fish production has increased by 6.6 per cent per year during the period 1985-86 to 1992-93. The growth in inland fishery was even higher, at 6.5 per cent per annum. India now occupies second position, next to China, in inland fish production. Although some large scale operators, including MNCs, have entered in this field fishery remains basically a small scale operation and its growth has benefitted the small man in the rural areas.

Work Force in Agriculture

Another aspect of the structural change in agriculture is the slow decline in the proportion of workers dependent on agriculture. While the decline in the share of agriculture in GDP of the country was quite marked, the share of the workforce dependent on primary sector, in which agriculture accounts for 95 to 97 per cent of workforce, has declined only marginally from 67.6 per cent in 1971 to 64.9 per cent in 1991. In absolute terms the number of agricultural workers increased substantially, from 122.2 million in 1971 to 188.9 million in 1991 (Table 3). There is a general stickiness in the exit of the workforce from agriculture the world over, but in case of India divergence in the movement of agricultural income and agricultural workforce is widening. It is clear that employment opportunities in non-agricultural sectors were not expanding commensurate to the increase in the work force. As a result a large number of workers earning low incomes are trapped in agriculture.

TABLE – 3

Distribution of Workforce (main workers) from 1971 to 1991

(Population in Millions)

Year	*Total Population*	*Total Work-force*	*Primary Sector*	*Agriculture (Cultivators and Agri-cultural Labourers)*	*Workers in Primary Sector as % of Total no. of Workers*	*Workers in Agriculture as % of Total no. of Workers*
1971	5480	1807	131.2	122.2	72.61	67.6
1981	6830	2207	153.1	146.9	69.37	66.6
1991	8460	2789	187.9	188.9	67.37	64.9

Source: CMIE, *India's Social Sectors,* February, 1996.

II

CHANGES IN THE ACCESS TO LAND

Agrarian Structure

Significant changes have taken place in the agrarian structure in the country as indicated by the changes in the pattern of land holdings. Strictly speaking, agrarian structure connotes more than the pattern of land holdings. During the course of development land as an input in agricultural production declines in importance and the non-land inputs acquire greater importance. In our country also this process, though slow, is quite evident. The difference between the developed countries and a developing country like India is that in our case the ownership and access to land determine to a large extent, the access to other non-land factors (particularly, credit) as well. In this respect land continues to play a pivotal role in agrarian societies such as ours.

It should be recognized, however, that even in such societies comparison of agrarian structure between different regions based on land holding pattern could be misleading because of significant differences in the quality of land from one region to other. Obviously, a hectare of land in Kerala is not equivalent to a hectare of land in Rajasthan. This handicap is relatively less serious when emphasis is more on inter-temporal comparison rather than on cross-sectional comparison. As we are interested in the former rather than the latter, changes in the pattern of land holdings, and rights in land, over time can be taken as indicative of the changes in agrarian structure.

Information on land holding pattern for the country as a whole and for various states is obtainable from two major sources: various rounds of National Sample Survey, and the quinquinnial Agricultural Censuses. The latest NSS round relevant for our purpose pertains to the year 1992. It gives information on ownership of land, but not on the operational holdings. On the other hand, latest Agricultural Census for the 1990-91 gives information on Operational Holdings but not on the ownership pattern. Unfortunately both are not strictly comparable (Sanyal, 1976). Between the two sources NSS is more reliable. We have used NSS data for examining the changes in the land holding pattern, but have supplemented our discussion on operational holdings by referring to the findings of Agricultural Census. For the present discussion we are using the categories holdings defined by the NSS rounds and the Agricultural Census, viz; Marginal farmers are those owning (or operating) areas between .01 to 2.49 acres, small between 2.5 to 4.99 acres, semi-medium between 5.00 to 9.99 acres, medium between 10.00 to 24.99 acres, and large owning (operating) 25 acres and above.

An examination of the relevant data on land holding pattern (Table 4, Table 5 and Table 6) suggest following major conclusions.

TABLE – 4

Size Distribution of Ownership Households

(In Percentage)

S. No.	*Size-Class (Acre)*	*Ownership Households 1971-72*	*1982-83*	*1992-93*
1.	Landless (00.00)	9.64	11.33	11.25
2.	Marginal (.01-2.49)	52.97	55.31	60.60
3.	Small (2.5-4.99)	15.49	14.70	13.40
4.	Semi-Medium (5.00-9.99)	11.94	10.78	9.30
5.	Medium (10.00-24.99)	7.83	6.45	4.50
6.	Large (25 & above)	2.12	1.43	0.88
7.	All Sizes	100.00	100.00	100.00

Source: N.S.S. various rounds.

a) An important feature of the overall change in the agrarian structure during the last few decades is that the trend towards landlessness has been arrested. The proportion of households depending on agriculture who do not own land, i.e., landless agricultural workers and the landless tenants (or pure tenants) stabilized around 11 per cent of the agricultural households in the decades of the eighties and nineties. Agricultural labourers households dominate this group; the proportion of the landless tenants (i.e. pure tenants) is small and, as we will see later, declining.

Although the proportion of landless agricultural labour households has declined for the country as a whole, the picture differs from state to state. For example, in 1971-72 Assam, Tamil Nadu and Kerala and the highest proportion of landless agricultural labour households. The 1982-83 data reveal that while Kerala and Assam dropped out from this list, the landless households increased significantly in Maharashtra and Gujarat. The same ranking continued in 1992, i.e., Maharashtra, Gujarat and Tamil Nadu were the three top states in this regard. It seems that landlessness is prevalent to a higher degree in industrially more developed states.

Above mentioned facts on landless agricultural labourers do not represent the extent of landlessness in strict sense of the term. Nearly 45 per cent of landless labour households lease-in land. However, extent of leasing-in land by the landless agricultural households is rather notional because the average size of the leased-in land per households is barely .3 acre, and seems to be more in the nature of home sites (Thorat, 1997). In any case, the proces of proletarianization in agriculture seems to have halted.

b) A noteworthy feature of agrarian structure in India is the downward slide; it is reflected in progressively smaller size of the average land holding in each size class. The average size of land holdings in India in the year 1971-72 was 3.77 acres, according to the latest NSS report on land holdings (for 1992-93) it further declined to 2.81 acres. As the skewness in the distribution as suggested by the gini coefficient, has not changed, it is safe to assume that the decline in the average size of land holding suggests a continuing tilt towards smaller holdings in all categories. It should be noted, however, that the pace of decline in the average size of holdings has decelerated in the recent years (Table 5).

TABLE – 5

Proportion of Area Owned (in percentage) and Average Area Owned (in acres) in Different Size Classes

S. No.	*Size-Class*	*Percentage of Area Owned* 1971-72	1982-83	1992-93
1.	Marginal	9.76 (0.69)	12.22 (0.70)	16.93 (0.69)
2.	Small	14.67 (3.57)	16.49 (3.55)	18.59 (3.41)
3.	Semi-Medium	21.92 (6.92)	23.38 (6.85)	24.58 (6.57)
4.	Medium	30.74 (14.79)	29.84 (14.62)	26.07 (14.26)
5.	Large	22.91 (40.76)	18.07 (40.04)	13.83 (39.07)
6.	All Sizes	100.00 (3.77)	100.00 (3.16)	100.00 (2.81)

Note: Figures in parenthesis give average area owned, in acres, in different size classes.

Source: Same as in Table IV

c) It is well known that Indian agriculture is dominated by the marginal and small holdings. During last two decades proportion of households in these holding groups in the total rural households depending on agriculture has further increased, from nearly 68 per cent in 1971-72 to nearly 74 per cent in 1992-93. An important development in this regard, which has largely gone unrecognized, is the remarkable increase in the area owned by the marginal and the small households. In 1971-72 the share of the marginal holdings and the small holdings in the total area owned was roughly 24 per cent, 9.76 per cent in marginal holdings and 14.67 per cent in small holdings. The latest figures (for 1990-91) suggest that nearly 36 per cent of agriculture land in the country is now owned by the small and marginal farmers, the two groups accounting for 17 per cent and 19 per cent respectively (Table 6).[3]

d) Semi-medium and medium farmers constitute the backbone of the Indian agriculture. Their proportion in the total number of holdings is declining, but the land owned by these categories of farmers has only marginally declined, from nearly 53 per cent (52.66 per cent) in 1971-72 to 51 per cent (50.65) in 1992. In fact, share of semi-medium farmers in the area owned has increased from 22 per cent to 25 per cent.

e) The large farmers on the other hand have declined in number, and the area owned by this category of farmers has also substantially declined. In 1971-72 nearly 23 per cent (22.91 per cent) of the total agricultural land was in large holdings. In 1992 the area under large holdings declined to about 14 per cent (13.83 per cent) of total land. They accounted for less than 1 per cent (0.88 per cent) of land owning households.

---

3. There is some indication suggesting, that there is a floor below which the marginal land holders do not operate the land. Thus, if we juxtapose the figures of the operational holdings given by the Agriculture Census for 1970-71 and those of ownership holdings given by NSS for the year 1971-72, we find that nearly 53 per cent of the owned agricultural holdings were in the category of marginal holdings. However, only 51 per cent of the operational holdings were in the same categories. This suggests that marginal farmers were not cultivating all the land which they owned. Similar picture is obtained if we compare area of operational holdings given by Agricultural Census (for 1990-91) and the area of ownership holdings given by the NSS round (for 1992). The marginal farmers accounted for 61 per cent of owned holdings, but 59 per cent of the operated holdings in this period. In terms of area, the marginal farmers in the first period owned 10 per cent of area and operated 9 per cent of area; and in the second period they owned 17 per cent of area but cultivated 15 per cent of land (see table 6).

f) Available records suggest a significant decline in the area under lease. These records are however, grossly inaccurate. There is a very high level of unrecorded tenancy. According to NSS survey for land holdings for 1992, nearly 69 per cent of all tenants and nearly 73 per cent of leased land was unrecorded (Thorat, 1997). An important development is a sharp decline in the proportion of holdings taken on lease. This is indicated by the fact that there is a remarkable increase in the proportion of wholly-owned holdings in the country. Whatever tenancy exists is shared by all size groups of farmers. In fact, the landless, marginal and small households are more active in the lease market both as lessor and lessee (Sharma, 1997). An interesting development is the prevalence of "reverse tenancy" in agriculturally developed states, i.e., in Punjab and Haryana, a tendency which was already noticed in other developed regions (e.g. Gujarat) in post green-revolution years (Vyas, 1970).

TABLE – 6

Proportion of Different Size Class of Holdings in the Area Operated

Size-Class	*Early Seventies*				*Early Nineties*			
	Ownership Holdings		*Operational Holdings*		*Ownership Holdings*		*Operational Holdings*	
	No.	*Area*	*No.*	*Area*	*No.*	*Area*	*No.*	*Area*
Marginal	53.0	9.8	51.0	9.0	61.0	16.9	59.0	15.2
Small	15.1	14.7	18.0	11.3	13.4	18.6	19.0	16.1
Semi-Medium	12.9	22.0	15.0	19.1	9.3	24.6	13.1	23.6
Medium	9.9	30.7	11.3	29.8	4.5	26.1	7.2	27.7
Large	2.9	22.9	3.9	30.8	0.88	13.8	1.6	17.5

Note: Figures of ownership holdings pertain to year 1971-72 and 1992. Figures for operational holdings pertains to year 1970-71 and 1990-91.

Source: Agricultural Census and NSS, various issues.

To sum up, the process of politarization in Indian agriculture has halted; more than one-third land is owned and cultivated under small and marginal holdings; and their share is progressively increasing; nearly 50 per cent of land is cultivated in semi-medium or medium holdings who have been able to hold on their own; less than 15 per cent of land is owned by large farmers and probably even smaller area is operated by them. Thus, the land cultivated in the small and marginal holdings is progressively increasing, that owned and cultivated by the medium holdings has remained stable, but the land owned and cultivated by the larger owners is progressively declining. These remarkable changes in agrarian structure were the outcome of institutional, technological and demographic factors. Market led processes had a relatively less important role to play, as the following account will indicate.

Factors Affecting Land Holding Structure

Market Processes

Even in developed countries market transactions in agricultural land are not numerous. In traditional societies such transactions are all the more limited because until a dire need arises a peasant would not like to sell his land. Provisions of various legislation enacted in recent years have also contributed to the freezing of land market in India; for example, a scheduled tribe land owner cannot sell his land to a non-scheduled tribe person. Inspite of these factors, at least till the mid 1950s there was some evidence of land being sold by small and medium land holders and purchased by large and absentee landlords (Rao, 1972). The classical pattern seemed to be: indebtedness due to natural calamities or social ceremonies leading to hypothecation of land with money lenders (who in many cases were land lords and or traders), and eventual sale of land to money lenders or bigger landlords.

During the post-independence period this process seems to have come to a halt. I have explained elsewhere the reasons for the discontinuation of this pattern (Vyas, 1980 a). Briefly, the fear of ceiling legislation acted as a brake to further expansion of holdings of big and large farmers. Opportunities for further intensification of farming in several parts of the country lured cultivators with large liquid resources away from purchase of land. Tenancy legislations in a number of States made the process of buying land by erstwhile tenants easy; this process is well documented for the western region of the country (Dantwala and Shah, 1971; Desai, 1974). For similar developments in other parts one has to rely on localized surveys and studies. Available evidence suggests that land market tended to work in favour of small and marginal landowners rather than against them.

Institutional Changes

It would be wrong to assume that market forces alone, or in the main, were responsible for obtaining the results noted above. The land market was supplementing the efforts of land reforms which played a much larger role in influencing ownership pattern. Directly, the imposition of ceiling on holding and allotment of surplus land among the landless led to diminution of bigger holding class and creation of small holdings. It is well known, however, that direct transfer of land was not a quantitatively significant phenomenon, the total area of surplus land redistributed among the landless till the beginning of the 1970s amounting to hardly one million acres (Thorat, 1997). Only in a few States (e.g., in Jammu and Kashmir, Kerala, and West Bengal) did the legislative intervention, mainly ceiling legislation, made remarkable impact on the size distribution of holdings. By and large, the indirect pressure exercised by legislation was more important. In spite of fictitious transfers and other devices employed by large landowners, enactment of land ceiling legislation led to large scale disposal of land by big landowners, particularly absentee owners, to forestall the effects of legislation. As the tenancy legislation gave the right of purchase of land to the cultivating tenant, this process was further accentuated.

However, the process did not unfold itself in a neat fashion. There were a large number of cases of ejection of small tenants as there were numerous cases of acquisition of land by tenants. During the 1950s and 1960s, a remarkable shuffle took place in the countryside. It is yet to be fully documented, though there is strong evidence to suggest that in large parts of the country small landowners and the landless were net gainers in this process. Small owners could retain their holdings against the machination of large farmers and they, as well as the landless, were the main beneficiaries once the larger farmers decided to dispose off part of their land in order to be on the right side of law. Movements such as *bhoodan* and 'land-grab', though by themselves did not benefit the small and marginal farmers in a measurable way, did contribute in creating a climate such that the large farmers thought it wise to dispose off parts of their land.

Demographic Pressures

While the increase in area under small holding group (and retention of area in the marginal holding group) could be largely explained by market and institutional processes, the increase in their number is basically due to population increase in cultivating households and lack of alternative employment opportunities in the countryside. An expansion of the household or, more commonly, death of the head of the household, leads to division of holdings among legal heirs. Unfortunately, there are no systematic studies of the household dynamics in the rural areas to arrive at a precise measure of subdivision of holdings over a period of time due to demographic factors. In the absence of such studies, one could only arrive at a rough approximation of changes in the number of agricultural holdings due to population pressure.

On the basis of what is decidedly a crude exercise, we have estimated the likely increase (from 1961 to 1971) in the number of holdings in different size-groups due to expansion in the number of households and partitioning of holdings, and arrived at the expected number of holdings. These numbers were then compared with the actual number as revealed in the 26th Round of NSS (Vyas, 1980b). It was found that in the case of marginal holdings the actual number of holdings was more than the expected number of holdings. This means that a large number of new marginal holdings were created, apart from those which came about due to partitioning of households. In other size-groups, the trend was just the opposite, suggesting net migration to lower holding size-groups with the expansion of the household. The increase in the number of marginal holdings, a substantial part of which is explained by demographic factors, could be either by what may be described as the "reverse ladder" process or by landless households acquiring small plots of land. From our discussion, the latter seems to be a more common occurrence. Similarly, a reduction in the number of large and big holdings could be due either to migration of households or, more probably, due to division of land holdings sliding them in the lower size-group. It bears repetition that the synoptic picture presented above conceals intra-size group changes; it also does not provide accurate description of the entry and exit from one size-group to other. Its chief merit is in underlining the importance of demographic processes in determining land holding pattern over a period of time.

III

PRODUCTION BASE – LAND AND WATER

Important changes have taken place in the production base of Indian agriculture, not all of which are conducive to sustainable development. These changes are reflected in the quality of land resources as well as in patterns of land utilisation, and in the availability and use of water for irrigation.

Land

Deteriorating Quality of Land Resources

India's total geographical area in 329 mha. of which nearly 141 mha or 43 per cent is subject to water and soil erosion.[4] In addition, nearly 34 mha. is affected by other types of land degradation, i.e. water logging, alkaline and arid soils, salinity, ravines and gullies etc. Thus, only 47 per cent of the land in the country can be considered problem free. Incidence of land degradation is particularly severe in Rajasthan (34.2 mha.), Madhya Pradesh (20 mha.), and Maharashtra (19.8 mha.). Other seriously affected states are Andhra Pradesh, Gujarat, Karnataka and Uttar Pradesh. These seven states account for three-fourth of the area affected by soil and land degradation.

Efforts to regenerate the affected areas have been slow and tardy. Hardly one-fifth (21.6 per cent) of the area affected by soil erosion and land degradation could be treated till 1992-93. Only a few states i.e. Sikkim, Maharashtra and Tripura have performed well in this respect. These states have been able to treat more than fifty per cent of the affected land. On the other hand, states such as Rajasthan and Madhya Pradesh

---

4. Data used in this section are taken from, *Water and Related Statistics*, published by Central Water Commission (June 1996).

are yet to treat more than three-fourth of their affected land (Table 7).

TABLE – 7

State-wise Estimated Total Special Problem Area, Area Treated & Balance Yet to be Treated

(Area in Lakh ha)

S. No.	Name of the State/UT	Area of Degraded Land Due To		Total Problem Area	Area Treated Till 1992-93	Balance Yet to be Treated	Percentage of Area Yet to be Treated to Total Problem Area
		Erosion	Special Problem Area				
1.	Andhra Pradesh	115.02	7.29	122.31	13.02	109.29	89.35
2.	Arunachal Pradesh	24.44	2.1	26.54	0.32	26.22	98.79
3.	Assam	22.17	7.82	29.99	2.29	27.70	92.36
4.	Bihar	42.60	22.92	65.52	14.92	50.60	77.23
5.	Gujarat	99.46	26.40	125.86	25.61	100.25	79.65
6.	Haryana	15.91	25.71	41.62	6.88	34.74	83.74
7.	Himachal Pradesh	19.14	-	19.14	3.29	15.85	82.81
8.	Jammu & Kashmir	8.83	0.1	8.93	2.84	6.09	68.20
9.	Karnataka	109.89	4.14	114.03	34.85	79.18	69.44
10.	Kerala	17.57	1.78	19.35	4.64	14.71	76.02
11.	Madhya Pradesh	196.10	11.07	207.17	47.58	159.59	77.03
12.	Maharashtra	191.81	6.65	198.46	106.44	92.02	46.37
13.	Manipur	3.74	3.60	7.34	1.14	6.20	84.47
14.	Meghalaya	8.37	2.65	11.02	1.20	9.82	89.11
15.	Mizoram	4.21	1.89	6.10	0.20	5.90	96.72
16.	Nagaland	4.05	6.33	10.38	1.02	9.36	90.17
17.	Orissa	45.78	32.25	78.03	8.34	69.69	89.31
18.	Punjab	10.07	22.23	32.30	9.00	23.30	72.14
19.	Rajasthan	167.29	174.92	342.21	18.31	323.90	94.65
20.	Sikkim	3.03	-	3.03	2.01	1.02	33.66
21.	Tamil Nadu	36.40	1.82	38.22	16.29	21.93	57.38
22.	Tripura	1.67	1.12	2.79	1.53	1.26	45.16
23.	Uttar Pradesh	71.10	60.05	131.15	37.60	93.55	71.33
24.	West Bengal	10.33	32.70	43.03	4.19	38.84	90.26
25.	Goa	2.00	-	2.00	0.15	1.85	92.50
26.	Delhi	3.49	0.01	3.50	1.35	2.15	61.43

Source: Water & Related Statistics: Information System Directorate: Central Water Commission, June 1996.

Apart from the soil degradation, vast areas in the country are also subjected to recurrent draught and floods. Nearly 99 districts in the country were identified as draught prone on the basis of the criteria suggested by the Irrigation Commission of 1972.[5] Some progress has been made in benefitting these districts, mainly through development of irrigation. Still there are 71 districts in the country which remain draught prone. These are mainly concentrated in the states of Rajasthan, Gujarat, Karnataka and Maharashtra.

Vast areas are also devastated by floods. On an average 7.6 mha. area was affected by the floods every year during the period 1953 to 1994. There were years when the area affected was much larger. Great loss of human life and vast damage to crops and property are reported year after year, due to floods. We do not seem to have made much progress in flood forecasting, leave aside flood protection.

Land Utilization

In view of the fragile nature of the land base, over large parts of the country care has to be exercised in the land use. Certain features deserve special attention in this respect. In the first place, India is one of the most intensively cultivated countries in Asia. Of the total reported area of 303.8 mha. nearly 140.3 mha or 46.3 per cent of land was under plough in 1970-71[6]. This proportion has not changed appreciably since then: the proportion of area under cultivation was 46.7 per

---

5. Irrigation commission (1972) defined an area as drought-prone if, (i) the rainfall happens to less than 75 per cent of the normal in 20 per cent of the years examined, or (ii) where the irrigation development falls short of covering 30 per cent of total cultivated area.

6. There has been some change in the area for which data are available, or in the 'reporting area'. In 1970-71 data was not available for nearly 25 mha. By 1991-92, this figure was reduced to 23.7 mha. or 7.2 per cent of the geographical area.

cent in 1992-93, the latest year for which the information is readily available (Table 8).

TABLE – 8

Trends in Land Utilisation

(Area in Million Hectares)

	1970-71	*1980-81*	*1992-93*
Reporting Area	303.76	304.70	305.01
Land under forests	63.91 (21.0)	67.47 (22.0)	68.7 (22.3)
Area Put to Non-Agricultural Uses	16.48 (5.4)	19.66 (6.4)	21.88 (7.2)
Barren & Un-Culturable Land	28.16 (9.3)	19.96 (6.4)	19.38 (6.3)
Permanent Pastures & Other Grazing Lands	13.26 (4.4)	11.97 (3.9)	11.30 (3.7)
Land Under Miscellaneous Tree Crops & Groves	4.30 (1.4)	3.60 (1.2)	3.67 (1.2)
Culturable Waste	17.50 (5.8)	16.74 (5.5)	14.64 (4.8)
Old Fallows Land	8.76 (2.9)	9.92 (3.3)	9.65 (3.2)
Current Fallows	11.12 (3.5)	14.83 (*4.9)	13.91 (4.6)
Net sown area	140.27 (46.3)	140.00 (46.0)	142.5 (46.7)

Note: Figures in parenthesis indicate percent to Reporting Area.
Source: Indian Agriculture in Brief, 26th edition.

Secondly, the stability in the area under cultivation hides two opposing tendencies. On the one hand, the area put to non-agricultural use, mainly for housing and industrial purposes, is increasing; it was 16.5 mha. in 1970-71 and increased to 21.9 mha. in 1993-94. On the other hand, the area classified as culturable waste is declining.[7] This

7. Culturable waste is the land once cultivated but not cultivated for five years in succession.

phenomenon is common to all the major states in the country. Unfortunately, the expansion in the land use for non-agricultural purposes is not taking place on the culturable waste land. At the same time agriculture is expanding on the waste lands, i.e. lands not particularly suited for agriculture. This suggests that the Indian agriculture is having a progressively less fertile land base.

Third, an intriguing development in this regard is the large area classified as fellow land. The land in this category comprise "current fellow" and "old fellow land". In a land scarce country existence of large areas of fallow land requires special attention. While the extent of current fallow can be broadly related to the pattern of rainfall, (i.e., inadequate rainfall forcing people not to cultivate a part of land), large area under this category needs attention. Similarly, the land classified as old fallow land or "other than current fallow" is hardly declining. One can advance the hypothesis that with higher investment required for non-land inputs, poorer farmers are forced to under utilise the land, (Reddy, 1991).

The fourth phenomenon of interest is the inadequate forest cover, which has stagnated at around 20 to 21 per cent of the reporting area since 1970-71 with only a marginal increase, of hardly more than 1 per cent, over last thirty years. If the norm of 30 per cent of area under forests is considered a desirable norm, then not only the country as a whole but also most of the states fall short of this desirable standard. Similar concern needs to be voiced in regard to pasture land. With the growing importance of animal husbandry sector, one would expect larger areas being devoted to the pasture land. Only justification for the decline in the pasture land could be an improvement in the quality of pastures. There is no evidence to suggest that this is happening.

The fifth noteworthy development is a remarkable shift in

the seasonal pattern of foodgrains production. The area under *kharif*, i.e. in the post-monsoon season, has progressively declined, from nearly 83 mha. in 1980-81 to roughly 75 mha. in 1994-95. The decline in the area under *kharif* crops has been witnessed in practically all major states. Correspondingly, the area under *rabi*, or the winter crops, has increased from approximately 43 mha to 49 mha. during the same period (Table 9). Over the period under review the pace of expansion of the area under *rabi* has accelerated. Most of the increase in the *rabi* area is due to the expansion of irrigation and the increase in the area cultivated more than once.

TABLE – 9

Foodgrains Area Under Rabi & Kharif Seasons

Crops	*Area (Million Hectares)*		*Yield Per Hectare (Kgs)*	
	1980-81	*1994-95*	*1980-81*	*1994-95*
Kharif	83.21	75.03	93.31	134.13
Rabi	43.46	48.52	119.51	186.41

Source: Indian Agriculture in Brief, 26th edition.

This shift in the seasonal pattern in agriculture has important implications in terms of changes in cropping pattern, and shift in the importance of different agricultural regions. Larger area under *rabi* has resulted in improvement of income of the cultivators and greater stability in crop production; former because of the higher yields in the *rabi* season and latter because *rabi* crops are generally grown in the irrigated area or the area with assured and adequate rainfall. The importance of this seasonal shift is illustrated by the increase in the area under oilseeds in Rajasthan and Madhya Pradesh. Mainly because of the expansion of *rabi* area these states have emerged as the principal producers of oilseeds in general and *rabi* oilseeds in particular. The tendency towards shift to *rabi* area has meant higher income for the producers. In most of the cases this also meant double or multiple cropping. Even in the areas where double cropping could not be introduced shift to *rabi* crops generally meant a shift towards higher value crops or higher yields of the same crop. Such a shift has also influenced marketable surplus and the pace and pattern of market arrivals.

Water

Like land water is the other essential component of the production base of agriculture.

According to the Central Water Commission, India receives average annual precipitation of 4000 Billion Cubic Meters (BCM). However, the total annual utilisable water resource of the country is estimated at 1122 BCM or 28 per cent of the average annual precipitation. The average availability of water is a misleading notion as there are remarkable variations in patterns of precipitation in different parts of the country. Arunachal receives more than seven times rainfall received by western Rajasthan or Saurashtra.

Bulk of this water is used for irrigation, which accounted for 83 per cent of the total water use in the country (in 1990). Use of water for irrigation has expanded phenomenally during the last 21 years or so. The net irrigated area increased from 31.1 mha. in 1970-71 to 53.5 mha in 1995-96. The expansion of the gross irrigated area has been even more rapid. The area irrigated more than once has increased from 7.1 mha. (in 1970-71) to 18 mha. (in 1995-96) (Table 10). Now approximately 38 per cent of the gross cropped area in the country is irrigated. In three states in the country more than 2/3 of the net sown area is now irrigated. These states are Punjab (93 per cent), Haryana (76 per cent) and Uttar Pradesh (66 per cent) (CMIE, 1999). The pace of irrigation expansion, particularly the expansion of the canal irrigation has slowed down in recent years, mainly because of slackening of public investment in agriculture with deleterious effects not only on the expansion of irrigation but also on the maintenance of irrigation systems (Dhawan, 1997).

TABLE – 10

Net and Gross Irrigated Area

(Area 000 Hectares)

Year	*Area Sown*				*Area Irrigated*				*Irrigated Area as % of Sown Area*			
	Net Change		*Gross Change*		*Net Change*		*Gross Change*		*Net Change*		*Gross Change*	
1970-71	140.8		165.8		31.1		38.2		22.08		23.0	
1975-76	141.6	0.8	171.3	5.5	34.5	3.4	43.4	5.2	24.3	2.3	25.3	2.3
1980-81	140.3	-1.3	173.1	1.8	38.8	4.3	49.9	6.5	27.6	3.3	28.8	3.5
1985-86	140.9	0.6	178.8	5.7	41.8	3.0	54.7	4.8	29.6	2.0	30.5	1.7
1990-91	142.8	1.9	182.5	3.7	48.0	6.2	63.2	8.5	33.6	4.0	34.6	4.1
1995-96	144.2	1.4	186.5*	4.0	53.5	5.5	71.5	8.3	37.10	3.5	38.3	3.7

* Provisional

Source: CMIE, Agriculture, September 1999, Statistical Abstract of India, various issues.

Another major change has taken place in the sources of irrigation. It is observed that wells provide 55 per cent of irrigation, followed by canals (35 per cent) and tanks (7 per cent), rest by other sources. The share of the area irrigated by wells is increasing progressively. The wells (both tubewells and other wells) now account for more than half of the area irrigated as against 38 per cent in 1970-71. This has resulted on the one hand, in raising the cost of watering the crops (due to expenditure on power to lift water), and has also introduced an element of inequity as the access to capital owned or borrowed, is necessary for well irrigation only exception being the small pockets where water markets have come into existence. At the same time it has ensured greater certainty in accessing water and more economic use of water.

Utilization of irrigation water by crops has also changed significantly. For example, 79 per cent of the total irrigated area was accounted by foodgrains and pulses in 1970-71. By 1992-93 this proportion has come down to 70 per cent. Within foodgrains, the share of rice in the total irrigated area is declining, while that of wheat is increasing. The other impressive gain is registered by oilseeds which now account for nearly 10 per cent of irrigated area (Water and Related Statistics, 1996).

While the physical expansion of irrigation is quite impressive, it is not clear whether use efficiency of water has also improved. Mounting cost of irrigation on the one hand, and lack of resources for operations and maintenance on the other augur ill for irrigated agriculture. Probably, additional irrigation facilities are not contributing to the increase in productivity in any remarkable way. In fact, the incremental contribution seems to be declining the problem of salinity and water-logging are becoming more acute.

The overwhelming impression given by the data on the availability and use of land and water resources in India is that the production base of Indian agriculture is weakening.

IV

THE INPUT STRUCTURE

Significant changes have taken place in the input structure of agricultural sector during last few decades. Till early 1950s the inputs mainly comprised the owned or leased-in land, family labour (with a few wage-paid labour during peak season), owned or hired bullock power, owned seed and organic manure from one's own livestock. This picture has remarkably changed. For example, the total value of the non land, non-labour, inputs, in 1960-61, was estimated at Rs. 1850 crores. By 1971-72 the figure rose to 4089 crores; in 1980-81 it was 15247 crores; the latest figure suggest that the value of inputs in 1992-93 was of the order of 49642 crores.[8] Thus, progressively the value of (mainly, purchased) inputs in relation to agricultural output is accelerating. Inputs which are mainly purchased now account for more than 34 per cent of the total value of the output as compared to 23 percentage in the year 1970-71.

Along with the increase in value of these inputs there has also been a change in the relative importance of various inputs. Although expenditure on livestock still accounts for the bulk of the total value of inputs, there have been significant changes in the importance of other inputs. For example, during the period under review the share of chemical fertilizers has increased from 2.6 per cent of the total value of inputs to 16.6 per cent; similarly, the expenditure on repair and maintenance of assets (mainly tractors) has increased from 4.4 to 7.7 per cent. Electricity and diesel oil which together accounted for hardly 3 per cent of expenditure in 1960-61 now comprise 10 per cent of the total value of inputs. The most rapid increase in value terms has taken place in chemical fertilizers (see table 11).

---

8. Inputs included are seeds, organic manure, chemical fertilizers, repairs and maintenance of assets, feeds of livestock, irrigation charges, market charges, electricity, pesticides and insecticides and diesel oil. This list does not include the interest on the capital invested by the farmers in developing their own irrigation sources. Figures quoted in this section, unless otherwise mentioned are from CMIE, 1996, and Input Survey for 1986-87.

TABLE – 11

Percentage Share of Inputs in Agriculture Sector

Year	*Total Inputs in Agriculture Sector (Rs. Crore)*	*Chemical Fertilizers*	*Repairs & Maintainance*	*Electricity*	*Diesel Oil*
1960-61	1850	2.6	4.4	2.2	0.7
1970-71	4089	8.4	2.8	2.4	5.5
1980-81	15247	15.1	5.0	3.9	3.0
1990-91	38971	16.4	7.7	4.3	4.9
1992-93	49462	16.6	7.7	4.3	5.7

Source: CMIE, India's Agricultural Sector, 1995.

Significance of this increase in the value of inputs should not be lost sight of. As we have mentioned earlier the share of agriculture in GDP has steadily declined remarkably over the period under review and to that extent agriculture's forward linkage with the rest of the economy has weakened considerably, but its backward linkages *via* the purchased inputs have significantly improved. Demand from agriculture for inputs from the industrial sector is becoming progressively more important.

An interesting aspect of the input structure is that the marginal and small farmers also use purchased inputs to a substantial extent. In fact, if we take into account two major inputs, namely, irrigation and fertilizers, the per hectare expenditure (accrued or imputed) on these inputs is larger on the marginal and small farms compared to the medium and large farms. For example, the net irrigated area to the net sown area was nearly 40 per cent for marginal holdings, and it goes on declining in the successive holding categories. It is only 19 per cent in case of the large holdings. It seems that the small and marginal holdings not only have proportionately larger extent of irrigation they also have larger areas irrigated more than once. The marginal farmers have nearly 20 per cent of their net sown area cropped twice or more than twice. The proportion of areas cropped more than once is 14 per cent in case of small holdings. The proportion of land cropped twice or more than twice on the large holdings is barely 10 per cent.

The same picture obtains in the use of fertilizers. Nearly two-third of the operated area of the marginal and small farmers is treated with fertilizers. The proportion is less than 50 per cent for the medium farmers and roughly 39 per cent for the large farmers. These data are based on the inputs survey of 1986-87; the results from the latest inputs survey are not yet available. But the comparison with the previous input survey, i.e. for 1976-77, also reveal both the phenomena, i.e., the increase in the proportion of the purchased inputs, and more intensive use of fertilisers and irrigation on marginal and small holdings. The same trends are likely to have continued, i.e., growing share of the purchased inputs, and relatively, more intensive use of these inputs on small farms, in the years following 1986-87 Input Survey.

Thus, the small and marginal farmers use their land more intensively with proportionately larger share in irrigation, and have proportionately more area treated by the fertilizers. To that extent the small land size is compensated by larger doses of irrigation and fertilizers. In other words, skewness in land holdings is corrected to some extent by relatively more equitable distribution of non-land inputs. And this process seems to be going on for last two decades.

An intriguing feature of the shift to more modern inputs is less than commensurate contribution of these inputs to the growth in agricultural productivity, especially since the beginning of the 1980s. Growth rate of aggregate agricultural productivity in India during the period 1980-81 to 1994-95 has been around 3 per cent. In contrast growth rate of fertilizers has been above 6 per cent and electricity above 12 per cent, though irrigated area increased by only 2 per cent per annum. (Karam Singh, 1997). The declining marginal returns to inputs can be explained only in two ways. One, the country has already reached a plateau in technology, in other words rising phase of production surface has already been obtained. Or, there could be another, and a related, explanation, namely, there is a break in the complementarity in the resource use, and as a result the overall contribution of these inputs is declining. The pricing policies, service delivery systems and the public investment may be responsible for the creating hurdles in exploiting complementarities. The first of these, i.e. inept price policies leading to inefficient resource use is illustrated by the adhocism in pricing of nitrogeneous, phosphatic and potassium fertilizers, which has resulted in an inappropriate mix of fertilizer use. The service delivery system biased towards 'progressive' regions and larger farmers has deprived backward regions and poorer classes to exploit the full potentialities of inputs. More so since larger number of farmers and marginal farmers are using purchase inputs, recent slackness in public investment, particularly in irrigation, power and other infrastructure, may have contributed to the diminished efficiency of the modern inputs.

V

CHANGES IN CROPPING PATTERN

The other major change which has taken place in the recent years is in the crop composition. We have already mentioned the growing importance of the subsectors of the agriculture, namely, animal husbandry, fishery, poultry raising, in comparison to the crops sector. Within the crop raising subsector important changes have taken place which have serious implications for agricultural producers, and which also affect relative importance of different regions.

Within the crops sector three major changes have taken place. In the first place the share of non food crops has increased in terms of area devoted to as well as value generated from these crops. For example, in the triennium ending 1971-72, nearly 25.7 per cent of the cultivated area was devoted to non-foodgrains. Their share increased to 32.4 per cent in the triennium ending 1992-93. In value terms the increase was not that substantial, as terms of trade tilted in favour of the foodgrains. Even then the share of non foodgrains in the total value of crops increased from 51.3 per cent to 53.4 per cent during the same period (Satyasai and Vishwanathan, 1996).

Second, noteworthy, development is that among the non foodgrains, other food crops i.e., sugar, oil seeds, spices and condiments and fruits and vegetables etc., are acquiring greater importance. They are now occupying a larger part of the cultivated area and account for larger share in value of agricultural production. The third important change has taken place in the share of so-called superior cereals among the foodgrains. Thus, the area under rice and wheat has expanded from 31.4 per cent of the area under cultivation in the triennium ending 1970-71 to 36.5 per cent in the triennium ending 1992-93. Correspondingly, the coarse cereals and pulses have declined in importance, both in terms of area and value. (Table 12).

Many of these changes were anticipated. I have elaborated on the nature and extent of diversification in agriculture elsewhere (Vyas, 1996). To recapitulate later, the farmers in this country, small and large, devote a part of the land for commercial crops in order to earn cash. In the 1970s and 1980s the policy of food self-sufficiency was pursued vigorously, and incentives were provided to the foodgrains production (e.g., better minimum support prices). During that period area under commercial crops stagnated. But soon this phase was over and from the mid 1970s gradual increase in the area under commercial crops began. With the globalisation of the economy, and the agriculture playing an important part in exports, incentive for raising commercial crops also improved. Fortunately, because of the improvement in the yields of foodgrains per capita availability of foodgrains remained stable even though there was fast growth in population, the latter increasing at the rate of about 2 per cent per annum. At least till the mid 1990s somewhat faster growth in commercial crops did not jeopardize the food security in the country at the macro level.

TABLE – 12

Proportion of Area under Food Crops Rice and Wheat to Total Cultivated Area

(Area 000 Hectares)

Year	*Cultivated Area*	*Area under Food-crops*	*Area under*		*Area under Non-food Crops*
			Rice	*Wheat*	
1970-71	177647	1243.2 (70.0)	37592 (21.16)	18241 (10.26)	334.8 (18.0)
1980-81	181309	1266.7 (70.0)	40152 (22.14)	22279 (12.28)	369.6 (20.0)
1991-92	180702	1278.3 (71.0)	42649 (23.60)	23262 (12.87)	599.5 (33.0)
1992-93	195677	1247.1 (63.0)	41637 (21.27)	24431 (12.48)	468.8 (23.0)

Note: Figures in parenthesis are percentage to total cultivated areas.

Source: CMIE, India's Agricultural Sector, A Compedium of Statistics, July 1996, Indian Agriculture in Brief, various editions.

The other change in the cropping pattern, namely, a larger share of non-foodgrains (i.e. sugar, edible oil, fruits and vegetable etc.) in the cropped area was a reflection of changes in the food basket. With increase in per capita income share of these items increased in the consumption pattern. This is more or less a universal phenomenon. In India the other change in food intake, i.e., the rising share of animal husbandry products, which is commonly experienced with increase in the household income was rather slow, mainly due to cultural reasons.

The shift within the foodgrains in favour of superior cereals, i.e., wheat and rice was basically an outcome of the nature of technological change. The high-yielding varieties which resulted in improving productivity in these crops further shifted comparative advantages in favour of growing these crops. The concern for food self-sufficiency helped in forging a supportive policy package along with the extension of the superior technology. In other words, the "green revolution" expressed itself in remarkable growth of wheat in the first instance and rice later on. The coarse cereals and pulses did not have the advantage of either technical or policy or institutional support for raising productivity. The area under these crops also shrunk. While the country could achieve food self-sufficiency with the growth in rice and wheat production the stagnation in coarse cereals and pulses have serious implications for the backward, rainfed, regions. It has particularly unfavourable implications for the poor consumers, especially in terms of the intake of protein. The stagnation, rather decline, in per capita availability of the pulses which is the principal source of protein for the poor, must have affected their nutritional status.

The nature of diversification from farm to non-farm sector and within the farm sector in favour of commercial crops, food crops other than foodgrains and within the foodgrains in favour of superior cereals have remarkably influenced the relative economics of different regions. The gains due to faster development of commercial crops and non-foodgrains food crops benefitted the southern and the western region, including rainfed areas of Rajasthan and Madhya Pradesh (especially due to the spurt in oilseed production). Break through in rice technology gave fillip to agricultural development in the eastern part. Besides, short maturing varieties of wheat and rice made significant impact on the cropping pattern in different states. For example, Punjab emerged as an important producer of rice, while eastern region improved its share in wheat production.

VI

SUMMING UP

The foregoing discussion has underlined the nature and the direction of change in agricultural sector in last 25 years or so. Following features stand out sharply in this review.

1. Although the share of agriculture in GDP has continued to decline its importance has not diminished. In fact, the linkages of agriculture with rest of the economy may become more important as infrastructure development takes place and rural and urban areas are better integrated. Direct contribution of agriculture in poverty removal because of its high employment elasticity, and indirect role it plays in providing wage goods and thus in containing inflation, is very substantial.

2. Within agriculture major changes are taking place in the importance of different activities. The share of ancillary sectors, mainly dairying, fisheries and poultry raising is becoming progressively more important. In

the crop sector the non-food crops have gained an edge over the food crops in terms of area as well as the value of output. Fortunately, this has not adversely affected the per capita availability of foodgrains in the country because of high yielding technology introduced in the foodgrains sector. Again, within the foodgrains sector the so-called superior cereals, i.e., wheat and rice, are gaining in importance. Both require adequate and ample water for irrigation. The dry regions where water is a major constraint, and they account for nearly 60 per cent of the cultivated area, only a part of area could benefit by switching to high value crops, such as oilseeds. Bulk of these areas have remained disadvantaged as the traditional dry land crops, mainly coarse cereals and pulses, have not gained in productivity and or value.

3. The input use over the period of time suggest that the share of the purchased inputs in the input structure has increased significantly. Part of it is due to the policy of subsidising these inputs. However, the subsidy induced increase in inputs has not resulted in more efficient use of inputs. Contrary seems to be true. The faulty pricing policies for different inputs have deprived agricultural producers the gains which could be obtained by more balanced use. The research and extension efforts have not contributed in developing and extending appropriate use of different inputs in specific environments. Slackness in the public investment in infrastructure, especially irrigation, also leads to the same results.

4. An important development is the continuous sliding down of the land holding structure, with progressively large areas of land going to the small and marginal holding categories. This, however, has not resulted into

an increase in proliternisation. Nor necessarily in lesser use of modern inputs. From available indications it is suggested that the use of inputs such as fertilisers and irrigation is more intensive on the small farms compared to larger farms. But because of meagre land base, and the low value cropping pattern, activity-mix, and the bias of the supportive systems they are not able to generate enough incomes.

5. There is some evidence that at the lower end, size of operational holdings, generally, do not go below a 'floor'. The extent of tenancy is probably declining. But all categories of farmers, including large farmers take part in the truncated, and often illegal, lease market. There is some evidence of reverse tenancy taking place in more prosperous regions.

6. A disquietening feature of recent development is the progressive degradation of soil and land base of Indian agriculture. It is reflected in the extent of soil deterioration as well as inefficient use, and in large areas inadequate availability, of water for irrigation. This, together with the fact that the forest cover is grossly inadequate compared to the requirements suggests that the production base is weakening. Unfortunately, the efforts made in this direction are grossly inadequate.

Where do we go from here?

Agricultural growth during the period under review was quite satisfactory. This was mainly due to the momentum generated by the technological breakthrough in wheat and rice production in the mid-sixties. This was helped by a price policy which ensured minimum support prices and thus took away, to a large extent, the market induced risk. The cheap input policies encouraged greater use of modern inputs. Demand conditions for most of the crops were quite favourable, as country was insulated from the secular decline in agricultural prices witnessed the world over in the sixties and the seventies. Institutions supporting agriculture particularly credit were extended vigorously. A strong lobby representing surplus farmers emerged on the political scene and was quite vigilant in safeguarding the interest of this section of producers.

This overall growth and thin crust of prosperity enjoyed by a small section of agricultural producers conceal growing weaknesses of the system. Technology-induced tempo of growth in agricultural output decelerated in the nineties. The burden of subsidies crowded out the investment in research, extension and infrastructure development. The support systems in extension, credit and marketing discriminated against the small producers. Slackening of public investment was particularly unfavourable to the backward regions. Two other corroding factors were the environmental degradation weakening the production base of the agriculture, and decay of the self-help institutions. These are serious developments and deserve concerted action of all concerned. We do have the requisite framework of institutions and enough experience in policy and programming. These advantages should be fully exploited to achieve the overarching objectives of strengthening production base and strengthening capabilities of the producers in a sector which is now facing new challenges both internally and in international sphere.

6

Emerging Issues in Indian Agriculture

A review of the performance of the agricultural sector since Independence, more precisely from the beginning of the planning era, reveals two features. Firstly on an overall basis, growth of agricultural production during the last three decades, though falling short of the country's requirements, has been quite remarkable in comparison with achievements registered in other large over-populated developing countries. Secondly, there are remarkable differences in performances of different states of the country in this regard. Not only some states lagged behind the national average throughout this period, there has been important qualitative differences in the growth rate. Some of the states which were doing well in the fifties performed poorly in the sixties slipped downward in the seventies. There are, of course, a few states which have shown either a consistently poor or a consistently superior record. Is there a pattern in these developments, or are these only random occurrences? Can we discern causal factors – institutional, technological, or organizational – which could explain the results? Are we in a position to predict the future path which agriculture is likely to take in different parts of the country?

(Paper presented at the Indian Statistical Institute Golden Jubilee Conference at Calcutta in 1981).

The author is grateful to Shri N.V. Namboodiri for his assistance in preparing this paper.

For the purpose of this discussion growth rates have been examined for the period 1950-51 to 1964-65 and the period 1965-66 to 1979-80. The justification for this division lies in the qualitative change which came about in the mid-sixties with the introduction of high yielding varieties of wheat and rice. The subsequent years saw a large scale conversion of the area under these cereals, particularly wheat, to the new varieties. There are few examples of a shift in the production technology of a particular crop in so short a period over such large areas. In less than a decade of introduction, 65 per cent of the area under wheat and 32 per cent of the area under rice were brought under high yielding varieties.

We may concentrate on foodgrains to sharply bring in focus factors responsible for the performance of the agricultural sector. Practically in all states, the proportion of gross area under foodgrains to gross cultivated area has remained very high and more or less stable. Within the foodgrains sector, area under various cereals and non-cereal foodgrains has changed, with an increase in the area and production of wheat, and a sharp decline in the area and production of other cereals and pulses. The share of rice in total production of foodgrains has remained stable around 40 per cent of the area under foodgrains.

Another reason for concentrating our attention on foodgrains is that major technological breakthroughs, so far, have taken place only in the case of foodgrains; an exception has been cotton. Finally we envisage that the relative importance of foodgrains will increase partly because of the acceptance of food self-sufficiency as an important goal of agricultural development and partly because importance of non-foodgrains will decline in the raw material base of Indian industries as well as in the export-mix. It needs to be underlined that we are speaking, in terms of relative importance of these two sub-sectors, the increase in demand in absolute terms, and hence pressure on various inputs for raising non-foodgrains agricultural commodities will continue unabated.

I

The overall rate of growth in foodgrains production in period I, i.e., from 1950-51 to 1964-65 was nearly 3.5 per cent (3.468 to be precise) per annum (see Table 1). A remarkable feature of the foodgrains economy in this period was that, except in Assam, Uttar Pradesh, and West Bengal, foodgrains production was higher than the population growth. During this period virtually all states could contribute to agricultural growth.

The factors which enabled a large part of the country to participate in growth process in a more equitable manner can be discerned from the exercise appended herewith (see Appendix 1). A simple econometric model with gross area, gross irrigated area and concentration ratio of owned holdings (as an indicator of access to land resource) as independent variables and foodgrains production as the dependent variable, could explain the major changes in production in different states and the relative importance of these factors.* Similar results were obtained when yield per hectare was substituted as a dependent variable. The relative importance of area expansion and irrigation-induced yield expansion is quite obvious.

On a more qualitative or judgemental plane, one would list the following factors to explain the growth of agricultural production in the first period: pressure of population on land; increased productivity on small holdings; and sizable expansion of irrigation facilities during this period. For reasons not yet quite clear, the smaller holdings had a higher proportion of

* We also introduced literacy rate (as a surrogate for investment in human capital). However, impact of literacy proved to be, statistically, non significant.

TABLE – 1

Annual Compound Growth Rates of Area, Production and Yield of Foodgrains

(percentage)

States	Production			Area			Yield		
	1950-51 to 1964-65	1965-66 to 1979-80	1950-51 to 1979-80	1950-51 to 1964-65	1965-66 to 1979-80	1950-51 to 1979-80	1950-51 to 1964-65	1965-66 to 1979-80	1950-51 to 1979-80
Andhra Pradesh	3.746	2.636	2.161	1.214	0.066*	0.277	2.532	2.570	1.885
Assam	1.091	1.070	1.384	1.013	0.951	1.269	0.078*	0.119*	0.115*
Bihar	4.315	2.269*	2.530	0.572	0.337*	0.349	3.743	1.932*	2.191
Gujarat	na	3.670	na	na	-0.641*	na	na	4.511	na
Haryana	na	5.290	na	na	1.403	na	na	3.887	na
Jammu & Kashmir	4.014	4.050	4.213	4.146	0.741	2.196	-0.132*	3.309	2.017
Karnataka	3.916	3.827	3.290	1.337	-0.077*	0.176*	2.579	3.904	3.114
Kerala	4.344	1.056	2.353	0.949	-0.286*	0.601	3.395	1.342	1.752
Madhya Pradesh	4.103	1.879	1.801	1.459	0.875	0.978	2.644	1.004*	0.823
Maharashtra	3.271[1]	4.920	na	0.501[1]	0.967	na	2.771[1]	3.953	na
Orissa	5.470	0.697*	3.017	1.482	1.517	1.586	3.988	-0.820*	1.431
Punjab	4.286[2]	7.306	na	1.971[2]	2.582	na	2.315[2]	4.724	na
Rajasthan	7.209	3.204	3.463	5.027	0.395*	1.930	2.182	2.809	1.533
Tamil Nadu	4.336	2.462	2.519	1.177	0.181*	0.395	3.159	2.281	2.124
Uttar Pradesh	1.361	2.419	1.983	0.570	0.259*	0.441	0.791	2.160	1.542
West Bengal	1.170*	2.450	2.097	0.427	0.943	0.884	0.743*	1.507	1.213
All India	3.468	3.142	2.678	1.373	0.581	0.763	2.095	2.561	1.915

*. Not significant at 5 per cent level na – Not Applicable

1. Includes Gujarat 2. Includes Haryana

Notes: These growth rates are calculated from indices of area (production or yield) with triennium ending 1969-70 as the base in physical units of area, production and yield.

irrigated land. Thus, the factors which affected agricultural growth in the pre-HYV period were within the reach of a large section of agricultural population.

II

The picture changes in a remarkable way in the second period. None of the first five states in period I could retain the same position in period II (Table 2). Only in the case of Rajasthan and Tamil Nadu was the change not so drastic. Different states took the top position as country's fastest foodgrains producing states in the post-HYV period. These were Punjab, Haryana, Maharashtra, Karnataka and Gujarat. The same picture is obtained when we shift our sights from rate of growth in foodgrains production to rate of growth in per hectare yields.

It is important to understand sources of growth in the second period. Nearly 82 per cent of growth in production during this period is accounted for by improvement in yield per hectare (as against 60 per cent in the first period) (Table 3). Therefore, the factors influencing the improvement in yield were of critical importance. As mentioned earlier we examined 4 factors to understand their relative importance in explaining the rate of growth in per hectare yield in different states. These factors, to recapitulate, were area under irrigation, quantity of fertilisers used, area under HYV seeds and, concentration ratio of the operational holdings (as a surrogate for access to land). Of these the concentration ratio in the operational holdings did not show statistically significant relationship with the yield one way or the other (See Appendix I). Irrigation showed a clear and positive association with the rate of growth in yield. It seems that irrigation as an instrument of public policy (most of the expansion in irrigation during this period was through the state-sponsored surface irrigation schemes) was used with

TABLE – 2

Ranking of States According to Annual Compound Growth Rates of Production, Yield, and Area of Foodgrains During 1950-51 to 1964-65 and 1965-66 to 1979-80

Rank	Production		Yield		Area	
	Period I	*Period II*	*Period I*	*Period II*	*Period I*	*Period II*
1.	Rajasthan	Punjab	Orissa	Punjab	Rajasthan	Punjab
2.	Orissa	Haryana	Bihar	Gujarat	Jammu and Kashmir	Orissa
3.	Kerala	Maharashtra	Kerala	Maharashtra	Punjab	Haryana
4.	Tamilnadu	Jammu and Kashmir	Tamilnadu	Karnataka	Haryana	Maharashtra
5.	Bihar	Karnataka	Maharashtra and	Haryana	Orissa	Assam
6.	Punjab	Gujarat	Gujarat	Jammu and Kashmir	Madhya Pradesh	West Bengal
7.	Haryana	Rajasthan	Madhya Pradesh	Rajasthan	Karnataka	Madhya Pradesh
8.	Madhya Pradesh	Andhra Pradesh	Karnataka	Andhra Pradesh	Andhra Pradesh	Jammu and Kashmir
9.	Jammu and Kashmir	Tamilnadu	Andhra Pradesh	Tamilnadu	Tamilnadu	Rajasthan
10.	Karnataka	West Bengal	Punjab	Uttar Pradesh	Assam	Bihar
11.	Andhra Pradesh	Uttar Pradesh	Haryana	Bihar	Kerala	Uttar Pradesh
12.	Maharashtra	Bihar	Rajasthan	West Bengal	Bihar	Tamilnadu
13.	Gujarat	Madhya Pradesh	Uttar Pradesh	Kerala	Uttar Pradesh	Andhra Pradesh
14.	Uttar Pradesh	Assam	West Bengal	Madhya Pradesh	Maharashtra	Karnataka
15.	West Bengal	Kerala	Assam	Assam	Gujarat	Kerala
16.	Assam	Orissa	Jammu and Kashmir	Orissa	West Bengal	Gujarat

Source: Derived from Table 1.

effectiveness. Although one could question the growing cost of irrigating land as well as the lack of comprehensive water resource planning in the absence of which investment in irrigation has not yielded optimum returns, the outcome, on the whole was quite, salutary. As with irrigation, fertilisers and area under HYV had a positive association with the growth of yield per hectare.

TABLE – 3

Relative Share of Area and Yield in the Output Growth - 1950-51 to 1964-65, 1965-66 to 1979-80 and 1950-51 to 1979-80

state	*percentage contribution of area*			*percentage contribution of yield*		
	1950-51 to 1964-65	*1965-66 to 1979-80*	*1950-51 to 1979-80*	*1950-51 to 1964-65*	*1965-66 to 1979-80*	*1950-51 to 1979-80*
Andhra Pradesh	32.4	2.5	12.8	67.6	97.5	87.2
Assam	92.9	88.9	91.7	7.1	11.1	8.3
Bihar	13.3	14.9	13.8	86.7	85.1	86.6
Gujarat	na	-17.5	na	na	117.5	na
Haryana	na	26.5	na	na	73.5	na
Jammu and Kashmir	102.3	18.3	52.2	-2.3	81.7	47.8
Karnataka	34.1	-2.0	5.3	65.9	102.0	94.7
Kerala	21.8	-27.1	25.5	78.2	127.1	74.5
Madhya Pradesh	35.6	46.6	54.3	64.4	53.4	45.7
Maharashtra	15.3[1]	19.6	na	84.7[1]	80.4	na
Orissa	27.1	217.6	52.6	72.9	-117.6	47.4
Punjab	46.0[2]	35.3	na	54.0[2]	64.7	na
Rajasthan	69.7	12.3	55.7	30.3	87.7	44.3
Tamilnadu	27.1	7.4	15.7	72.9	92.6	84.3
Uttar Pradesh	41.9	10.7	22.2	58.1	89.3	77.8
West Bengal	36.5	38.5	42.2	63.5	61.5	57.8
All India	39.6	18.5	28.5	60.4	81.5	71.5

Source: Derived from Table 1

1 Includes Gujarat

2 Includes Haryana

The most remarkable feature in period II is an increase in the share of purchased inputs in the input base for agricultural production. From 1970-71 to 1978-79 purchased inputs in agriculture were growing at the rate of 11 per cent per annum at constant prices; bulk of this increase was accounted for by chemical fertilisers. For the country as a whole purchased inputs now account for 14 to 15 per cent of the value of agricultural output; their importance in the input structure is even higher (Table 4). Clearly, in the faster growing states this proportion will be still larger. An important implication is that, apart from the access to land, access to credit has become a key factor in Indian agriculture. This will be more true for the small farmers who would not have their own cash surpluses. Their dependence on the credit institutions makes the role of these institutions quite critical.

It is important to dwell on the question of access to land in some detail. It is interesting to observe that the concentration ratio of operational holdings in all the bottom five states (West Bengal, Kerala, Madhya Pradesh, Assam and Orissa) is lower than the concentration ratio for the country. And in all these cases it has further declined in 1976-77 compared to 1970-71 (See Table 5).

It is not the concentration of holdings, therefore, which in the Indian context determines the agricultural performance in a particular state. It seems that the more critical factor is the capacity to generate surplus or to have access to organised sources of credit. It is remarkable that the average size of operational holdings in all the bottom states barring Madhya Pradesh is smaller than the all-India average. Further, excepting Madhya Pradesh and Assam, the decline in the average size of holding is more than the same for the country. Conversely, barring Madhya Pradesh the proportion of holdings above 2 hectares is lower in these states than in the country. In each of the five states claiming top position in terms of yield per hectare in the second period, proportion of holdings above 2 hectares is significantly larger than that for the country (Table

TABLE – 4

Trends in the Value of Inputs to Agriculture and the Gross Value of Agricultural Output, 1970-71 to 1978-79

Year	seed	organic manures	irrigation charges	electricity	pest. & insecti-cides	diesel oil	chemical fertilisers	total columns (4) to (8)	all inputs (9)+(2) +(3)	gross value of agricultural output	column (11)/ column 10
					Rs. in crores at 1970-71 prices						
1970-71	694.8	292.0	51.7	59.1	40.5	226.0	343.0	721.0	1707.8	17531	10.26
1971-72	697.2	292.2	36.3	64.7	43.2	267.6	462.3	874.1	1863.5	17552	9.42
1972-73	668.8	285.6	60.9	77.2	48.6	303.1	506.7	996.4	1950.8	16315	8.36
1973-74	694.2	299.9	64.5	82.2	57.6	338.9	487.8	1031.0	2025.1	17619	8.70
1974-75	699.3	289.7	83.1	102.9	129.0	344.6	521.2	1180.8	2169.8	17248	7.95
1975-76	724.1	302.2	119.0	118.4	167.7	385.1	502.4	1292.6	2318.9	19373	8.35
1976-77	706.4	295.2	133.0	131.3	150.6	433.7	656.3	1504.9	2506.5	18276	7.29
1977-78	747.7	305.1	130.5	137.7	127.1	450.1	775.0	1620.4	2673.2	20441	7.65
1978-79	763.4	309.7	137.4	162.6	141.2	524.1	842.4	1807.7	2880.8	20920	7.26
annual compound growth rates	1.23	-0.17	16.53	12.90	19.28	9.61	9.47	10.97	11.02	2.48	

Source: National Accounts Statistics, 1970-71 to 1978-79, Central Statistical Organisation, Ministry of Planning. Government of India, January, 1981.

6). Although concentration of operational holdings in these states was, by and large, higher than in the bottom states; what is worse, in there out of five states it had further deteriorated. Two conclusions are obvious. Firstly, there is a minimum size of holding below which in most of the regions of country it is difficult to generate surpluses and perpetuate the process of growth. Secondly, skewness in the distribution of holdings, at this stage, is not proving a handicap in accelerating the pace of growth in agriculture. In other words, on the institutional side, our sights should shift from redistribution type of land reforms to the reforms which facilitate consolidation of rural holdings in viable units of production.

TABLE – 5

Change in Average Holding Size, and the Inequalities in Land Operated

State	*average holding size (area operated in ha.)*		*percent decline*	*Gini concentration ratio of land operated*	
	1970-71	*1976-77*		*1970-71*	*1976-77*
Andhra Pradesh	2.51	2.34	6.77	.599	.575
Assam	1.47	1.37	6.80	.530	.525
Bihar	1.52	1.11	26.97	.604	.573
Gujarat	4.11	3.71	9.73	.509	.493
Haryana	3.77	3.56	5.04	.527	.547
Karnataka	3.20	2.98	6.87	.539	.542
Kerala	0.57	0.49	14.04	.541	.539
Madhya Pradesh	4.00	3.58	18.50	.569	.561
Maharashtra	4.28	3.66	14.49	.528	.512
Orissa	1.89	1.63	13.76	.491	.469
Punjab	2.89	2.74	5.19	.555	.582
Rajasthan	5.46	4.57	16.80	.593	.609
Tamil Nadu	1.45	1.25	13.79	.538	.533
Uttar Pradesh	1.16	1.65	9.48	.548	.533
West Bengal	1.20	6.99	17.50	.478	.459
All India	2.28	2.00	12.28	.619	.618

Source: Derived from *Basic Statistics Relating to the Indian Economy*: Vol.2. States, Centre for Monitoring Indian Economy, Bombay, October, 1981.

TABLE – 6

Percentage Distribution of Operational Holdings - NSS 17th Round and 26th Round

State	percentage distribution of operational holdings (ha.)					
	NSS 17th round (1961-62)			NSS 26th round (1971-72)		
	below 1	1-2	above 2	below 1	1-2	above 2
Andhra Pradesh	45.13	17.96	35.91	47.37	19.11	33.52
Assam	38.57	37.65	23.73	52.70	29.93	17.37
Bihar	55.51	22.49	22.00	58.80	23.33	17.87
Gujarat	22.48	16.98	60.54	27.91	21.41	50.68
Jammu and Kashmir	48.42	29.42	22.16	54.65	30.74	14.61
Karnataka	26.19	17.44	56.37	28.75	22.80	48.45
Kerala	90.58	11.47	7.95	86.32	8.86	4.82
Madhya Pradesh	21.36	20.37	58.27	25.94	20.27	53.79
Maharashtra	31.07	14.39	54.04	24.34	21.69	53.97
Orissa	40.22	28.54	31.24	34.50	25.89	19.61
Punjab+Haryana	28.77	13.89	57.34	14.58	18.78	66.64
Rajasthan	17.67	18.80	64.13	19.59	19.63	60.78
Tamil Nadu	54.81	23.45	21.74	69.88	21.45	18.67
Uttar Pradesh	44.53	27.14	28.33	49.37	27.64	23.59
West Bengal	44.91	29.67	25.42	61.14	22.53	18.63
All India	41.67	41.67	36.66	45.16	22.45	32.39

Source: NSS No. 144, 17th Round for 1961-62, and NSS No. 215, 26th Round for 1971-72, Tables on Land Holdings, Government of India.

III

It is generally assumed that there are good prospects of continuing growth in agricultural production at the rate of 3 per cent per annum or more. The underlying reason for this optimism is our capacity to expand irrigation facilities on 2 to 2.5 million hectare of land every year. It has been shown in the previous sections that irrigation has been the main engine of growth in the past. It will continue to play that role in future. However, apart from the rising cost of irrigating an acre of land and our indifference towards proper management of water supplies, there are major problems which the country has to resolve if agriculture growth at the desirable rate has to be assured along with fair distribution of gains among agricultural producers. They are: contribution to agricultural production from a substantial part of the country may be lagging behind as the growth may be accounted for by a few well-endowed regions; share of purchased inputs may continue to rise in importance in the total input structure while the marketing and credit systems may not be able to cope with the requirements of the large mass of the small and marginal farmers; linkages with non-agricultural sector may not be adequate so as to enable gainful employment of surplus population in the non-agricultural sectors. In the following paragraphs we will elaborate these issues.

Regional Inequalities

Already there are disturbing symptoms which suggest that if not corrected the problem of regional inequalities will further aggravate and in turn will give rise to tensions and disruptions. In spite of the remarkable spread of the high yielding variety technology there are large number of areas in the country where agricultural growth has been very tardy. In early 1970s (average of triennium 1970-73) there were about 90 districts which had per hectare yield level of less than 800 kg. per hectare (see Table 7). It is remarkable that in Madhya Pradesh, which accounted for roughly 11 to 12 per cent of the foodgrains production in the country, 31 out of 44 districts the per hectare yield of foodgrains was below 800 Kg. Most of the high yielding districts were concentrated in the top five states identified earlier, Gujarat being the only top state with a large number districts in the poor-per-hectare-yield category. It is interesting to observe that although a part of Haryana, one of the top states, is also arid and semi-arid, there was only one district where per hectare yield of foodgrains was less than 800 Kg. There was major concentration of the low yield districts in dry regions of the bottom five states. From whatever fragmentary evidence one has, the situation does not seem to have improved in any remarkable manner.

TABLE – 7

Spacial Distribution of Yield Levels of Foodgrains

State	*foodgrains in yield level in kg./hectare, triennium ending 1972-73*						
	below 200	*200 to 400*	*400 to 800*	*800 to 1200*	*1200 to 1600*	*above 1600*	*total*
	number of districts						
Andhra Pradesh	-	-	8	5	3	1	17
Assam	-	-	-	6	2	-	8
Bihar	-	-	5	8	2	-	15
Gujarat	-	1	10	7	-	-	18
Haryana	-	-	1	3	2	1	7
Himachal Pradesh	-	-	-	-	1	-	1
Jammu and Kashmir	-	-	1	1	1	-	3
Karnataka	-	-	5	4	8	2	19
Kerala	-	-	-	-	6	1	7
Madhya Pradesh	1	-	31	12	-	-	44
Maharashtra	1	11	9	2	3	-	26
Orissa	-	-	5	6	-	-	11
Punjab	-	-	-	-	2	9	11
Rajasthan	3	4	8	11	-	-	26
Tamil Nadu	-	-	-	4	1	7	12
Uttar Pradesh	-	-	7	36	6	-	49
West Bengal	-	-	-	8	6	1	15
Total	5 (1.7)	16 (5.5)	90 (31.2)	113 (39.1)	43 (14.9)	22 (7.6)	289 (100.0)

Source: G.S. Bhalla and Y.K. Alagh "*Performance of India Agriculture. A Districtwise Study*", Sterling Publishers, New Delhi, 1979, p. 62.

It is quite clear that we do not yet have a superior technology which the farmers in dry areas can adopt within the framework of the present organization of production. If we want these areas to contribute in a significant manner to the agriculture production of the country more thought will have to be given to organizational aspects. For example, one of the improved practices which can make substantial impact on dry agriculture is to prepare the land and sow the seeds before the onset of monsoon so that the small saplings can get benefit of rains. But an obvious problem in popularising this innovation is to ensure availability of drought power during the pre-monsoon period to cultivate the hard land. Similarly, earlier attempts to ensure proper water conservation have, by and large, failed because they presumed coordinated action by cultivators covered by an identified watershed. Such examples can be multiplied. Ecology of these regions does not permit growth augmenting innovations on small, individual, farms.

It is clear that the growth of agriculture in the dry areas will not be possible within the framework of the extant agrarian organization. We will have to think in terms of new forms of collective action in organizing production, delivery of inputs and services and mode of extension. While it is possible to retire some marginal areas from agriculture and concentrate on the non-agricultural activities there, it is not a feasible solution for the bulk of dry regions which account for forty per cent of the gross cropped area. Organization of non-agricultural activities in these areas is as difficult, if not more, as the organization of agricultural production. Besides, if the agricultural production in these areas continues to stagnate, there is only a limited chance of compensating the emerging gap in production and requirements of foodgrains by accelerating production on the so-called progressive areas. And until agricultural productivity rises, the income problem of the agricultural producers in dry area will become intractable.

Delivery Systems

With the growing importance of purchased inputs, the role of institutions delivering credit, marketing and extension services becomes more important. These institutions are, by and large, geared to serve medium to large farmers. The failure of the delivery system to make an impact on the underprivileged sections can be mainly ascribed to our exclusive attention on the agencies which deliver the services and neglecting characteristics of the households who receive. For any effective service organization the capacity of its clientele to receive and absorb services is of critical importance. In recent years major innovations in the delivery of input and services were carried out through organizational changes in marketing, credit and extension services. There was little corresponding action to delineate the features of the recipient groups and adapt programmes to their specific requirements. This is not surprising since most of our delivery efforts are manned by the bureaucracy which has a strong bias for uniformity.

An important precondition for efficient functioning of the delivery system is the strength of the recipient system. The delivery system, today, is geared to serve the medium and large farmers and performs fairly successfully vis-a-vis these groups. It will be unrealistic to assume that a small or marginal farmer or a landless labourer can have similar, useful, interaction with the manager of a cooperative bank or a marketing society or a specialist in agriculture. The consideration of numbers as well as the power is relevant here. We have tried in the past, at least in one instance, to deliver all inputs and services in a planned, budgeted, manner to each household in the selected areas through the Intensive Agricultural District Programme (IADP). Yet the very size of the clientele proved to be a factor against this type of approach. With the exception of two or three districts the programme failed to make an impact. For any meaningful interaction the number of beneficiaries dealing with a delivery outlet has to be reduced. The only practical way to do is to organize people in homogeneous groups. These groups in turn will be able to disburse facilities in a equitable manner among the participating members. Besides, only by organizing themselves can be poor generate requisite pressure and bargaining power to make things work in their favour.

Inter Sectoral Linkages

It has been shown else where that even if we take an optimistic view of future rate of growth say, four per cent per annum, and further assume that the small farmers will not be neglected in this process, the problem of rural poverty cannot be tackled only by agricultural growth.[1] Expansion of employment opportunities in non-farm sector is of critical importance. While the preliminary results from the 1981 census show that some dent might have been made in the occupational pattern of the work force in the rural area, no major change is in evidence and agriculture dominates as the source of employment. Other indicators of the forward and the backward linkages also do not suggest a different outcome. It is important to observe that in areas where such linkages are in evidence, for example in Punjab, the rate of growth has been phenomenally high. If we accept that not many states will be able to reach a tempo of growth exhibited by a state like Punjab or Haryana, we will have to look carefully to the strategy for forging a strong relationship between agricultural and non-agricultural growth.

Two considerations will be important in this connection. One is the question of physical infrastructure, it is quite clear

---

1 Ifzal Ali, et. al., "Indian Agriculture at 2000: Strategies for Equity", *Economic and Political Weekly*, March 1981, pp. 409-413.

that the states which have progressed rapidly in non-agricultural sphere possess apart from a strong agricultural base well developed physical infrastructure, particularly in communication and power. Table 8 will show the relative position of different states in this regard. The second important aspect is the distribution of purchasing power among the rural households. I had shown elsewhere that nearly 50 per cent of the households in the rural areas in this country accounts for roughly 90 per cent of foodgrains production, the picture for the agricultural production as a whole cannot be much different[2]. This implies that the bottom 50 per cent of the rural households have claim on the agricultural incomes roughly of the order, of 10 per cent or so. Much of this income is likely to be imputed income. Unless a case nexus is built between a much larger section of rural population and other producers it will be difficult to sustain a viable growth.

There are some areas, for example Kerala, which have a relatively better infrastructure and investment in human capital, as reflected in the high rate of literacy and better health care, yet the progress of the non-farm sector in these regions is not as rapid as one would have expected. The missing link there probably is a satisfactory rate of growth in agricultural production. The lesson which can be drawn from the experience of the past is that for strengthening inter-sectoral linkages a judicious combination of three factors, i.e. a reasonably rapid growth in agricultural output, development of physical infrastructure and the investment in human capital is necessary. They will demand a better technology for arid and semi-arid areas, better organization of both the delivery systems and the recipient groups, and well planned effort to improve physical and social infrastructure. Above all the need

---

2. V.S. Vyas, "Mainsprings of Agricultural Growth in India", Dr. Panse Memorial Lecture, August, 1977.

for institutional changes which facilitate consolidation of the small farmers assets and mobilization of their collective strength, will become paramount.

TABLE – 8

Relative Position of Different States with Respect to Roads and Power

state	*surfaced and unsurfaced roads (kms. per 100 sq. kms. of area)*	*villages electrified as % of total number of villages*	
	1977	*1972*	*1981*
Andhra Pradesh	38.3	34.0	64.9
Assam	76.6	3.0	25.6
Bihar	46.6	12.0	30.9
Gujarat	26.9	26.0	68.5
Haryana	67.1	90.0	100.0
Jammu & Kashmir	7.8	11.0	70.4
Karnataka	65.4	38.0	62.6
Kerala	232.2	100.0	100.0
Madhya Pradesh	22.8	12.0	35.9
Maharashtra	53.3	38.0	77.2
Orissa	74.2	8.0	40.0
Punjab	90.5	52.0	100.00
Rajasthan	17.6	12.0	45.3
Tamil Nadu	129.6	82.0	99.1
Uttar Pradesh	63.9	21.0	37.6
West Bengal	157.9	9.0	37.5
All India	48.8	21.0	47.0

Source: "Basic Statistics Relating to the Indian Economy – Vol.2, States". Centre for Monitoring Indian Economy, Bombay, October 1981.

APPENDIX

Factors Influencing Foodgrain Production and Productivity Pre- and Post-HYV Period

In order to examine whether the relative share of different factors in foodgrains production and productivity has changed during the pre- and post-HYV periods (i.e., pre-1964-65 period and post-1964-65 period) we have tried to find out the relationship between the change in some important determining variables on the one hand and foodgrains production on the other with the help of cross-section data, with state as a unit. Two separate exercises are done for pre- and post-HYV periods; for the first period data for the triennium ending 1964-65 was used, for the second period data for triennium ending 1979-80 was utilised.

In all, 15 states have been covered in this exercise. (Punjab and Haryana had to be clubbed together). These states represent over 97 per cent of the total foodgrains production during both periods. Gross foodgrains production and the yield per hectare were regressed on the variables specified below by means of a double-log function. The results are given in Appendix Tables 1 and 2.

Specification of Variables Used in the Cross-section Study

X_1 : Gross area under foodgrains (in '000 hectares)

X_2 : Gross irrigated area under foodgrains (in '000 hectares)

X_3 : Concentration ratio of land distribution (ownership holdings)*

---

* For triennium ending 1964-65, the land distribution data are from NSS No. 144, 17th Round, 1961-62. For triennium ending 1970-80, land distribution data are from NSS No. 215, 26th Round, 1971-72.

X_4 : Area sown under high yielding varieties of all foodgrains (in '000 hectares)

X_5 : Fertiliser consumption (in '000 tonnes of nutrients)**

X_6 : Ratio of gross irrigated area to gross cropped area under foodgrains

X_7 : Fertiliser consumption per hectare of gross area under foodgrains

X_8 : Area under high yielding varieties as per cent of total Area under foodgrains.

— Foodgrains production ('000 tonnes)

— Foodgrains yield (Kg./ha.)

RESULTS

In all, we have fitted six regressions: three with gross foodgrains production as the dependent variable (Appendix table 1) and three with foodgrains yield per hectare as the dependent variable (Appendix Table 2). As the R^2 and F values suggest, all these regressions appear to be statistically significant. As reflected in the 'd' values, we did not find any auto-correlation.

Gross Foodgrains Production: The most important variables explaining the foodgrains production in both periods, viz. triennium ending 1964-65 and triennium ending 1979-80, (throughout this discussion figures for 1964-65 represent triennium ending 1964-65 and figures for 1979-80 represent those for triennium ending 1979-80) were gross area under foodgrains and gross irrigated area under foodgrains. However,

** It was assumed that 75 per cent of the total fertiliser consumed is accounted by foodgrains.

Note: Of these variables only X_1, X_2, X_3 and X_6 are relevant for triennium ending 1964-65.

during 1979-80, the relative contribution of gross area had declined compared to 1964-65, while the relative contribution of irrigated area had gone up (Appendix Table 1, columns 2 and 3). The concentration ratio of land holdings had positive but non-significant elasticities during both periods.

For 1979-80, when other variables such as area under high yielding varieties and total fertiliser applied to area under foodgrains were introduced, the relative contribution of gross area and irrigated area declined as their contribution was probably subsumed by the area under high yielding varieties and fertiliser consumption (Appendix Table 1, column 4). Both area under HYVs and fertiliser consumption had positive elasticity coefficients but only the former was found statistically significant. The above results clearly indicate that there was a shift in the relative importance of factors contributing to agricultural growth, i.e., a shift from gross area and irrigated area under foodgrains to other factors of production such as fertilisers and the use of HYV seeds in the second period.

Yield per hectare: Yield per hectare of foodgrains was regressed on irrigation ratio and the concentration ratio of ownership holdings in 1964-65 and 1979-80. The relative contribution of irrigation had gone up in 1979-80 in comparison with 1964-65. The concentration ratio showed an inverse relationship, though still non-significant, with per hectare yield of foodgrains in 1979-80. When we introduced variables such as per hectare fertiliser consumption and the HYV coverage in 1979-80, irrigation still emerged as the single most important factor in explaining yield variation, followed by HYV coverage and fertiliser consumption. The concentration ratio showed an inverse but non-significant relationship with per hectare yield.

APPENDIX TABLE – 1

Changes in the Relative Share of Factors Influencing Foodgrains Output – Triennium Ending 1964-65 and 1979-80

variables/parameters		*triennium ending 1964-65*	*triennium ending 1979-80* I	II
(1)		*(2)*	*(3)*	*(4)*
constant		1.3141 (.7398)	2.1338* (.7855)	1.9154 (.7125)
gross area under foodgrains	(X_1)	.6187** (.0717)	.4620** (.0945)	.3788** (.0941)
gross irrigated area	(X_2)	.2729** (.0861)	.3863** (.1010)	.2419* (.1152)
concentration ratio	(X_3)	.3894 (.4426)	.4616 (.3855)	.1956 (.4596)
area under HYV's	(X_4)	-	-	.0282* (.1490)
fertiliser consumption	(X_5)	-	-	.0385 (.0265)
R^2		.961	.956	.973
F - statistics		90.48	74.98	65.14
d		1.73	2.31	1.92

(In row 2 and 3, variable X_4 and X_5 are omitted).

* Significant at .05 Level

** Significant at .01 Level

Standard Errors are in the parantheses

'd' - Durbin - Watson Statistics

APPENDIX TABLE – 2

Changes in the Relative Share of Factors Influencing Foodgrains Yield - Triennium Ending 1964-65 and 1979-80

variables/parameters		*triennium ending 1964-65*	*triennium ending 1979-80*	
			I	*II*
(1)		*(2)*	*(3)*	*(4)*
constant		7.2162** (.2278)	7.5918** (.2196)	6.2662** (.5419)
irrigation ratio	(X_6)	.3619** (.0720)	.5023** (.1021)	.3052** (.1157)
concentration ratio	(X_3)	.0019 (.3603)	-.4489 (.3157)	-.3063 (.3451)
fertiliser consumption	(X_7)	-	-	.0879* (.1586)
area under HYVs as per cent to total area under foodgrains	(X_8)	-	-	.1992 (.1586)
R^2		.678	.672	.808
F - statistics		12.65	12.29	13.55
d		1.69	2.49	2.15

(In row 2 and 3, variable X_7 and X_8 are omitted).

* Significant at .05 Level

** Significant at .01 Level

Standard Errors are in the parantheses

'd' - Durbin - Watson Statistics

7

Ensuring Food Security

Role of the State, Market and Civil Society

FOOD SECURITY: CONCEPT AND STATUS

BANISHING hunger and ensuring food security to all citizens has been accepted as the primary responsibility of the state towards its citizens, and is repeatedly endorsed at various national, regional and international fora. The concept of food security is interpreted in a variety of ways. However, physical and economic access to food at the household level, at all times, to ensure healthy and active life is the crux of food security. In practice, food security is, generally, equated with the absence of hunger, or at best provision of pre-determined number of calories at the household level. This notion of food security and the resultant policies and programmes have failed to achieve the principal goal of food security, i.e., enabling households to lead a *healthy and active life*.

These days, hunger understood as starvation is not a pervasive phenomenon in our part of the world; not even in

---

(Presidential Address to III Asian Conference of Agricultural Economists, Jaipur in 2000).

Author owes much to the discussions held with a number of colleagues on this topic. Special thanks are due to S.S. Acharya, Barun Kanjilal, Ramesh Chand, Sunil Ray, N.K. Singh and Vidya Sagar. Usual disclaimers apply.

the poorer countries of the region. Incidence of hunger, defined as the absence of two meals a day, is limited to small number of people mostly in isolated pockets and inaccessible places, that too during certain parts of the year. For example, in India according to National Sample Surveys people who claimed that they did not have two square meals in a day constituted 19 per cent of total rural population in 1983 and were reduced to 7 per cent in 1993. Even while recognising difficulties in interpreting meaning of "square meal"– basically, a culturally, socially and psychologically determined notion – one can safely assume that stark hunger is not a widespread phenomenon in most of the Asian countries.

Inadequate consumption of calories is much more common. Average dietary energy supply in calories, derived from national food balance sheets and population data, show that in the early 1990s although enough food was available globally, nearly 840 million people in the developing world had inadequate access to food, i.e., below the minimum level of energy requirements. There has been substantial degree of progress in this regard since the beginning of the 1970s, primarily as a result of progress in East Asian (including China) and parts of South Asia (including India and Pakistan). On the world wide basis average daily per capita dietary energy supply increased from less than 2300 calories in 1961-63, to 2440 in 1969-71, to 2720 in 1990-92, and is expected to reach a value of 2900 calories by 2010 AD (WDR, 1993).

For several developing countries, the 1970s was a decade of improvement in this regard with rapid progress continuing up to about the mid-1980s. The pace of improvement slackened thereafter. Since then several countries and even whole regions failed to make progress, and some have even experienced reversal. Even though the global availability may increase to 2900 calories per capita per day by 2010, large number of people in developing countries may continue to face acute problem of food insecurity. The population with inadequate access to food may decline from the 21 per cent of the population of the developing countries in the mid-1990s to 12 per cent in 2010, but it is still likely to number 680 million people. We may note that because of gross inequality in distribution, the average figure of the food availability at the regional or national level, and more so at the global level, are not very meaningful[1].

Food security becomes a reality only at the household level–in fact, at the level of each member of the household. As far as household food security is concerned, with the consensus emerging favouring the "entitlement approach, principally developed by Amartya Sen (Sen, 1981) to explain the causes of famine, and its consequences for different groups of people – in other words, asymmetry of its impact – we have taken a major step forward. This approach, as now well known, is a significant departure from earlier explanation of famine solely in terms of decline in food availability. The application of this approach to explain endemic hunger and food insecurity is not yet perfected (Osmani, 1995). The entitlement thesis (which posits relationship between endowments of the households and their entitlement) can provide rich insights in understanding food insecurity once the concept is widened to include not only legally enforceable entitlements, but also the market induced and civil society bestowed entitlements.

The second area, where the consensus has emerged is the recognition of the weakness of the calorie-based definition of food security. One need not dwell at length on the inadequacy

1. Against the average intake of 2153 calories per capita per day in India (1993-94), the bottom four deciles had an intake of less than 2000 calories per capita per day (Suryanarayana, 2000).

of the calorie norm as an indicator of food security. In brief, the major problem with the calorie norm is to determine what could be considered as adequate number of calories. In India, as in several other developing countries of this region, where this norm is taken as the basis for defining poverty line, i.e., those having calorie intake above certain level being defined as non-poor and the rest as poor, a serious, but inconclusive, debate continues with different scholars maintaining different standards of adequacy. In any case, it is clear that the norms of adequate calories will vary depending on the external environment and the nature of activity of an individual. Thus, calorie requirement for a person in humid climate may be different from that of the one in dry and harsh climate. Similarly, calorie requirement of a person pursuing sedate operations will be different from the one engaged in manual labour.

Another serious lacunae of calorie norm is that calorie adequacy cannot be equated to healthy and active life. This is evident from the fact that while more and more people are able to access 'adequate' calories, this is not reflected in a sizeable reduction in malnutrition. Dietary energy supply measurements based on average availability of calories at the household level, besides failing to reveal intra household distribution of food does not reflect true nutritional status. Even if we assume that "adequate" calories are available to every member of the household there is no certainty that available calories will meet the requirements of protein energy, and micro nutrients, such as iron, iodine and Vitamin A. The most commonly used indicator of Protein Energy Malnutrition (PEM) is the percentage of children whose weight for age falls below a reference value. Prevalence of malnutrition in children under-5 judged by this indicator has declined in developing countries from 46 per cent in 1975 to 34 per cent in 1995, but progress has not been uniform. The number of under nourished children (in 1995) is estimated at 54 million in Latin America, 121 million in Africa, and 363 million in Asia. In Asia, south and central Asia has by far the highest malnutrition levels, in percentage terms as well as in absolute numbers. In these sub-regions, about 44 per cent of under-5 children are malnourished, accounting for half the total number of malnourished children in developing countries, Without an assurance of nutritional adequacy food security has very little meaning (United Nations, 2000).

There is a broad agreement that all other things remaining the same, higher level of malnutrition would lead to higher burden of disease in a society, and vice versa. For example, in general, malnourished children have a significantly higher incidence of diarrhoeal diseases, even after controlling for adverse social, economic and environmental factors. Further, untreated diarrhoea is precipitated by malnutrition, and is often the underlying case of marusmus and kwashiorkor. Similarly, morbidity associated with Acute Respiratory Infections (ARI) among children is systematically associated with malnutrition. Malnourished children with severe ARI have a mortality risk two or three times higher than that of healthy children.

There is growing consensus on the need to widen the definition of food security. *Calorie norm, at best can provide a threshold but not the standard for food security.* Food security acquires a meaning where it also connotes nutritional security at the household level. It is a different matter that nowhere, in developed as well as developing countries, this notion of access to nutritionally adequate diet is operationalised (Vyas, 1997). The main reason for the absence of nutritional security, or for that matter even the narrowly defined (calorie based) food security, is that we have not taken a balanced view on the respective role of the state, markets and civil society in ensuring food security in true sense of the term. I will mainly dwell on this aspect in the following presentation.

II

THE ROLE OF THE STATE

Whichever way food security is understood, the state has an important role to play. The state's role in strengthening food security is more prominent in ensuring availability of food and ensuring its access by the households, particularly the poor households. State interventions are of direct as well as indirect nature. For example, investment in research and development in agriculture or the investment in infrastructure, or institution of land reforms will have an indirect but significant impact on the availability of food. This is what Dreze and Sen (1989) have called "growth-mediated security". In the short term more direct impact is exercised by trade policies, price policies and by public distribution of food. There is a vast literature on each one of these topics. I do not wish even to summarise this very rich discussion. I will like to draw your attention to some of the issues on which one may say that 'jury is still out'.

One of these important issues pertains to agricultural trade policy and food security. There is a pressure on all developing countries to wean away from the policy of food self sufficiency which was till lately the overarching objective of agricultural policies of several medium and large countries in this region. The widespread move towards globalisation on the one hand, and secular decline in the food prices at the international level on the other, have been advanced as the arguments to forsake food self sufficiency as a national objective and organise production on the basis of comparative costs. But such proposition is flawed on several counts. In the first place, the notion of comparative advantage often represented by the border prices is, at best, a static concept. It does not take into account the dynamic role of technological and institutional measures. It also assumes quick and frequent shifts in cropping pattern by domestic producers to adjust to year to year changes in international prices. Secondly, wide swings in inter year and intra year fluctuations in the international prices, greater in magnitude than the fluctuations in the domestic prices, enhance risk and uncertainty for the domestic producers as well as consumers. Advocacy of unrestricted exposure to international markets ignores the fact of the dependence of a large majority of rural producers on foodgrains production as their main source of livelihood; it over estimates the resilience of the system to compensate these producers from heavy and sudden dislocations. These assumptions are not borne out by the facts, not at least in a large and poor country such as India (Tyagi, 1990; Nayyar and Sen, 1994; Ramesh Chand, 2000).

As I have mentioned elsewhere, food self-sufficiency is not an article of faith (Vyas, 1998). Once our livelihood and consumption patterns change, with small number of workers engaged in food production and small percentage of expenditure spent on food, and more resilience is imparted to the economic actors, we can think of reviewing the policy of food self-sufficiency. To take a doctrinaire approach on 'free' trade in foodgrains would amount to jeopardising one of the essential attributes of food security, i.e., adequate availability of foodgrains at reasonables prices, and will further compromise the prospect of livelihood for those who are inherently food insecure. At the same time food self-sufficiency should not be interpreted as an invitation to autarky. It simply connotes a trade strategy which would not expose the vulnerable sections of producers as well as consumers to avoidable shocks from external trade. Thus, it does not preclude 'switch' trade to meet requirement for particular grains; nor it excludes international trade in food grains at the margin.

On some aspects of price policy there is a greater unanimity. It is now well established that low and stable foodgrain prices are a potent tool to reduce poverty, reduce vulnerability of the poor to external shocks, and presumably, enhance food security (Vyas, 1998b, 1998c). Difficulty is faced in implementing this policy in countries where bulk of the foodgrain producers are also poor. Obviously, if there are urban biases, or the farmers are penalised due to macro economic distortions, say, in exchange rates, appropriate policies at the macro level are called for. However, politicians in most of the countries, rich and poor, have taken the easy option of raising foodgrain prices for the producers, lowering issue prices for the poor, and subsidising the gap between the high procurement prices and low issue prices. This policy is under severe pressure in the prevailing economic environment where containment of fiscal deficit is given high importance. More often than not, it is the poor whose interests are sacrificed in the pursuit of fiscal discipline, especially in countries with competitive politics and powerful vote banks. Richer farmers with marketable surpluses claim, and get, high prices in the name of the poor farmers though the latter do not have marketable surplus to benefit from high administered prices; in fact, as net buyers of foodgrains they are the loosers.

The more enduring way to resolve the dilemma arising out of the 'poor producer poor consumer' syndrome is to raise agricultural productivity and thereby improve the producers' income terms of trade, and afford food at reasonable prices to the poor. This was the policy pursued in the early years of the Green Revolution in the 1970s, in several countries - certainly in India - with remarkable beneficial effect on the producers as well consumers.

For raising agricultural productivity non-price factors are of critical importance (Desai, 1997). Concerted efforts have to be made to raise the level of technology, provide rural infrastructure, strengthen supportive institutions, and invest in developing human capabilities. These are difficult and non-glamorous tasks. But a state committed to the objective of sustainable and pro poor growth has hardly any other option.

Third important area of state intervention is the public distribution of food grains. A number of countries in Asia have organised programmes of food grains distribution, free or, more often, at concessional prices. If the state has taken the responsibility of banishing Hunger, supply of food to those who cannot afford to get it at the market place, is the logical corollary. There are critics of these programmes who suggest that public distribution of food grains impose heavy burden on the exchequer and the really "down- and- out" are not reached by these programmes. They also maintain that the same amount of resources which are devoted to public distribution of food grains could be utilised for creating employment opportunities, or strengthening poverty alleviation programmes. Unfortunately, the record of poverty alleviation programmes in terms of efficient use of resources or in terms of reaching the poorest of the poor is not much better. The real problem is the difficulty in targeting. Because of loose targeting, fiscal burden increases and the deserving persons do not get the benefit. Coupled to that is the inefficient functioning of the state agencies responsible for food procurement and distribution. The solution to these problems is not to abandon the public distribution of grains but to plug the loopholes. As I will state later, both markets and the civil society have role to play in this regard.

With the food distribution schemes in existence for years in a number of countries of Asia we should be able to draw lessons. I would like to underline four important lessons. One, there is a need to distinguish between the objective of containing rise in the food grains prices in general, and giving succour to the really disadvantaged sections. To achieve the former objective (of containing rise in general price level) the nature of operations would be analogous to 'open market operation', which would necessitate operations of buying and selling of grains on a fairly large scale, while a target group oriented food distribution programmes will require more modest quantities to handle. Second, while rigorous screening is important, there will always be a small section of population who will need direct assistance to obtain food. No civilised society can ignore such unfortunate groups. Third, experience has also shown that concessional food distribution can be so organised as to help in alleviating poverty in a sustainable way - by ensuring nutritional security along with food security through schemes such as 'school meals' programmes; by strengthening the production base by linking food distribution to schemes such as land reclamation, watershed development, afforestation, etc. Finally, a centralised bureaucratic system will never be able to reach the poorest of the poor, and will have built-in inefficiencies. This, the last conclusion, or lesson suggests decentralisation of the food distribution programmes and participation of the beneficiaries in a meaningful way.

ROLE OF MARKET

At present, discussion on the role of markets in economic development is at the centre of stage. Not long time back market was advanced as alternative to state, in any case to bureaucratic interventions for initiating and sustaining economic growth. In more recent years the question is not posed in terms of alternative paradigms, i.e., state oriented versus market-oriented growth, and a more balanced approach can be discerned (as reflected in the discussion on this topic in successive World Development Reports of the World Bank). This discussion has its own value, but by over emphasising the role of market the debate has relegated the *functions* of market to the background. To begin with the basics, the market has three functions of adding time, place and form utilities to products and services. These primary functions are more important for agriculture where production is seasonal, localised and needs processing before it can be consumed.

If food grains markets perform these functions efficiently every one will benefit and prospect of annihilating food insecurity will brighten. Reverse is true if markets are not functioning properly, with additional disadvantages to the poor. Are food grains markets functioning properly, i.e., are they incorporating time, place and form utilities in an efficient manner?

I will like to plead my ignorance about the functioning of the food grains markets in countries of Asia, except for India. However, a collection of studies discussed in a seminar organised by Asian Productivity Council, suggests that many of the problems pointed out in the Indian context are also faced by other developing countries of Asia (APO, 1997). An efficiently functioning market would be able to provide food grains in all seasons at stable prices only with the additional cost of storage (which would include wastage and spoilage, as well as interest on the capital invested). If the price in the off-season is more than the storage cost the market can be considered inefficient. Similarly, if the cost of food grains at different locations is more than the transport costs, or the prices in different locations are not moving in the same directions and with similar pace, the market is not performing its functions efficiently. Earlier studies in India (Cummings, 1967; Lele, 1967), concluded that agricultural commodity markets are well integrated with a high degree of pricing efficiency. Their methodology was seriously questioned (Blyn, 1973). In a more recent, and methodologically more rigorous exercise

Wilson and Swami (1999) have shown that there is increasing degree of market integration in recent years in the case of rice and wheat, but that is not true for *jowar* (sorghum) which is the poor man's crop. It should be noted that all these studies are conducted in more or less organised markets. The picture is different in the unorganised markets in remote areas where physical access itself is a problem[2]. Market efficiency worked out by earlier writers ignored two ground level realities, i.e., high transaction costs to be incurred by the poor, and discriminatory prices faced by the poor, especially in areas where markets are not developed.

For understanding the reasons for such inefficiencies, the market failure paradigm as developed by Stiglitz and others is helpful. This paradigm was developed specifically for analysing credit markets but can help us in understanding imperfections in the food grains markets as well. The factors responsible for imperfections in the markets faced by the poor are: unequal bargaining power of different economic agents, asymmetry of information and, moral hazards. When it comes to markets in foodgrains for the poor another contributory factor to market imperfection has to be recognised, i.e., the high transaction costs. The poor face all these handicaps in the food grains markets. Weak bargaining power of the poor produces and the poor consumers is a fact of life, whether one subscribes to the notion of interlocked markets or not.

Sources of information for the poor are weak due to illiteracy and lack of communication and also due to the isolated locations where the poor are concentrated. Difficulty in enforcing 'contracts' both for the buyers and sellers create

2. A narrow interpretation of 'entitlement thesis' would suggest that given the 'endowments' a household could access food from any place. In other words, entitlement could be equated to accessibility. The aspect of physical accessibility is lost in this interpretation. This aspect of missing markets provide rationale for self-provisioning.

moral hazards. In any case, the poor buy and sell in small quantities and intermittently and as a result transactions costs are high, which thwart competition. Thus, apart from poverty market imperfections make the poor more vulnerable in terms of food security.

In any discussion of food security functioning of the food grains markets is an important factor. An efficiently functioning market which adds time, place and form utility is particularly helpful to the poor, given their vulnerability as producers as well as consumers. Removing imperfections in the markets can contribute to food security, and their prevalence exacerbates food insecurity. The measures which impart efficiency in the functioning of the markets, e.g., regulatory provisions, organisational improvements, attempts towards information dissemination, and removal of locational handicaps mainly by investment in infrastructure and improvement in connectivity, are factors contributing to food security and their importance should be fully appreciated. While the role of state in providing and upholding legal framework and in strengthening market infrastructure is recognised, role of civil society to correct market distortions is not fully appreciated.

ROLE OF CIVIL SOCIETY

In the ongoing controversy on the respective role of state and markets in economic development – occasionally, also on poverty alleviation – the role of civil society is seldom recognised. The debate is in terms of strengths and limitations of these two institutions. As a result, alternatives proposed are either in the nature of counterbalancing power of state by market initiatives, or correcting imperfections of markets by state regulations. Even when the role of civil society is discussed it is couched in highly abstract terms, e.g., 'moral economy' versus 'political economy',– or as Hayami has put graphically, in terms of 'traditional – yoke' versus 'evil market' (Hayami, 1990). In the current debate neither the characteristics of the civil societies in the countries of Asia are spelled out nor the important developments in the political organisation of these societies are recognised[3].

My own familiarity with the social structures impinging on the poverty alleviation is very rudimentary, though I am aware that some of the eminent sociologists in India (M.N. Srinivas, S.C. Dube, A.R. Desai, Yogendra Singh to name only a few), have dwelt on the social underpinning of economic transactions. But such analysis has not been incorporated in 'mainstream' discussion on poverty alleviation or food security. It is equally important that we recognise recent developments in the political organisations in our societies, as these have major implications for ensuring food security to the poor. To illustrate, a fairly wide spread development in Asian countries is the decentralisation of state functions and devolvement of the powers of state at progressively lower levels.

Before we discuss the implications of democratic decentralisation for food security, it will be useful to face two important questions. One, what is the unit of civil society we are considering. We can talk about the global society, or the civil society coterminus with the nation or a region, or it could be a village community. While the exact unit of reference will depend on the functions of civil society one is examining, in the context of present discussion our main focus is on the role of the small communities say, a village. The larger unit may be important for some roles, e.g. for advocacy role, but for implementation of food security programmes, especially

3. It is important to remind ourselves of the sagacious advice of Gunnar Myrdal "For social scientists it is a sobering and useful exercise in self-understanding to attempt to see clearly how the directions of our scientific exertions, particularly in economics is conditioned by the society in which we live and most directly by the political climate (Myrdal, 1972, 1:9).

for the poor, it is the ground level institutions which are relevant. Second, it is not only the small size of the groups, their homogeneity, especially in terms of asset holding, latter as a proxy for economic power, is equally important[4]. As heterogeneity is the rule rather than exception, for availing food security our unit for consideration could even be smaller than a village community, i.e., a number of small size, homogeneous groups within a village.

I will attempt to discuss the role of the civil society, i.e. the village communities, in Indian context. An important development in this country is the amendment of the Constitution which now recognises local bodies as distinct tier of government. The basic unit of decentralisation is the village council, with the village assembly, *gram sabha,* wielding substantial powers. It functions in several respects as an institution of direct democracy. An implication of such decentralisation, known as *Panchayati Raj* system in this country, is that at the grass root level the state is becoming coterminus with the civil society. This has imparted new role to the institutions of civil society at the village level to which we have not given adequate attention.

In the context of democratic decentralisation, civil society at the village level acquires three distinct functions, vis-a-vis the State. It could act as an agency of the higher levels of government in implementing various development programmes of the state, more important for our present discussion being the programmes of poverty alleviation and public distribution of foodgrains; it can respond to the policies and programmes as they impinge at the local level, disseminate useful

---

4. One of the reasons of the success, at least in the initial period, of the now famous Amul Milk Co-operatives is that in the area where activities of these co-operatives were started, in Kaira district of Gujarat state, one buffalo per household was the rule. There were only a handful of farmers who had two or more buffaloes.

information and perform the watch-dog function; it can take a pro-active role in ensuring food security to the disadvantaged sections of the community. A few words on each of these roles may be useful.

In the first phase of decentralisation the agency functions are more important. The local level institutions can claim superiority over the higher level institutions on the ground of ensuring lower transaction costs, assuring greater transparency, and coping with the problems of "free-riders". For these reasons programmes such as public distribution of food grains can be entrusted to the local level institutions, with higher level institutions at the district, state and union levels taking up the balancing role, i.e., bridging the gap between demand and supply of food grains at respective levels. Due to intense social interaction at the local level distribution can be made more transparent, thereby minimising leakages and corruption. Most of the criticisms of public distribution system, PDS, in this country is on these two grounds, i.e. it is very costly and it ignores the vulnerable sections. Involvement of the grass root institutions will be a major step forward in meeting the objective of PDS.

Another important function of the grass root organisations is to respond to the state initiatives and point out the lacunae in their functioning. Various measures initiated by the state to ensure food security to the poor do not benefit them because of bureaucratic hurdles or procedural tangles. Village level institutions can take up watch-dog as well as advocacy functions and point out the defects and fight the malpractices[5]. While the devolvement of agency function at the village level ensures lower transaction cost, their role in advocacy and

5. The role of a grassroot organisation, MKSS in Rajasthan in ensuring minimum wages to the labour employed on the famine relief works, and its *Jan sunwai* (peoples' hearing) to monitor expenses incurred on the rural public works is a good example of such advocacy-cum-watch-dog role.

surveillance also contributes to the lowering down the "moral hazards".

The third role of the civil society, i.e., pro-active role in ensuring food security is an ethical role, moored in the principles of mutuality and fellow feeling. In this respect the entitlement approach by emphasising legal entitlement, detracts from the ethical and moral imperatives for food security. To dismiss sentiment of mutual obligation as remnant of a dying culture or expression of a romantic world view, is to ignore a large number of efforts being made by philanthropic and religious institutions to provide succour to less advantaged people. If it is considered an obligation of the state to ensure that hunger is banished from the society, should the civil society be totally immune from the suffering of the fellow human beings? It is true that in the past the social order which ensured such help to the unfortunate members was feudal in character, and had several defects. Ingenuity lies in overcoming such features without forsaking the basic obligations of the society towards its members.

It is not only in relation to the state that the civil society institutions play an imortant role, they also play an equally important role *vis-a-vis* market. Several features of market imperfection can be corrected by these institutions. By organising themselves as producers and or consumers the poor can enhance their bargaining power, and also contribute to reducing transaction costs. Such groups can afford to obtain necessary information and correct asymmetry in information. These institutions can frame and implement rules to manage common property resources, and can develop a surveillance system to discourage "free riders". By offering collective security they can minimise the moral hazards.

Several communities in this country, and I am sure in other Asian countries also, are performing these important roles in reducing chronic food insecurity. Of course, there are many more examples of the civil society organisations coping with the problems of transient food insecurity induced by external shocks such as drought, floods other natural calamities, or for that matter tragedies in individual households. In this country there are institutions of civil society still in existence in several parts of the country, known as *Dharm Gola* or by other similar names, which help poor to tide over the problem of seasonal food shortages.

There is another aspect of the role of the civil society institutions, which imparts true meaning to food security, i.e., influencing consumption in the direction of 'healthy and productive life'. If food security is to be translated in terms of nutritional security, role of civil society institutions become all the more important. The "moraluation" that the society can exercise will be any time more effective than the regulations imposed by state authorities[6]. There are several examples in this country of voluntary organisations, especially the organisations of Gandhian persuasion, who could influence people to abjure from taking liquor or tobacco or take up vegetarian diet. It allowed households to reallocate their resources in nutritionally more desirable items. Besides, as the example of several countries in our own region have shown, civil society institutions can tackle some difficult problems which are important for sustainable food security, such as population control, more effectively than what the state with political fiat or markets with the systems of incentive and disincentives can achieve. It is true, while much of the authority of civil society institutions at the grass root level has been eroded with the increase in population, penetration of the market and explosion of wants, some of these institutions

---

6. As one leader of a NGO put it, "It is more difficult to influence consumption pattern than to organise production efforts".

still wield moral force and appeal to the basic goodness of the human beings.

Task of ensuring food security to all is a difficult task. It will become more difficult if we tilt the balance in favour of one of the three important institutions, the state, market or civil society, and make only one of them responsible for ensuring food security. Recognising the role of each one of these institutions and to make them complementary to each other is essential to ward off hunger and ensure food security in true sense of the term.

8

Food Security in South Asia

Issues and Options

BANISHING hunger from the face of earth as an objective has been repeatedly articulated in various national, regional and international fora. It was clearly enunciated in the World Food Conference (1974), which declared that "every man, woman and child has the inalienable right to be free from hunger and malnutrition." The 1996 World Food Summit sought, and received, commitment from the FAO member nations to banish hunger in its starkest form among half of today's hungry population by the year 2005. This is already a step-down from the World Food Conference (1974), where the resolution on objectives and strategies of food production, declared that all governments "should accept the goal that *within a decade* (emphasis added) no child will go to bed hungry, that no family will fear for its next day's bread, and that no human being's future and capacities will be stunted by malnutrition."

Translating this commitment into concrete action requires information on the characteristics of those suffering from food insecurity, as well as the options available to them. Further, the role of public policy in this regard has to be carefully

---

(Slightly edited and shortened version of a report titled "Food Security in South Asia", submitted by the author to the Asia Pacific Regional Office of the Food and Agricultural Organization of the United Nations, Bangkok in 1997. The author benefitted from comments and suggestions by Dr. Donito Antiporta of FAO. Usual disclaimers apply.)

examined. It is the latter aspect of food security, i.e., public policy, to which this paper is addressed.

The locus of public intervention is the nation state, whose activities have a profound impact on the success or failure of the efforts to eradicate hunger at the household level. As nations progressively become integrated in regional and global groupings, regional and in many cases global initiatives acquire an added importance in several national efforts. It is in this perspective that we are examining the scope for national policies in providing food security in the countries of South Asia.

This paper draws heavily on the findings of case studies of five countries of South Asia.[1] Section 1 introduces the South Asian Region, provides justification for selecting this region for an intensive study on food security (FS) and spells out the similarities and dissimilarities of the selected countries. Section 2 traces the progress in achieving this goal in the five selected countries and points out what may be termed as the *unfinished agenda*, while Section 3 critically examines the public policies responsible for the given state of food security in respective countries. Section 4 draws lessons from past experiences and suggests needed reorientation in the policies.

I

FACTORS INFLUENCING FOOD SECURITY IN SOUTH ASIA

The concept of food security has evolved over a period of time. Until the early 70s, adequate availability of foodgrains

1. The case studies on which this paper is mainly based include: Sustainable Food Security in Bangladesh (Kamal Nayan Kabra); Food Security in India – Lessons for Other Developing Countries (Vijay S. Vyas); Food Security in a Land-locked Economy: Nepal (Vidya Sagar), Household Food Security, Poverty and Growth in Pakistan (V.N. Mishra); Food Security in Sri Lanka: Achievement, Approaches and Unfinished Agenda (S. Mahendra Dev).

at the national level was considered a good measure of food security. Emphasis was placed on food self-sufficiency at the national level, principally through domestic production. The 1974 World Food Conference added another dimension to food security when it emphasized, apart from the overall availability, stability of food supplies within and over the years. Later, and mainly due to the writings of Amartya Sen, the question of 'access' and 'entitlement' gained prominence. An agreed definition of food security suggests that *all households should be able to avail at all times of adequate food for a healthy living*. This interpretation of food security, apart from emphasizing the elements of availability, stability and access, also includes – while giving due attention to "healthy" living – the nutritional dimension. This paper looks into the four dimensions of food security.

The food security concept now in vogue stops at the examination of food security at the household level. It does not look at the food security issues within the household, i.e., the intra-household distribution of food. With the recognized gender bias prevailing in all societies this is a serious omission. Unfortunately the available data do not permit us to go below the household level.

Judged by the criteria of food insecurity and poverty, South Asia has the dubious distinction of being the worst affected region. A large majority of the poor and the food-insecure people live in this part of the world (World Bank, 1990) and the incidence of malnutrition is very serious (UNICEF, 1996). The region is also backward in terms of other social development indicators (UNDP, 1996). Any effort of ensuring food security to the poor households should naturally look at the countries of this region.

The countries covered by this study (Bangladesh, India, Nepal, Pakistan and Sri Lanka) apart from their geographical proximity, share a common history. Mainly due to the hegemony of British Colonial power for nearly two centuries these countries have common structures and socio-political institutions.[2] There are marked similarities in their judicial and bureaucratic systems, as well as in their approach to education and health services and several other fields of public intervention. There is much that they can learn from each other. Also, there is vast scope for cooperation and complementary action. At the same time, and it bears repetition, action programmes in the area of poverty reduction and food security have to be grounded primarily within the countries, while regional collaboration may supplement country-level action.

The countries are medium to large, with the population varying from 17 million in Sri Lanka to 884 million in India (in 1991). The countries range in size from 6.6 million ha (Sri Lanka) to 329 million ha (India), each characterized by diverse and distinct regions. The northern part of Bangladesh is geographically different from its coastal areas; India is divided in 15 distinct agro-ecological zones; Nepal has three demarcated zones of Mountains, Hills and Terai; Pakistan's Indus plains are in sharp contrast to the arid regions of Sindh or hilly and semi-arid areas of the northwest; Sri Lanka's landscape is clearly defined by its dry and wet zones. These regional variations have to be taken into account when designing a meaningful programme for food security as the regions within the countries are distinct, and are subject to varying degrees of vulnerability.

Another remarkable feature, which has an important bearing on food security initiative, is that large areas in several of these countries are disaster-prone. Bangladesh and coastal parts of India are threatened quite frequently by cyclones and floods. Recurring droughts are a common feature in the arid and semi-

2. The British influence on Nepal was indirect but nonetheless powerful.

arid parts of India and Pakistan. Incidence of natural calamities is more severe on the food insecure households. The respective governments also have to devote large resources to cope with frequent natural disasters.

In terms of human development, all these countries, with the exception of Sri Lanka, rank low. The UNDP Human Development Report states that of the 174 countries for which the Human Development Index (HDI) was calculated, the selected countries were ranked as follows: Bangladesh 143, India 135, Nepal 151, Pakistan 134, Sri Lanka, 89 (UNDP, 1996). More disaggregated indicators of human development, i.e., infant mortality rate, maternal mortality rate, illiteracy or life expectancy at birth tell the same story. The handicaps in the area of health and nutrition are further compounded with inadequate and inequitable access to health services. These countries have well developed institutional and administrative structures, but are weak in physical infrastructure. Some have witnessed frequent political upheavals and periodic negation of democratic institutions. But the commitment for poverty eradication and social justice is shared by important political groups in these countries. In some respect this commitment has not gone beyond rhetoric, yet the fact that the national consensus in these countries favours assigning high priority to poverty eradication should not be underestimated.

There are some similarities and significant differences in the economic structure of these countries. Two of the poorest countries, Bangladesh and Nepal, are located in this region. India occupies a middle position in economic terms among the countries; Pakistan and Sri Lanka are slightly better-off. But all these countries are classified "poor" by the World Bank. A redeeming feature is the respectable rate of growth in GNP registered during last decade - 5 per cent or more per annum in India and Pakistan, and around 4.5 per cent per annum in the remaining three countries. Furthermore, with the exception of Sri Lanka, all other countries improved their performance in the 1980s compared to the 1970s, although much of this growth was negated by the growth in population. As a result the per capita growth in GNP was modest even in the relatively faster growing countries such as India and Pakistan (Table 1).

TABLE – 1

Growth in GNP and per capita GNP

Item	*BGD*	*IND*	*NEP*	*PAK*	*SRL*
Annual growth rate of GNP (1980-93)	4.5	5.0	4.6	6.1	4.6
Annual growth in agricultural production (1980-91)	2.7	3.2	4.9	4.2	2.3
Annual growth in population (1980-91)	2.2	2.1	2.6	3.1	1.4
GNP per capita annual growth rate					
1965-80	-0.3	1.5	-	1.8	2.8
1980-93	2.1	3.0	2.0	3.1	2.7

Sources: FAO Yearbook, Production, 1994; Human Development Report, 1996.

Agriculture plays a pivotal role in the economies of these countries, although its share is declining, and has come down to nearly 25 per cent of GDP in Pakistan and Sri Lanka. It is a dominant sector in terms of employment in all five countries. Agriculture also claims a high share in the total trade even in countries with lower share of agricultural income in GDP, i.e., in Pakistan and Sri Lanka (Table 2).

TABLE – 2

Role of Agriculture in National Economies in the Selected Countries, 1991

Item	*BGD*	*IND*	*NEP*	*PAK*	*SRL*
Agriculture's share in GDP (1993)	30	31	43	25	25
Percentage of labour force in agriculture (1991)	65	65	94	52	48
Agriculture trade as share of total trade (1991)	10	17	21	16	32

Sources: Human Development Report, 1996; FAO Trade Yearbook, 1994.

Agrarian structure in these countries is dominated by small farms (i.e., holdings of less than one ha), which account for a large proportion of cultivating households. The share of these holdings exceeds 55 per cent of total holdings except in Pakistan where they account for 17 per cent. Their share in total cultivated land is also not insubstantial, at nearly 20 per cent in Sri Lanka and Bangladesh, and 15 and 17 per cent in India and Nepal respectively. An exception to this common feature is Pakistan where only 2 per cent of agricultural land are marginal holdings.

In addition to the marginal and small farmers there are a large number of landless households, accounting for 20 per cent of all rural households in Bangladesh, 30 per cent in India, 18 per cent in Nepal, 30 per cent in Pakistan, and 22 per cent in Sri Lanka (Jazairy et al, 1992). These two categories (marginal farmers, and landless labourers) and a large number of traditional craftsmen constitute the bulk of food insecure households in the rural areas of the region. These are not only large populous countries; the population pressures on land are also very heavy. Per capita holdings are small and agriculture is characterized by intensive cultivation. The scope for further expansion of agricultural land is virtually exhausted in most of the countries in South Asia, and in most of their regions.

The countries in South Asia have a high rate of population growth, high concentration of poor households, low per capita income, and a modest rate of GDP growth. Agriculture is the dominant sector of their economies and, agrarian structure is dominated by landless labourers, small and marginal farmers, and the scope for extensive agriculture is more or less exhausted. Given these and several other social and political handicaps it will be instructive to see what they could achieve in ensuring food security for their people. Hence this review on the four dimensions of food security as listed above, i.e., availability, stability, access and nutritional status.

II

PROGRESS IN ENSURING FOOD SECURITY

Availability of Foodgrains

An impressive achievement shared by most South Asian countries is in the availability of foodgrains at the macro level. There has been significant improvement in the per capita availability of food, in terms of calories, over two decades (1969-71 to 1990-92) in India, Pakistan and Nepal,[3] and a marginal decline in Sri Lanka. Only in Bangladesh was there a significant decline in the overall food availability. Such availability by itself is not a sufficient condition for food security for the poorer households. At the same time, adequate availability of foodgrains will facilitate more equitable distribution, while the reverse will occur if there is an overall scarcity of foodgrains. Table 3 shows the availability of food in terms of calories.

TABLE – 3

Changes in foodgrains availability (calories per capita per day)

Country	*1968-71 (I)*	*1990-92 (II)*	*II and % of I*
Bangladesh	2118	1995	94.2%
India	2037	2331	114.4%
Nepal	1910	2144	112.3%
Pakistan	2177	2339	107.4%
Sri Lanka	2267	2233	98.5%

Source: FAO, Food Security Situation (mimeo, 1996).

---

3. It may be mentioned that pertinent data on different aspects of food security is of varying reliability in different countries. The case of Nepal is an extreme but by no way a solitary example. In this overview paper for inter-country comparisons, we have relied mainly on the FAO publications.

The second important aspect of food availability is a change in diet composition of various population groups, indicating a rise in the share of non-cereal consumption in general and animal products in particular (Nepal seems to be an exception to this general trend). This suggests an increase in the availability of calories at a faster rate than the availability of foodgrains, particularly cereals. At the same time, changes in the diet composition, i.e., shift to superior cereals and animal husbandry products suggest that the *cost of calories* has increased.

Changes in diet composition generally take place with the rise in per capita income, due to higher income elasticity of demand for superior cereals and for non-cereal food (fruits, vegetables and animal husbandry products). Records of different countries are not uniform in this respect, but improved availability of foodgrains and of the quality of food is a common feature of most countries in this region (Table 4).

TABLE – 4

Food supplies from Vegetables and Animal Sources (in kcal), 1980 and 1990

	BGD	*IND*	*NEP*	*PAK*	*SRL*
Total (1)					
1980	1902	1959	1863	2144	2341
1990	1994	2297	2302	2431	2205
Vegetable Products (2)					
1980	1847	1840	1725	1853	2231
1990	1936	2136	2166	2109	2099
Animal Products (3)					
1980	54	119	138	261	110
1990	59	162	135	323	106
(3) as % of (1)					
1980	2.84	6.07	7.41	12.17	4.70
1990	2.96	7.05	5.86	13.29	4.81
(2) as % of (1)					
1980	97.11	93.93	92.59	86.43	95.30
1990	97.09	92.99	94.09	86.75	95.19

Source: FAO Production Yearbook, 1994.

However, per capita availability of low-cost nutritious food, especially pulses, has declined in a number of countries, e.g., India and Pakistan. This raises the question whether the improvement in quality of diet is also true to the poorer groups.

An important aspect of national food availability is the move towards national food self-sufficiency. During the 1960s and 1970s in some countries, particularly in Bangladesh, food aid (which was used for food-for-work programmes) accounted for a significant portion of food supplies. The volume of supply from this source has progressively declined, and now accounts for a limited proportion of total supplies. Countries have to depend on domestic production or on trade for their food.

Agricultural development policies in South Asian countries were directed to augment food supply from domestic sources on a priority basis. There were sound economic and political reasons to stress the augmentation of foodgrains production (Vyas, 1994), and most of the countries have made significant progress in achieving this objective. One indicator of this tendency is the decline in the share of imports in foodgrains availability (Table 5).

TABLE – 5

Production, import, export of cereals and pulses in the triennium ending 1993 (in 1000 mt)

Country	*Production (I)*	*Imports (II)*	*Exports (III)*	*Net availability (IV)*	*I as % of IV*
Bangladesh	293037	1484	-	30788	95.2
India	211227	1139	938	211428	99.9
Nepal	5430	53	28	5455	99.5
Pakistan	23003	2145	753	24395	94.3
Sri Lanka	2472	1086	1	3558	69.5

Sources: FAO Production Yearbook, 1993; FAO Trade Yearbooks, 1993.

Even when the countries in South Asia were unable to meet the requirements for foodgrains from their domestic production their capability to import the necessary supplies was enhanced due to their improved merchandise exports. The picture does not change much even if we include import of agricultural inputs. The share of foodgrains imports together with the imports of agricultural inputs still remains around 2-4 per cent of total merchandise exports in India and Nepal, and between 8 and 9 per cent in Pakistan and Sri Lanka. Only in Bangladesh do these imports account for over 12 per cent of merchandise exports (Table 6). The overall picture which emerges is that through domestic production, and whenever necessary from imports, the countries in South Asia progressively improved the level of food availability at the macro plane over the past two decades. They could also improve, at the aggregate level, the availability of qualitatively superior foodstuff.

TABLE – 6

Import of foodgrains and agricultural inputs as percentage of total merchandise exports (average for the years 1991-93), (in US$000)

Country	*Total foodgrain Imports (I)*	*Total Agri. Input Imports (II)*	*Total merchandise exports (III)*	*I as % of III*	*II as % of III*	*I+II as % of III*
Bangladesh	209901	247203	19111677	10.98	1.29	12.3
India	2806627	206395	202195333	1.39	1.02	2.41
Nepal	10600	17756	3161333	3.35	0.56	3.91
Pakistan	3754997	133580	6676800	5.62	2.00	7.62
Sri Lanka	2047477	228315	2448000	8.36	0.93	9.30

Source: FAO Trade Yearbook, 1993.

Stability

The other noteworthy achievement in this regard is the strengthened capacity of these countries to cope with the yearly fluctuations, and thus periodic shortfalls, in foodgrains production. During last two decades, there were few instances of death from starvation even though some countries faced severe droughts, floods and cyclones which resulted in large shortfalls in agricultural production. This becomes more notable as the proportion of the food aid, which was never substantial except in the case of Bangladesh, became negligible over the period. A steady supply at the national level was possible in a number of countries by better management of available food stocks, integration of domestic food markets and judicious use of buffer stocks as well as of trade channels. General Poverty Alleviation Programmes (PAP) and specially designed relief programmes further helped. Thus, the shortfall in foodgrains production was not translated as shortfall in foodgrains availability even when the former was of large magnitude.

Partly because of foodgrains availability in domestic and international markets as well as judicious price policies, the real prices of foodgrains did not rise to any significant extent from the mid-70s to the early 90s. For a large proportion of the households, particularly in Nepal and Bangladesh, domestic production or in-kind wages accounted for a large part of food supply. Households which practised self-provisioning were not directly affected by the level of foodgrain prices. Foodgrains prices did not exacerbate the incapacity of even other sections of the population to obtain food. This factor further assisted the poor and food insecure households.

The same cannot be said about the seasonal fluctuation in foodgrains supplies which was reflected in sharp price fluctuations. Part of such fluctuations is inevitable, even desirable, in agricultural products. Excessive fluctuations however hurt the poor. Instability in foodgrains prices over the seasons could not be muted. Seasonal fluctuations in foodgrains prices were more severe compared to intra year fluctuations in the general index of prices. These fluctuations hit the households which were not in a position to stock foodgrains. The incidence of such fluctuation was particularly serious on the marginal and small farmers, wage labourers, and impoverished craftsmen and workers in the informal sectors whose employment varied over the seasons.

Access to Food

The most important aspect of food security is household access to food. Some progress has been made in this direction. The clearest evidence is provided by the reduction in the proportion of households below the poverty line. In most of these countries poverty line is defined in terms of expenditure on food *plus* other essential expenditures; the former can be translated in terms of calorie intake at the household level. The ratio of the households below the poverty line is therefore a sensitive indicator of the state of food security. Methodologies in estimating poverty ratios differ; therefore, the estimates of poverty also differ. Some broad indications are however available from Table 7, which indicates a general

TABLE – 7

Trends in poverty: Estimates of poverty ratio

Country	*Early 1970s*	*Late 1970s*	*Early 1980s*	*Late 1980s/early 1990s*
Bangladesh	—	73.0	58.0	47.0
India	56.4	53.1	56.0	33.7
Nepal	—	40.0	40.0	49.0
Pakistan	—	38.93	20.0	24.9
Sri Lanka	27.7	22.7	21.9	27.0

Source: Report of the Independent South Asian Commission on Poverty Alleviation, SAARC, November, 1992.

decline in the poverty ratio during last two decades in all five South Asian countries. However, a hard core of poverty, ranging from 25 per cent in Pakistan to 49 per cent in Nepal, still persists. Clearly, some countries are doing better in this regard.

Direct evidence on household food intake is not easy to find in the absence of surveys designed for this purpose, which are not common in these countries. India is an exception to this rule due to its regular National Sample Survey (NSS), which indicated an improved cereal intake by the households in the bottom income deciles. This is corroborated by direct inquiries into the extent of hunger. The NSS data in this regard suggest a reduction in the overall level of hunger to less than 10 per cent by 1990. However, severe incidence of hunger did prevail in some parts of the country, e.g., the eastern parts, and in the bottom income deciles, going up to 30 per cent in the last decile. Similar evidence is available in Bangladesh and Nepal. Not much should be read in such self-perceived assessment of hunger or satiety, but it is reasonable to infer that overall level of hunger has declined although the incidence of hunger in the backward areas and lower deciles is still quite severe.

Nutritional dimension

These countries have failed not so much in abolishing hunger but in their inability to control widespread malnutrition. The UNDP Human Development Reports reflect the dismal state of nutrition and nutritional related aspects (Table 8).

TABLE – 8

Indicators of malnutrition

Item	*BGD*	*IND*	*NEP*	*PAK*	*SRL*
Pregnant women aged 15-49 with anaemia, %, 1975-91	58	88	-	-	-
Low birth weight infants, %. 1990	50	33	-	25	25
Maternal mortality rate (per 100,000 live births), 1993	850	570	1500	340	140
Infant mortality rate (per 1,000 live births), 1993	106	81	98	89	17
Under-five mortality rate (per 1,000 live births), 1994	117	119	118	137	19
Underweight children under five (%), 1985-95	66	53	-	40	38

Source: NDP, Human Development Report, 1996

To sum up, the countries of this region did reasonably well in maintaining an adequate supply of foodgrains at the national level. There were fluctuations in foodgrains production but public policies muted these fluctuations by proper supply management such that shortfalls in domestic foodgrains production did not severely reduce the supplies. Seasonal instability in the supplies as well as seasonal fluctuations in foodgrains prices could not be corrected to the desired extent. The headcount ratio of poverty suggested a decline during the 70s and 80s though at a slow pace, and presumably food insecurity has been eliminated in some sections of population. The South Asian countries could provide access to food to progressively larger number of households, yet severe pockets of hunger remained. Hardly any dent was made on malnutrition, which continued to be a serious problem.

III

PUBLIC POLICIES TOWARDS FOOD SECURITY

A number of measures towards food security were implemented by the selected South Asian countries. Important among these are macro policy interventions, including policies on population growth. The others include the following:

- Agricultural growth in general and growth in foodgrains production in particular;
- Agricultural price policies;
- Poverty alleviation programmes; and
- Public distribution of foodgrains.

Macro Policy Interventions

The success in ensuring food security, or the lack of it, was conditioned by macro-economic developments as much as specific policies and programmes addressed to resolve this problem. Macro-economic policies in the countries in this region were pursued in the context of progressive liberalization, rather than debureaucratization, careful sequencing of reforms (starting from the industrial and financial sector reforms), and concern for stable price levels (i.e., curbing excessive inflation). An important aspect of these reforms was to remove the special treatment given to domestic industries by way of tariff, quotas and licenses, which had tilted the terms of trade in favour of industry and to the disadvantage of agriculture. The vigour with which the policies were pursued differed from one country to another, but the main thrust of the macro economic reforms was similar.

An important feature of the macro-economic development in the countries of South Asia is that none of them achieved spectacular growth in national income. With rapid growth in income it is easier to "spread" the effects of growth. GDP did grow rapidly in some regions within these countries leading to a remarkable decline in poverty in those areas and to that extent, in food insecurity.

The case of Punjab State in India is an example. With an annual growth rate of nearly 7-8 per cent during the 1970s and the 1980s, the poverty level in that State declined to less than 20 per cent of the rural households. Most of the South Asian countries had to cope with food insecurity with an overall annual rate of growth of 4-6 per cent. When translated in per capita terms the growth rate was hardly 2-3 per cent per annum.

Another important feature of economic growth in South Asia is the relatively low level of inflation. During most of the 70s and the 80s, inflation remained in the early tens, coming down to single digit in a number of years. This distinguished the growth experience of this region from that in the developing countries of Africa and Latin America.

Population Growth

Apart from a modest improvement in the rate of growth and low rate of inflation the other factor which contributed to food security was the slowdown in population growth in four out of five countries. Sri Lanka had already achieved a low annual rate of growth of population (1.3 per cent, which comes close to China's 1.2 per cent) reflecting its high standards in education, health and nutrition. Bangladesh, India and Nepal also slowly moved in that direction. Pakistan only marginally improved in this regard, even though the rate of population growth in this country was already very high (3.1 per cent per year). The result was that even when economic growth in general and agricultural growth in particular was satisfactory, especially in the context of South Asia, progress was quite slow when translated into per capita growth.

Agricultural Growth

Faster development of their agricultural sector enabled the countries in South Asia to make some dent in poverty and food security. Majority of workers in these countries derive their livelihood from agriculture, and the food expenditures account for a high proportion of the total expenditure of the poor households. The experience of these countries suggests that direct and indirect effects of agriculture growth are positive in terms of poverty reduction (Ahluwalia, 1985). Other things being equal, the key to the success of the low-income food-deficit countries in ensuring food security lies in the extent to which they are able to increase their agricultural production. In the 1980s the record of the countries of South Asia, with the exception of Bangladesh and Sri Lanka, was encouraging, both in terms of agricultural and food production. But in the early 1990s their agricultural growth started faltering (Table 9). It is important in this context to review the contribution of agriculture, or its lack, by assessing changes in agrarian structure, technology and the price policies in influencing growth.

While discussing agricultural production growth, we should stress that the agrarian structure in these countries was dominated by the households that own and/or cultivate small and marginal holdings.[4] However, the area cultivated by the small farmers differed by country. Bangladesh and Nepal represented a predominantly small holder agriculture. Pakistan on the other extreme had small holdings accounting for a

4. Sri Lanka, and to an extent India, had also a large estate or plantation sector. However, food production even in Sri Lanka was attributed almost exclusively to the small holdings.

negligible (2 per cent) share in the cultivated land. It was also characterized by high inequity in the landholding pattern. With the exception of Pakistan, the distribution of agricultural holdings in the countries of the region did not suggest any remarkable hegemony of the large farmers.

TABLE – 9

Annual growth rate of GDP, GNP per capita, agricultural production, food production and population in five South Asian countries

Item	*Years*	*BGD*	*IND*	*NEP*	*PAK*	*SRL*
Average annual GDP growth rate	1980-90	4.3	5.8	4.6	6.3	4.2
	1990-94	4.2	3.8	4.9	4.6	5.4
Average annual population growth (%)	1980-90	2.4	2.1	2.6	3.1	1.4
	1990-94	1.7	1.8	2.5	2.9	1.3
Average annual growth of GNP per capita (%)	1980-93	2.1	3.0	2.0	3.1	2.7
	1985-94	2.0	2.9	2.3	1.3	2.9
Average annual growth rate of agriculture	1980-90	2.7	3.1	4.0	4.3	2.2
	1990-94	1.9	2.9	1.3	2.7	2
Average annual growth rate of food production per capita (%)	1979-93	1.5	1.2	-0.1	1.2	-1.8

Sources: World Development Report, 1996; Human Development Report, 1996.

All these countries introduced redistributive land reforms, i.e., ceilings on landholdings and redistribution of surplus land, together with other agrarian reform measures, such as protection of tenants, consolidation of holdings etc. These reforms did not accelerate growth in agricultural production. It is instructive to refer in this context to the example of China where the introduction of structural reforms in the countryside, i.e., introduction of the "households responsibility system," led to a steady upsurge in agricultural production from the late 70s to the mid-80s.

The main reason for the negligible impact of agrarian reform on production in the South Asian countries – apart from several lacunae in legislation and in implementation – were the weaknesses in the supportive systems, i.e., input supply, extension, credit and marketing. These institutions were basically geared to the requirements of medium to large farmers and bypassed the small landholders (Vyas, 1994). Agricultural growth in South Asia was largely attributed to the medium to large farmers who had viable landholdings and access to support institutions.

While the structural reforms did not have a measurable impact on agricultural growth, the other policy measures did have a salutary impact. Public interventions to raise agricultural production could be divided into two categories: [a] the non-price factors and [b] the price factors. In all these countries the non-price factors contributed significantly to agricultural growth.

The most important among the non-price factors was technology. From the mid-60s onwards, high-yielding varieties (HYV) of wheat, and later of rice, became popular. HYV technology had a significant impact on the production of wheat and rice, more so in the former. Because of improved factor productivity, this technology also contributed to increased income.

HYV technology was a package which included assured supply of water and adequate application of fertilizers, together with improved seed. Being input-intensive, it required better access to credit. Because of natural limitations and institutional inadequacies, not many agricultural producers could directly benefit from this technology. A large number of producers in the rainfed, non-irrigated areas or inaccessible regions where inputs could not be brought easily, and agricultural producers who could not avail of credit, did not benefit from the Green Revolution. Whatever its impact on income distribution, HYV technology increased domestic production of cereals in the countries of South Asia.

An equally important contribution of the public policies was in terms of public investment in improving rural infrastructure, particularly in extending irrigation. This also attracted private capital formation which was supplementary in nature. Capital formation in agriculture, led by public investment, plays a major role in agriculture growth in the region. Unfortunately, with misplaced emphasis on curtailing government expenditure, public investment in agriculture has slackened in the 1990s, resulting in the faltering growth of agriculture.

Most of the countries in this region also introduced price incentives by subsidizing inputs and guaranteeing remunerative minimum support prices. With an improvement in minimum support prices, the terms of trade between agriculture and non-agriculture sector which were heavily biased against agriculture started improving. The macro economic reforms, particularly since the beginning of the 1990s, also contributed to this process. Favourable agricultural prices and guaranteed minimum support prices created a conducive environment for the adoption of input-intensive high-cost technology. This indirect effect of price policy was more important than the direct impact of the rise in agricultural prices on agricultural production. As is well established, the aggregate supply response *vis-a-vis* the rise in prices is weak in agriculture.

In the context of food security, price policy is a double-edged sword. The countries in South Asia used price policy to create an environment conducive for the producers. However, that also meant high prices for the consumers of foodgrains. It should be noted that few agricultural producers in these countries have a marketable surplus and few therefore benefit from the high prices. Others who depend wholly or partially on the market for their food supply pay a heavy price. The bulk of such "net buyers" which include landless agricultural labourers and marginal farmers, i.e. the poor majority of the rural areas, are losers in the first instance.

The impact of high prices on these sections, however, could be neutralized to the extent that rise in prices leads to higher production and larger employment, and agricultural growth leads to improved demand for non-agricultural goods and services and consequent rise in non-farm employment. Such developments, however, did not take place to any remarkable extent.

Poverty Alleviation Programmes

Another important influence on ensuring food security was the Poverty Alleviation Programmes (PAP). The South Asian countries have a long tradition of such programmes[5] which are normally divided into three categories: those that provide social safety net; those intended to create assets for the poor households; and those that generate wage employment. The success of these programmes varied from country to country but was not spectacular.

The programmes which could provide safety nets to the destitute, disabled or poor households in other indigent categories, were not prominent in these countries. Only in recent years, and not in all countries, were the programmes (such as help to the widows, old persons and other disabled) instituted. One programme in this category which is gaining popularity is the mid-day meal programme for the school going children. In many countries either foodgrains are distributed free or cooked food is provided to those attending schools.

---

5. In India and Sri Lanka, they have existed for more than three decades. Other countries launched several poverty alleviation programmes in the 70 and the 80s.

Such programmes not only supplement food available to the poor households but also encourage children to attend school.

All these countries have accepted the responsibility of coping with food scarcity during emergencies such as natural disasters, when food is distributed free among the affected households. The record of disaster management in the South Asian countries has been praiseworthy. As noted earlier there have been few deaths from starvation, though the frequency and intensity of natural calamities remain unabated.

The more sustainable programmes of poverty alleviation and food security are those which involve the distribution of assets among the needy households, or provision of gainful employment. Land redistribution among the landless has not achieved its objective to any remarkable degree in the countries of South Asia. The emphasis is now on the distribution of reproducible assets (livestock, tools and implements, credit) among the poor. The Integrated Rural Development Programme (IRDP) of India, and its variants in other developing countries are becoming important in this context. Evaluation studies on such programmes, especially the IRDP reports in India, indicate that their contribution in eradicating poverty has not been significant. Another finding is that they only benefit those poor households with a minimum of wherewithal. Resourceless households are unable to take advantage of these programmes, although there are exceptions, like the Grameen Bank in Bangladesh or SEWA in India which reach the "unreachables" (Report of the South Commission, 1996).

For the asset-less poor households the selected countries sponsor a variety of employment schemes, most of which are variants of the food-for-work programmes. The employment generated by these programmes is not substantial (except in regions such as Maharashtra State of India where an Employment Guarantee Scheme is operating). Lack of funds has limited the countries from launching employment guarantee programmes for all needy sections. Even where employment programmes with limited coverage are launched, public works are generally non-sustainable because of the inadequacy of complementary capital inputs. However, the countries have devoted large amounts from their regular budget for the PAP (as in the case of India and Sri Lanka) or have imposed special taxes to fund these programmes (as in Pakistan). The scope of such programmes and their geographical coverage are widening, and their effectiveness in sustaining employment is improving. Measures such as decentralization of planning and implementing such works (as in Sri Lanka) and dovetailing these works with the natural resource development (as in India) have improved their effectiveness.

Public Distribution of Foodgrains

The South Asian countries have a long tradition, dating back to the Second World War, of distributing food to the poor households at below-market prices. An earlier arrangement was rationing foodgrains; and in later years, maintaining a regime of dual prices and giving the poor the benefits of lower-than-market price.

All countries in this region have instituted Public Distribution Systems (PDS) to achieve this objective. PDS is run through food procurement in the domestic market at a pre-announced procurement price, although imports have been resorted to in some countries, e.g., Bangladesh and Sri Lanka. Foodgrains are distributed through PDS (or 'fair-price' shops) at the "issue price" which is generally lower than the market price. As the gap between procurement and issue prices is usually narrow, the State subsidizes the PDS operations.

A major objection raised against this method of ensuring food security is that it becomes difficult to target supplies to the poorer households, and the arrangement becomes, in effect, universal. The poor get only marginal assistance. The cost of running such a "universal" system becomes prohibitive. At the same time, the experience in Sri Lanka which switched from cheap food delivery through PDS to the "food stamps" system suggests that such an alternative did not ensure food security to the needy households. Furthermore, with inflation the effective purchasing power through food stamps (which had a fixed nominal value) was severely eroded. Even in countries where PDS in its original form continues, the difference between the market price and the issue price is reduced to curtail subsidies on food and save budgetary resources. Such a move takes away the benefits of PDS as far as the poor are concerned. Apart from the income transfer to the poor which the cheap foodgrains imply, PDS also acts as market outlet in areas where private trade is reluctant to operate. Finally, it can discipline the market by providing effective competition to private trade.

The countries of South Asia used all the above discussed modes to ensure food security to poor households. The efforts were in right direction, but because of faulty implementation, the benefits accruing to the poor were not commensurate to the resources expended.

Three major criticisms against these programmes are as follows:

- These are not cost effective programmes.
- They have generally benefited the near-poor but not the abject poor.
- As they do not involve genuine participation of the poor, they encourage a dependency syndrome.

There are important lessons to be learned from the experiences of the South Asian countries in ensuring food security for the poor households. These lessons are summarized in the next section.

IV

LESSONS FROM THE SOUTH ASIAN EXPERIENCE

The experience of the past two decades in South Asia has thrown some important lessons to ensure food security to the poorer households. It may be recalled that these countries are medium to large in terms of size and population. A large section of their households, ranging between 22 and 49 per cent, is still below the poverty line. Economic growth is modest and rate of population growth is high. Agriculture is the mainstay of their economy. These countries are either food deficient or barely self-sufficient. The lessons drawn from the experience of these countries are as follows.

In medium to large developing countries a large degree of food self-sufficiency is desirable to ensure food security.

Agriculture is the dominant sector of these economies, in terms of its contribution to national GDP, share in international trade and share in employment. Foodgrains production is the dominant sub-sector of their agriculture, except in Sri Lanka where plantation crops are equally important. Growth in agricultural output, particularly in foodgrains production is important from the point of view of availability, stability, as well as access to food for the large masses. The countries in this region could make a dent in the problem of food insecurity by raising the level of domestic foodgrains production, particularly of cereals. At lower income levels, cereals and other vegetable products are the main source of calories. It is only at a later stage of development that non-cereal foodgrains, i.e., animal husbandry and fisheries products, gain in importance.

The option of importing foodgrains in any but marginal quantities is not an easy option for most of these countries, due to the foreign exchange constraint which can be relaxed in most non-oil exporting economies only by a higher level of agricultural production and export. At their present stage of development, substantial foodgrains imports would drain their meager foreign exchange earnings. Added to this is the inadequate and poor state of infrastructure, e.g., port, transport, warehousing, etc., which result in higher cost of imported food.

On the supply side, the bulk of the surplus foodgrains is located in the developed countries. Foodgrains prices in the international markets are likely to rise once the developed food-exporting countries implement the conditions proposed in the Uruguay Round and dismantle the subsidy regimes. The prospects of food aid are not bright and they are becoming progressively dimmer. Raising domestic production of foodgrains is the only viable alternative to ensure adequate availability.

From the point of view of availability and to ensure stability, major reliance will have to be placed on government stocks. The countries need sufficient quantities in "buffer stocks" to support stabilization programmes in the face of fluctuating production. Fluctuations in foodgrains production would put a severe pressure on the poor households. Importing foodgrains would drain the meager foreign exchange resources. Within the countries, foodgrains production will have to be given high priority in inaccessible regions which face serious problems in the event of production shortfalls in any particular year.

The main argument for augmenting domestic agricultural production rests on the fact that a large proportion of the workforce is employed in agriculture. Their gradual withdrawal is generally conditioned on the availability of surpluses from agriculture for investment in non-agricultural sector. The direct and salutary impact of growth of agricultural output would be on the income and employment of these workers. Growth in agricultural production will also generate secondary effects as the demand for non-agricultural goods would rise and provide conditions for faster growth of non-agricultural sectors. Implicit in the policies pursued by these countries in recent years, especially after their disenchantment with the "forced industrialization" approach to economic growth, is a notion of agriculture-led growth. Because of their comparative advantages (dynamic, if not current) this model is valid even in an era of progressively integrating world economies.

The route to food self-sufficiency should be through improved agricultural productivity.

These countries have reached the limits of extensive cultivation, and the scope for further expansion of cultivated area is not very bright. In fact, there is a need to withdraw some of the marginal lands as cultivation has been extended to areas which are ecologically unsuitable for crops. At the same time, the possibility of encouraging foodgrains production by raising productivity is quite substantial, primarily because the yield levels of most crops grown in these countries are still fairly low. The countries have used non-price as well as price measures to induce farmers to produce more. The experience has shown that the route towards increasing agricultural productivity in a sustainable and equitable manner lies mainly in the *improvement of technology and institutions*.

The large scale adoption of superior technology e.g., the spread of HYVs in areas suitable for their adoption, has increased the chances for raising agricultural production. But there is now a growing apprehension that "technology shelf" is almost empty. It is important to raise the level of yield-augmenting technology. It is also clear that a few precautions not exercised in the past, have to be taken to make agricultural growth sustainable.

These include, first and foremost, a *greater concern for environmental and ecological factors*. Care has to be taken that the natural resource base for agriculture is not damaged. This particularly applies to the efficient use of water resources. Raising productivity in water use in a cost-effective way is as important as increasing land productivity.

Secondly, *research and development efforts should be geared towards evolving labour-intensive yield-augmenting technologies*, i.e., the type of technologies which could be more easily adopted even on the small resource-poor, farms.

Thirdly, to the extent feasible, *research should be geared to develop more robust varieties*, i.e., those which can stand the vagaries of nature.

Fourthly, *systematic efforts should be made to bring the fruits of technological advances for crops grown in the poor regions by the poor farmers.*

Finally, to the extent possible, *research on, and extension of, nutritionally superior crops and varieties should be encouraged.*

Many of these considerations were ignored in the past, with the result that only a small section of producers benefited from advances in technology and that too in a manner that was not sustainable.

There is an equally important need to strengthen the delivery systems.

The agrarian structure in these countries is dominated by small and marginal holdings. On the other hand, the delivery systems, i.e., institutions for input supply, credit, marketing, and extension, serve medium to large farmers rather than those with small farms. Once their operations are brought to the level of the marginal farmers, the transaction costs of these institutions rise. This makes them bypass the small farmers. A congruence between the recipient system characterized by the small and marginal farmers, and the delivery systems geared to the requirements of large holdings, does not exist. This has to be provided principally through institutional innovations.

Genuine cooperative institutions could meet the requirements of the small farmers. However, cooperatives in most of the countries have degenerated into inefficient state enterprises in which people have no participation nor involvement. Strengthening these institutions should be taken as a priority task. Similarly, NGOs have an important role in achieving the objective of "reaching the unreachable" but their efforts, with the exception of a few NGOs, are sporadic and non-sustainable.

Price policies should not be used as a vehicle for transferring incomes.

While the importance of non-price factors should be fully appreciated price policies have an important role in attaining food security. The countries in this region generally used price policies for a purpose, i.e., for income transfer, for which it is not the right instrument. In recent years they have instituted high procurement prices as an instrument to raise agricultural output. Such policies benefit only those farmers with marketable surplus. High prices by themselves may not be effective in raising agricultural production as the aggregate supply response of agriculture is low. High foodgrain prices will hurt the small and marginal farmers as other poor households in the rural and the urban areas depend on the market for the bulk of their food requirements.

The main function of prices is to act as the signal for

allocation of resources, to which function it is legitimate to add the "*insurance*" *function by declaring and implementing the Minimum Support Prices.* Beyond these two functions, price policies should not be pressed to improve producers' incomes. In other words, by encouraging technological improvement and reforming institutions, efforts should be made to raise crop yield in cost-effective ways and thus achieve higher productivity and enhanced production. The important objective should be to improve the *income terms-of-trade* rather than the *barter terms-of-trade*.

There is a lively debate in these countries on what may be considered as "fair price" for agricultural produce. The mainstream thinking in these countries is that to define fair prices as those equal to "border prices" is not tenable in most of the circumstances (Nayyar and Sen, 1994, Vyas, 1994, Acharya, 1997). Apart from the well-known defects of border prices as the operational guide for domestic price policy interventions, the view of "comparative advantage" on which the notion of border price principally rests, is basically a static one. Once a dynamic view of comparative advantage is taken, border prices lose their role as the only, or even the principal guide, for domestic price policy.

Other considerations become important. A reasonable stability in market prices, an environment conducive to the adoption of superior technologies, an insurance element provided by measures such as minimum guaranteed prices, need for procuring grains for public distribution system, a reasonable incentive element for producers, *plus* the state of international prices - these are the factors to be plugged in to develop the price policy guidelines. Any mechanistic view is neither feasible nor desirable.

An important aspect of price policy as practiced in these countries in recent years is to remove the discrimination against agriculture. This was done, rightly, by correcting distortions in the exchange rate and in industrial policies. By bringing the value of currency closer to its value in the market, the disincentives of certain types, e.g., for exports, were removed. Similarly, by dismantling tariff and quota regimes which kept industrial prices unduly high, the terms of trade were made favourable, at least less unfavourable, to agriculture. Success achieved by the countries in these reforms has helped agricultural producers without causing distortions in the economy.

Public investment in agricultural sector has a unique role and it should not be slackened.

Agricultural growth as suggested above requires strong infrastructure support, R&D efforts and enhanced institutional capability. These are capital-intensive efforts. One of the undesirable features of the recent developments in these countries is the slackening in the pace of public investment in agriculture. The limited resources available are being diverted to subsidize inputs or output of agriculturists. Subsidies are "crowding out" investments on agricultural development. Such subsidies may be important in the initial phase of introduction of an input or a cultural practice, and only for a limited period of time. Today it has been realized that subsidies should be "capped" and be time-bound.

Growing shortfalls in public investment in agriculture cannot be compensated by private investment. In any case, private sector investment in agriculture is generally complementary to public investment; private investment is attracted when public investment makes returns on private investment attractive. Generally, private resources will not be invested in lumpy or long-gestation or low return activities, or in activities where benefits cannot be ascribed to an identified group or individuals i.e., in investments which create public goods or externalities. Much of the investment in agriculture is precisely of this nature. A certain proportion of the State's revenue has to be earmarked for public investment in agriculture. This should be emphasized because of the recent tendency of withdrawal of the State from economic activities. Such withdrawal has convincing logic in certain types of economic activities, but the investment in creating infrastructure etc., is not one of those. The state cannot abdicate its responsibility of creating basic infrastructure, strengthening research and extension and development of institutions for enhancing human capabilities.

Rural development programmes should be continued and strengthened.

Experience in South Asian countries shows that growth in GDP, unless the rate is very high, will be unable to generate measurable "spread-effects." Wherever the trickle-down effect has taken place, the rate of growth of the economy has been substantial. Apart from the rate of growth, its *composition* also matters. In this respect the growth led by agriculture is more effective in fulfilling the objectives of poverty alleviation and food security. However, it is not realistic for a large portion of the poor households in these countries to assume that economic growth would make them food-secure. These countries need to have direct public interventions to eradicate poverty.

Output growth in agriculture and non-agricultural sectors does not generate sufficient employment. Employment elasticity of agricultural growth is low, and is probably declining. For small and marginal farmers as well as landless labourers and poor artisans, employment opportunities outside agriculture are becoming progressively more important. Looking to the slow growth in the non-farm sector, employment opportunities cannot be provided on the requisite scale in non-farm activities for some years to come. Thus, other opportunities either in the form of self-generated or wage employment have to be created by public programmes, mainly in the infrastructure building activities. All the countries in this region recognize this fact and have launched various schemes to provide employment. The outcome is positive but the costs are high. It is important to bring down costs and ensure that employment is self-sustaining. This needs, apart from a more comprehensive micro-level planning, the use of labour to strengthen the agriculture base and enhance the value of natural resources. In the absence of such long term strategies the "employment for the sake of employment" would prove to be unaffordable in time to come.

The scope of poverty alleviation programmes should include not only a rise in wages or in current income. It should also aim at providing assets and skills to these sections. The poor households will be able to respond to economic stimuli only if their capacity is enhanced. Without access to productive assets, which also include the marketable skills, the poor cannot contribute to, and benefit from, the growth process.

Public distribution of foodgrains in a reformed way is essential for ensuring food security to the poor.

All the countries in this region have had long experience in public distribution of foodgrains. These programmes have helped a segment of the vulnerable households. As pointed out by several critics, the public distribution system in these countries suffer from severe defects. Needy households are not covered under PDS, or they avail only a part of their foodgrains requirement from PDS. It is the non-poor urbanites, civil servants etc. who take the maximum advantage of the system.

The objectives of PDS will be served only when it is targeted to the poor. This is difficult to achieve in societies where the poor constitute a large segment of the population and the non-poor are only marginally better off. Efforts to link PDS with some measure of income, for example, denying PDS supplies to the income-taxpayers, etc., have not been successful. The only realistic way to target PDS for the poor is by some method of self-selection. Combining PDS with rural employment programmes and to make it an adjunct of PAP is one promising way.

The other feature of PDS which prohibits the poor from taking maximum advantage of the system is the recent tendency to push up the issue price of the foodgrains distributed through PDS in order to reduce food subsidies. The margin between the market price and the issue price is being narrowed, and in many instances there is hardly any difference between the two. As such tendencies go against the very logic of public distribution, there should be a substantial margin between the market price and the issue price. A corollary to this strategy is to be watchful about the likely leakages due to the price differential between the PDS issue price and open market prices.

Efforts should be made to economize on the cost of PDS by looking closely into existing arrangements for procurement, storage and distribution, and by ensuring that the really needy groups are informed of such arrangements. In order to achieve the latter, PDS for example can be related to the extent of poverty in a region, or to the groups who volunteer for rural employment work. Another way is for the commodities and varieties which are generally consumed by the poor to be distributed through PDS. The alternatives to PDS, including food stamps, have not succeeded in ensuring food security for the disadvantaged section.

The dimension of nutrition should be added to the food security issue.

The case studies of the five South Asian countries show that *deprivation in terms of hunger* is not a widespread phenomenon. *Malnutrition* is the more pervasive deficiency. Also, while there has been improvement in ensuring food to the people, little progress has been done to improve their nutrition. A major cause of malnutrition is poverty which has to be tackled by rapid growth, preferably in the agricultural sector, and by the PAP.

But poverty by itself does not explain the high prevalence of malnutrition. There is a need to supplement poverty alleviation programmes with specific nutrition enhancing programmes. Dissemination of information is an important part of such efforts. The countries have learned that an effective way to deal with the issue of malnutrition - which also partially takes care of the intra-household distribution of food - is to give mid-day meals to the schoolchildren. This helps strengthen their nutrition, and also acts as an incentive for the spread of education. Similar innovative ways should be developed to reach women in the poor households on whom the incidence of malnutrition is the most severe.

Nutrition is not just a matter of adequate intake of calories or protein or micro-nutrients. Two other factors are important to extend food security to nutrition security: *availability and access to health services, and environmental hygiene and sanitation.* Provision of these should also form a part of the food security agenda.

Most of the corrections, as well as new initiatives, in public policies have to be instituted at the national level. However, there are some areas where regional cooperation may make these efforts easier as well as more effective.

9

Poverty Alleviation and Nutrition Enhancement

The Missing Links

THE countries of South Asia have registered a rate of growth in GDP ranging between 4 to 6 per cent per year during the last decade and a half. Their record is not as spectacular as that of the countries of south-east Asia, but it can be considered fairly respectable when compared to other developing regions of the world. Part of this growth was muted because of high growth in population. In this respect also there is an improvement as the rate of growth of population in these countries is decelerating. Rate of growth of population in Sri Lanka is now closer to that in China, 1.3 per cent as against 1.2 per cent per year in China (for the years 1990-94). India and Bangladesh have also made significant strides in this regard. Even in Pakistan which had one of the highest rates of population growth among the developing countries, exceeding 3 per cent per annum, there is a declining trend (World Bank, 1996).

A distinguishing feature of the growth in these countries was a rapid increase in agricultural production. During the

---

Paper prepared for the Symposium on Nutrition and Poverty organized by the United Nations Administrative Committee on Coordination - Sub-Committee on Nutrition in 1997 at Kathmandu. Discussion in this note refers to five large countries of South Asia: Bangladesh, India, Nepal, Pakistan and Sri Lanka.

1980s average annual growth in agricultural production exceeded the growth in population in all the countries of the region, with the exception of Sri Lanka. During the first half of the nineties, while Sri Lanka improved its position in this respect, Nepal and Pakistan lagged behind (see Table 1). As is well known the growth triggered by agriculture is more participatory and has better "spread-effect". Within the agricultural sector, food production increased quite substantially. As a result per capita foodgrain production rose in three out of the five large countries of South Asia: Bangladesh, India and Pakistan; it slightly declined in Nepal. Sri Lanka was the only country where per capita foodgrain production declined measurably. The faster growth in foodgrains production apart from directly benefitting the producers of foodgrains also contributed significantly to food security at the macro level.

TABLE – 1

Annual Growth Rate of GDP and GNP, Agricultural Production, Food Production and Population in Five South Asian Countries

	Years	*Bangladesh*	*India*	*Nepal*	*Pakistan*	*Sri Lanka*
Average annual GDP growth rate	1980-90 1990-94	4.3 4.2	5.8 3.8	4.6 4.9	6.3 4.6	4.2 5.4
Average annual population growth (%)	1980-90 1990-94	2.4 1.7	2.1 1.8	2.6 2.5	3.1 2.9	1.4 1.3
Average annual growth of GNP per capita (%)	1980-93 1985-94	2.1 2.0	3.0 2.9	2.0 2.3	3.1 1.3	2.7 2.9
Average annual growth rate of agriculture	1980-90 1990-94	2.7 1.9	3.1 2.9	4.0 1.3	4.3 2.7	2.2 2
Average annual growth rate of food production per capita (%)	1979-93	1.5	1.2	-0.1	1.2	-1.8

Source: World Development Report, 1996
Human Development Report, 1996.

The countries of this region have recognized that economic growth by itself cannot solve the poverty problem which afflicts a sizeable section of their population. There are large number of households in these countries who do not possess productive assets nor have requisite skills to respond adequately to the stimuli provided in the market place. Special programmes have to be mounted for enabling these people to obtain necessary wherewithals, including minimum food, clothing and shelter, and to enable them to participate in economic growth process. Mainly due to these considerations practically all the countries in South Asia have initiated several Poverty Alleviation Programmes (PAP). A sizeable part of their budget is spent on these programmes. In spite of the pressure on the reduction in government expenditure to balance the budget, which is an important ingredient of the new economic policy and to which all these countries are subscribing, the proportion of government expenditure on poverty alleviation programmes has not diminished. There is a national consensus in all these countries for according poverty alleviation programmes a high priority in the economic agenda.

The poverty alleviation programmes have taken a variety of forms and differ in content and organizational structures. All these, however, can be grouped under three major categories. In a number of countries particularly in India and Sri Lanka emphasis was placed on providing productive assets to the poor. The beginning was made with redistributive land reforms. However, it was soon recognized that because of the prevalent social and political environment land redistribution would not succeed beyond a limited extent. The emphasis now is on the provision of reproducible assets (animals, tools, equipments, etc.), and to organize training programmes for the poor to equip them for the better utilization of these resources. Besides, there is an emphasis on providing easier access to credit by the poor households. The instruments such as mandatory lending by the banking institutions in the social sector and discriminatory rate of interests in favour of the small borrowers are introduced as a part and parcel of PAP. Different types of asset distribution programmes exist in practically all countries of the region.

The other important category of the poverty alleviation programmes is in the nature of the employment generation programmes. Genesis of these programmes can be traced to the food-for-work programmes and the famine-relief programmes which were introduced in the region in the post-Second World War period. These programmes are now more clearly oriented towards alleviation of poverty through fuller and more sustainable employment among the poorer households, particularly among those households who do not possess productive assets or are not entrepreneurial enough to make use of such assets. In a number of countries, particularly in Bangladesh and India, employment generation programmes have acquired an important place in their efforts for poverty alleviation.

The third general category of poverty alleviation programmes is aimed at providing a social safety net to the vulnerable sections. Unlike the developed countries, in the countries of this region social security programmes aimed at providing income entitlement to the children, women, aged persons, unemployed, etc., are not yet very significant. The most important safety net provided to the poor is entitlement for cheaper food through Public Distribution System (PDS). PDS creates a dual market and enables the poor to obtain foodgrains and other necessities below the prices prevailing in the "open" market. Although in none of the countries of the region PDS is fully successful in reaching the targeted groups and meeting all their requirements, yet as an instrument for ensuring food security it is gaining, progressively, more importance. The countries are trying to make their public distribution systems more effective, mainly, by adopting a more target-group oriented approach. Other variants of PDS (i.e., other than the issue of foodgrains by 'fair price' shops), are also being tried. For instance, Sri Lanka has introduced the Food Stamp plan, which gives greater freedom to the beneficiaries in the selection of timing, quantum and outlets for acquiring food. Targeting is attempted by focussing on particular occupational groups (e.g., wage paid labour on employment projects) or particularly disadvantaged regions (e.g., tribal or drought prone areas).

A satisfactory rate of growth of GDP, faster growth in agriculture and public interventions in terms of poverty alleviation programmes have all contributed to the reduction in the proportion of the households below the "poverty line". The decline in the poverty ratio in this region is not as dramatic as, say, in China or Indonesia, but in each country of the region excepting Nepal there has been significant decline in the ratio of the poor households, if not in the actual numbers. Only in Nepal poverty ratio increased from about 40 per cent to 49 per cent. Bangladesh has brought down the poverty ratio from more than three-fourth in the early eighties to nearly half of the total number of households by the end of the eighties. India has brought the poverty ratio down from 50 per cent to closer to one-third during the same period, and both Pakistan and Sri Lanka now have around one-fourth of their households who could be defined as poor (Table 2). This is a significant achievement which should not be underestimated, more so when one realizes the unfavourable initial conditions: rapidly rising population, pervasive poverty, low level of GDP, abysmal lack of infrastructure, inexperienced administration, divisive social structures and such other handicaps. A national consensus on alleviation of poverty and deliberate public interventions for poverty alleviation overcame to a measurable extent the bottlenecks in achieving this goal.

TABLE – 2

Trends in Poverty: Estimates of Poverty Ratio

Country	*Early 1970s*	*Late 1970s*	*Early 1980s*	*Late 1980s/ Early 1990s*
Bangladesh	—	73.0	58.0	47.0
India	56.4	53.1	56.0	33.7
Nepal	—	40.0	40.0	49.0
Pakistan	—	38.93	20.0	24.91
Sri Lanka	27.7	22.7	21.9	27.0

Source: PRAG, 1997
Report of the Independent South Asian Commission on Poverty Alleviation, SAARC, November, 1992.

Important as this achievement has been there is no reason to be complacent. Even in the relatively better performing countries in the region, nearly one-fourth of the households are below poverty line. The situation is worse in the poorer countries such as Bangladesh and Nepal, and in the backward areas of even the relatively prosperous countries. Besides, the poverty alleviation programmes are subjected to three major criticisms. In the first place, cost of implementing these programmes is very high. This leads some of the critics to suggest that the amount earmarked for PAP could be better utilised by investing it in the general developmental activities. There is no evidence to suggest that the cost of administering these programmes be it IRDP, employment programme, or PDS is going down. The second worrisome aspect is that the poorest of the poor have not benefitted much from these programmes. The people who have crossed the poverty-line are those who were closer to the poverty-line. Third, in the absence of the genuine participation of the poor themselves, these programmes have generated a 'dependency syndrome'.

Thus, significant progress has been made in alleviating

poverty yet certain concerns persist. The important among these concerns is that the reduction in poverty has not been sufficiently reflected in the reduction in malnutrition.

II

The increase in foodgrains production at the national level on the one hand, and the poverty reduction on the other has, generally, resulted in an improvement in average calorie intake at the national level. Thus, in 4 out of the 5 selected countries calorie intake per capita per day has improved in 1990 compared to 1980; Sri Lanka is the only exception (Table 3). Picture is not as encouraging when it comes to the calorie intake among the poorer sections. For India, the latest National Sample Survey data (for 1994) shows that 35.7 per cent of the urban population and 27.8 per cent of the rural population have per consumer unit calorie intake of less than 80 per cent of the prescribed norms. In Bangladesh the bottom 5 deciles' calorie consumption is lower than the normative requirements. In Sri Lanka, again, nearly 45 per cent of the households are not receiving the minimum required calories. It is estimated that in Nepal 36 per cent of the population consume less than the minimum dietary energy requirements (PRAG, 1997).

TABLE – 3

Kilo Calories Per Caput Per Day - National Average

Country	1970	1980	1990
Bangladesh	2196	1902	1994
India	2082	1959	2297
Nepal	1912	1863	2302
Pakistan	2200	2144	2431
Sri Lanka	2304	2341	2205

Source: FAO Year Book, Production, 1994.

It is a sad fact that in all these countries hunger does persist among the households on the lower rungs of income ladder. The direct evidence of calorie intake in the poorer households obtained through specially designed surveys suggests that a moderate increase in per capita intake of calories has taken place even among the poorer section in at least three of the five larger countries of the region, i.e., India, Pakistan and Sri Lanka. In the remaining two countries, i.e., in Bangladesh and Nepal, hardly any dent was made in the problem of protein-energy malnutrition (PEM).

All the five countries suffer from serious nutritional deficiencies, such as vitamin A deficiency, iron deficiency, iodine deficiency etc. The same is true about other micro nutrients. For example, the intake of protein was less than 50 gms a day in Bangladesh and Sri Lanka while India barely met the adequacy level. Calcium was supplied in insufficient quantities in all the countries of South Asia with the exception of Pakistan. India had a relatively better record in this regard. The iron deficiency was most critical in Bangladesh where it was less than 10 gm. i.e., well below the adequacy level. There was no clear indication of improvement in the per capita iron intake. The intake of thiamine showed increase in India and Pakistan but its intake in Bangladesh and Sri Lanka was less than adequate. Situation of riboflavin was no better than that for other micro nutrients, with Bangladesh showing a markedly deficient situation, while Sri Lanka's position was only marginally better. In case of vitamin C, Bangladesh registered a signification reduction over the last decade (UN. ACC. 1993). It should be remembered that these figures are in terms of average availability. Arguably the deficiencies of micro-nutrients are much more severe among the poorer households.

The net result of these deficiencies was reflected in various indicators of malnutrition. The most significant indicator in this respect is the infant mortality rate (IMR). In this respect situation in Sri Lanka (with IMR at 18 per 1000 live births in 1992) was far superior compared to other countries of the region. Bangladesh and Nepal with IMR at 108 and 99 are at the other extreme. India and Pakistan with IMR of 82 and 91 occupy the middle position. Within these countries the situation in some parts was better than others (for example, infant mortality rate in Kerala was fairly low). An equally sensitive indicator of malnutrition is the percentage of underweight children under age five. The evidence available towards the end of 1980s suggests that at least in 3 out of 5 large countries of the region, for which data are available, i.e., Bangladesh, India and Pakistan, not only the proportion of under-weight children was high, the improvement in the situation over a period of 10 years was, at best, sluggish. The decline in the percentage of underweight children ranged between 0.4 per cent per year in Bangladesh to 0.9 per cent per year in Pakistan. In India the decline was at the rate of 0.7 per cent per year (UN.ACC., 1993). The other important indicators of malnutrition, e.g., women's mortality and morbidity, paint a similar picture (Table 4).

It is clear that while a few countries have succeeded in improving calories intake at the household level, even these were not successful in attacking the problem of mal-nourishment and ill-health, particularly among the children and women. With rampant malnutrition and consequent ill-health prevailing in the large sections of population, the calorie intake could impact on the health only inadequately due to what may be called the "sieve effect". In other words, the body is not capable to digest the food intake in a manner which would lead to better strength and stamina.

Availability of food, even the availability of nutrients, at the household level is, however, one of the determinants

TABLE – 4

Basic Health Indicators

	Year	*Bangladesh*	*India*	*Nepal*	*Pakistan*	*Sri Lanka*
HDI ranking		146	134	151	128	97
Life expectancy at birth	1992	55.6	60.4	53.5	61.5	71.9
IMR (per 1000 live births)	1992	108	82	99	91	18
Underweight children under age five (%)	1990	66	—	51	42	42
Average annual change in prevalence underweight in percentage points (per year)	1980s	-0.4	-0.7	—	-0.9	—
Malnourished children under age five ('000)	1992	11480	69345	1665	3725	762
Low birth weight infants (%)	1990	50	33	—	25	25
Maternal mortality rate (per 100,000 live births)	1980-92	600	460	830	500	80
Pregnant women aged 15-49 with anaemia (%)	1975-91	58	88	—	—	—
Population with access to (%)						
Health services	1985-93	45	85	—	55	93
Safe water	1988-93	84	79	42	68	60
Sanitation	1988-93	31	27	6	38	50
Births attended by trained health personnel (%)	1983-93	5	33	6	35	94
One year olds fully immunised against:						
TB (%)	1990-93	95	92	73	87	86
Measles (%)	1990-93	71	82	59	71	89
Population per doctor	1988-91	12500	2439	1666	2000	7143
% of government budget on health	1990	4.8	1.6	—	0.7	—

Source: PRAG, 1997

UNDP, Human Development Report, 1995

UN, Second Report on the World Nutrition Situation, Country Trends, Methods and Statistics, Vol. II, March 1993.

(though an important one), in enhancing nutrition. There are two other relevant factors: [a] availability and access to health services and [b] quality of care. Starting with the availability of health services, it may be mentioned that the investment in these services is inadequate. Hardly 0.7 per cent of the government budget in Pakistan is earmarked for health services. It is 1.6 per cent for India and 4.8 per cent for Bangladesh. These data pertain to year 1990. However, there is no evidence to suggest that there had been any remarkable improvement in this regard during last few years. Vast sections of population do not have the benefit of a qualified doctor, or even a nurse. The basic components of an efficient health service are not in place (Table 4).

More than the amount of expenditure, or the availability of certain basic facilities, the policies in regard to the provision of health services leave much to be desired. Health system is, basically; urban oriented; there is much greater emphasis on curative rather than preventive aspects; health administration is highly bureaucratized and centralized; administrative costs are unduly high. The situation has become worse because of the inadequacy of sanitary services, difficulties in obtaining potable water, and extensive pollution. The poor have to bear more than their share of these deficiencies.

As regards the quality of care at the household and community level, the socio-cultural factors militate against the care of children in general and girl child in particular. In traditional societies with better social cohesion and wider prevalence of joint families the children, probably, received more attention. Now the traditional safety-nets are much weakened with the disruption of social loyalties and disintegration of joint family system. These factors coupled with widespread poverty and economic compulsion to earn a living, have created a situation in which women do not have enough time to bestow care and attention on their children. The lack of scientific knowledge on child rearing adds to the handicaps. The health systems as organized in these countries do not contribute to enhancing the level of awareness on health and nutrition. There are, however, certain public interventions, the most notable being the ICDS programme in India and the mid-day meal programmes in a number of countries in the region, which have been quite noteworthy in their contribution to child health care. However, the cost incurred on these programmes is disproportionately high compared to advantages that they bestow.

III

Poverty is perhaps the single most important determinant of individual, family and, community health status. The eradication of poverty is an important measure, though not the sufficient one, to improve nutrition. For achieving nutritional goals the countries in the region will have to strengthen simultaneously all the three determinants of nutrition, i.e., household food security, availability and access to health services and, quality of care. A comprehensive approach is needed even while pursuing the goal of poverty alleviation. The manner in which poverty alleviation programmes are designed need to be reviewed. While targeting these programmes at the poorest level of the societies the nutritional aspect needs to be built in.

For example, a large number of programmes aimed at asset acquisition by the poor, e.g., IRDP in India, comprise projects to distribute animals (dairy cattle, poultry birds, pigs, etc.) to the poor households. Raising vegetables and fruits or small scale fishery could be made part of PAP. As these enterprises contribute, at least partially, to self-provisioning, nutritional education can be imparted along with the resources for these projects. Enhancing nutrition is relatively easy in the programme for rural employment generation. Wherever a kind component is provided as a part of the wages on the rural works, more nutritious food can be made part of the kind payment. Similarly, in the organization of PDS incentives can be provided by way of, say, discriminatory pricing, to encourage off-take of more nutritional grains and other food stuff.

A few lessons from the experience of PAP in South Asia may be emphasized in order to make them effective tools for nutrition enhancement as well.

1. Poverty Alleviation should be treated in a comprehensive way. PAPs will have to incorporate the features of health care if they are to make positive and lasting impact on malnutrition. An integrated view on poverty alleviation which gives equal importance to household income together with education, health and nutrition, will better contribute to the economic performance of the poor households.

2. Poverty Alleviation would be sustainable, only if proper attention is given to the preservation and enhancement of natural resources, on sanitation and on environmental hygiene. Programmes which are indifferent to the degradation of land, or pollution of air and water, cannot be sustained for long, nor can they impart requisite strength to the beneficiaries.

3. Poverty Alleviation Programmes should be appropriately targeted. Even in the countries which have relatively better record in poverty alleviation, the near-poor rather than the abject poor have taken the advantage. The problem of malnutrition, including the incidence of PEM, is more severe at the bottom rung of the poverty ladder. Undoubtedly, it is more difficult

to reach the 'unreachable'. Alternative delivery system, e.g., NGOs or the local level governments, could, probably, be more effective.

4. Poverty Alleviation should emphasise the quality of care. Strong emphasis on the care for the under-privileged, for the women and for children should inform the philosophy of PAP and should be reflected in the design and the content of the programmes.

10

India's Rural Development Strategies

Lessons in Agricultural Growth and Poverty Alleviation

DURING the course of the last two decades India's agricultural production nearly doubled, yet there was no remarkable improvement in the standard of living of the poorer half of the rural population. A critical review of India's growth strategy may provide important lessons on both of these aspects. India not only avoided a stagnation in agricultural production, as limits to expand the sown area were reached but, by all indications also instilled a dynamism in the growth process. The same country, however, could make only minimal progress in providing adequate food, clothing, housing and other bare essentials of decent human existence to a large proportion of its population. The persistence of widespread poverty is all the more intriguing given professed egalitarian bias of Indian policy makers, as is the record of agricultural growth itself considering the pervasiveness of India's small and fragmented farms, illiterate and resource poor peasantry and severe social and institutional handicaps. In this paper

---

Paper prepared at the invitation of International Association of Agricultural Economists, for IAAE/CAAE/CAAS Symposium, Beijing, China in 1987.

we examine the facets of India's growth performance and draw some important lessons from this experience.

I

AGRICULTURAL PERFORMANCE

Main Characteristics of Agricultural Growth

In the post Independence era (i.e. since 1947), and more so since the early sixties, the driving force for agricultural growth in India was the urge for food self-sufficiency. A severe drought in 1964/65 which was preceded by four years of stagnation in agricultural production reduced the availability of the domestic foodgrains to a percariously low level. India's experience in procuring foodgrains from abroad was not a happy one. Indian policy makers felt that political strings were being attached to the food supply deals. In any case, nation's attention was drawn to the low productivity of resources committed to agriculture. During the same period many other developing countries were passing through a similar "food crisis". What distinguishes India's record is that once a decision to attain food self-sufficiency was made, the nation's considerable resources - human, material and institutional – converged on reaching this goal. As a result food self-sufficiency (understood in the rather narrow sense of substituting food imports by domestic production) was largely achieved in less than two decades. In the following paragraphs, we review the main features of agricultural growth and briefly examine the principal policy interventions to achieve this objective.

For an examination of India's agricultural strategy, the period since Independence may be broken into two phases. The years preceding the introduction of the High Yielding

Varieties (HYV) Program, (i.e., from 1947/48 to 1965/66) may be called Phase I and the years following this program, Phase II. In this paper we will be concentrating more on the post-HYV period, (i.e. on Phase II.)

For a period of 17 years, from 1967/68 to 1985/86, agricultural production increased at a (compound) rate of 2.7 per cent per annum. During the same period, the growth rate of population was 2.24 per cent per annum. There was a slow but continuing improvement in per capita production. By itself India's agricultural growth rate was an impressive but not an exceptional performance. What makes India's performance remarkable is the fact that the growth was achieved in progressively larger measures by improvements in productivity of the most important and constraining factor, namely, land. This is reflected in the increases in yield per hectare. During this period, area under crops was increasing at a rate of 0.4 per cent per annum, while the yield per hectare was increasing at a rate of 2.0 per cent per annum. A large proportion of increment in the area was accounted for by an increase in the area-sown-more-than-once (mainly in the perennially irrigated areas) or, in other words, by greater intensity of land use. As far as *net* sown area is concerned, it increased by barely 1 per cent over the *whole* period, from 140.8 million hectare (in 1970-71) to 141.8 million hectare in 1982-83.[1] A doubling of agricultural output on virtually the same land area makes India's performance truly remarkable.

Apart from the emphasis on augmenting yield, there are other distinguishing features of India's agricultural development strategy which need to be recognized.

---

1. Various issues of *Indian Agriculture in Brief*, published by the Directorate of Economics and Statistics, Ministry of Agriculture, Government of India. Statistics quoted in this paper, unless otherwise stated, are from this publication.

a) Greater emphasis was placed on increasing production of food crops as against non-food crops; among the food crops on the cereals; and among the cereals principally on wheat. The following table provides necessary details.

TABLE – 1

Compound Growth Rate of Production of Principal Crops 1967/68 to 1985/86 (in percent per annum)

All crops	2.68%
Food grains	2.74%
Cereals	2.97%
Wheat	5.66%

Source: Indian Agriculture in Brief

(b) The strategy of food grains production was centered around HYV of seeds of wheat and rice. HYVs of wheat and rice were released on a large scale in 1966/67; by 1981/82, nearly 75 per cent of the area under wheat was planted with HYVs. The increase of area under rice was less spectacular, nonetheless during the same period approximately 50 per cent of area under rice cultivation was brought under HYV rice varieties.[2] The speed at which high yielding varieties, particularly for wheat, spread in India was unprecedented.[3]

(c) HYVs give best results with assured water supply and adequate application of fertilizers. It was no surprise, therefore, that HYVs spread most rapidly in areas

2. Data from *Development and Spread of High Yielding Wheat Varieties in Developing Countries*, and *Development and Spread of High Yielding Rice Varieties in Developing Countries*, both by Dana G. Dalrymple, United States Agency for International Aid, 1986.

3. See *India's High Yielding Varieties Programme in Wheat, 1966-67 to 1971-72*, by V.S. Vyas, Centro Internacional de Majoramiento de Maiz y Trigo, Mexico City, 1975.

where already significant expansion in irrigation area had already occurred and farmers possessed the means to purchase inputs such as fertilizers. Initially only a few districts, mainly in the Punjab, Western Uttar Pradesh and Coastal Andhra Pradesh, satisfied these requirements. Thus, the base on which the production potential was being developed was relatively narrow.

Two further points concerning India's agricultural growth strategy need to be made. First, agricultural growth in India took place in the face of serious internal and external handicaps. Second, developments taking place in the economy during the last few years give reasonable assurance that the current pace of growth in agriculture can be sustained for quite some time to come.

Agricultural developments since the mid-sixties, commonly referred to as the Green Revolution, are not distinguishable from the experience during the previous decade and a half in terms of rate of growth in production. The growth rate of agricultural production was actually higher at 3.1 per cent per annum during 1949/50 to 1964/65, in Phase I, compared to 2.7 per cent during Phase II (1967/68 to 1985/86). What distinguishes the latter period, as mentioned above, was the much higher contribution of yield increases to total output growth (2.0 per cent in Phase II compared to 1.3 per cent in Phase I). It would be readily appreciated that augmenting production by increasing yield per hectare is a much more difficult task than increasing output through area expansion. The former involves timely delivery of modern inputs to millions of small and fragmented farms served by poorly developed infrastructure of transport and communication; organization of massive extension services to spread appropriate agronomic practices among a very large number of illiterate producers; strengthening credit and marketing institutions which can interface with numerous small farmers having paltry resources. India had, and continues to have, all these handicaps. In addition, the external environment was also placing serious strains on the country's resources at a time when it had just emerged from the century's worst drought. Seen in this background, India's successes in agricultural production can be better appreciated.

Another salient feature of India's agricultural performance is its capacity to sustain the momentum of the New Technology. Three critical factors helped determine the success of HYV based New Technology: (i) enlargement of area under irrigation, (ii) continuous adaptation of old HYVs and release of new varieties, and (iii) provision of modern inputs, particularly fertilizers. Irrigation is the keystone to this program. Since the mid-sixties area under irrigation has increased at an impressive rate of 2.1 per cent per year. One-third of the country already benefits from irrigation or assured rainfall. An expansion of irrigation over, say, 1.5 to 2.0 million hectares every year has more or less been institutionalized. Use of improved seeds and fertilizers goes in step with irrigation expansion. Research in varietal improvement and strengthening of delivery systems have generated their own momentum.

If there are no major natural calamities, seriously misdirected economic policies or a substantial deterioration in the external environment, the established trend in production can not only be maintained, it can be accelerated. Slowly but steadily New Technology is spreading over larger areas, and this process can continue.[4]

---

4. Evidence assembled by G.S. Bhalla, Yoginder Alagh, and S. Mahendra Dev suggest that 84 districts comprising 25.6 per cent of cropped area have reached a productivity level of Rs. 1300 or more in triennium 1975-78. During the triennium 1962-65 the number of such districts was 48, accounting for 12.6 per cent of cropped area. See, Yoginder K. Alagh "Regional Dimensions of India Agriculture", paper presented at the Conference on Indian Economy, Boston, 1986 (mimeo) Table 4.

Agricultural Policies

The policy measures which enabled India to usher in the Green Revolution have relevance for other developing countries. We will briefly review policy interventions in three important areas: technology development, price policies, and changes in agrarian structure through land reform.

Technology Development

India had started systematic efforts in developing agricultural technology right from the beginning of this century. However, these efforts were given a fillip after Independence. Three major organizational developments are noteworthy in this connection: first, the establishment of an apex organization, the Indian Council of Agricultural Research (ICAR); second, the establishment of state level Agricultural Universities patterned after the United States' Land grant Colleges; and third, the launching of All India Coordinated Research Schemes in commodities and farming systems. These three moves complemented one another. ICAR could take an overview of research needs of the country and set a national research agenda. The Agricultural Universities, to whom the state level research tasks were assigned, could take a more disaggregated, regional view. Integration of teaching and research tasks also ensured a close liaison between basic scientific research and applied agricultural research. The All India Coordinated Research Programs for different commodities and located in different soil-climatic zones, enabled experiments to be carried out in different environments, and thus provided cross sectional results to scientists working on different aspects of a commodity in different locations. By the early sixties, when high yielding semi-dwarf varieties of wheat and rice were being developed at CIMMYT and IRRI the agricultural research establishment in India was in a position to select, cross and adapt useful varieties.[5]

Mainly because of efficient organization of research and improved extension methods, productivity of investment in research turned out to be fairly high. Studies made in the early to mid-seventies indicate that the annual rate of return on the investment in agricultural research was above 60 per cent.[6]

In addition to the strengthening the organizational structure the Indian government gave special attention to improving the working conditions of the agricultural scientists and raising their emoluments. An All-India Service of Agricultural Scientists was created which enabled the scientists to reach the top positions in the bureaucratic hierarchy which earlier were the preserve of generalists. Apart from opening up new avenues of promotion, this arrangement accorded prestige and recognition to the agricultural scientists.

In the mid-sixties, with a developed research apparatus and qualified manpower, policy makers were in a position to decide on the major research thrusts. They opted for encouraging research in high yielding wheat and rice varieties. It was possible at that time to give greater support to research in high yielding varieties of maize or pearl millet or sorghum, all of which were showing some signs of a breakthrough. In the case of wheat and rice, however, chances of success were considered to be high. Since the country was facing a difficult food situation, this probability weighed heavily on the decision makers. As we shall see later, it also had distributional implications.

---

5. Due to limitation of space, we are not dealing here with a number of supportive moves in extension.

6. Quoted by Vernon W. Ruttan, based on the research of Evanson and Jha (1973) and Kahlon, Bal, Saxena and Jha (1977). See *Agricultural Research Policy* by Vernon W. Ruttan, University of Minnesota Press, Minneapolis, 1982, Table 10.3, p. 243.

Agricultural Price Policy

The price policy pursued in India played a major role in the spread of New Technology. It ensured stable and remunerative prices for those crops where advances in technology promised a yield breakthrough. The price policy was designed, at the same time, to ensure that consumers also received the benefits of gains in productivity, it was also complemented by an organizational structure which guaranteed the implementation of policy pronouncements at the field level.

Since the early sixties Indian policy makers recognized the gravity of the food problem. The Food Corporation of India (FCI) was established in 1964 to facilitate proper management of public distribution system in foodgrains. Soon it acquired the capacity to procure, transport, store and distribute foodgrains in huge quantities. The magnitude of its operations are indicated by the fact that by the late seventies FCI was procuring nearly 12 to 13 million tons of foodgrains every year, distributing almost an equal amount through a large number of fair price shops, and holding a buffer stock of approximately 20 million tonnes. (By 1986 the stocks reached a level of 23 million tons.) Through a net work of its own procurement centres and by utilizing the state governments' facilities as well as farmers' cooperatives, FCI enabled producers in the 'surplus' areas to dispose off their grains at the prices announced by the Government.

The Agricultural Price Commission (APC) constituted in 1965 was another important component of the food management system. Although it was located in the Ministry of Food and Agriculture, it was accorded autonomous status. Some of the outstanding economists of the country were invited to serve on the Commission. Bureaucratic and political leadership gave serious consideration to the Commission's recommendations. A tradition of mutual trust and respect was built. With APC as the thinking organ and FCI as the implementing arm, the country was well placed to manage its difficult food economy.

Since the mid-sixties price policy was geared to support the adoption and spread of New Technology. During the first few years of its existence, APC recommended minimum support prices as well as procurement prices for important agricultural commodities. The minimum guaranteed prices for major commodities were announced before the beginning of the sowing season. The minimum guaranteed price was generally adequate to cover the cost of variable inputs for a particular crop. Towards the beginning of harvesting season, procurement prices for important foodgrains (e.g. wheat and rice) were announced. FCI would procure any quantity of wheat or rice offered by any producer at this price level. Procurement prices were closer to the anticipated 'normal' market prices. In addition to an eye on the 'normal' price, several other considerations were taken into account in arriving at the procurement price such as international prices, input prices, prices of competing crops, and above all, the most important factor in determining procurement prices, was the cost of cultivation.

In the latter years (i.e. the beginning of the seventies), the distinction between minimum support price and procurement price was abolished, with the procurement price becoming the only relevant instrument of price policy. This was a defensible proposition in a situation of overall scarcity, but proved to be a burden and a liability once the state of self-sufficiency and, in some commodities, a state of surplus, was reached. This is due to the fact that the procurement prices guaranteed a *cost-plus* return to the producers and implied that the state will purchase all wheat (or rice) offered for sale at that price. Nonetheless, the price policy played a major role in steering the country away from a state of acute shortage toward that of relative adequacy. This role was played effectively because three important considerations were always kept in the forefront.

First, the agricultural price policy was effectively supported by the country's policy on technology. By announcing remunerative and guaranteed prices for the crops for which new technologies were available (e.g. wheat), producers were encouraged to adopt the technology without fearing a crash in prices due to increased output. For example, from the mid-sixties to early seventies, during which time production of wheat more than doubled (from 10.4 million tons in 1965-66 to 24.7 million tons in 1972-73), the minimum support prices for wheat were first increased and then stabilized (around Rs. 76 per quintal). Since then, prices for wheat have risen by approximately 3 per cent per annum mainly to neutralize increases in input prices. The same instrument of guaranteed prices was used for the spread of HYVs of rice, once such varieties were available. Thus, since the mid-seventies when a superior technology for rice was established, a boost was given to rice prices with the guaranteed price of rice rising at the rate of approximately 7 per cent per annum, much faster than the price of inputs, the general index of prices or for that matter procurement price of wheat.

The second distinguishing feature of the price policy was its role in stabilizing returns to the farmers in the face of fluctuations in commodity production. The objective was not to neutralize fully the impact of production changes on the market place, but rather to soften the blow. As D.S. Tyagi has shown, if the price flexibility coefficient is taken into account, year-to-year fluctuations in prices in the face of variability in crop production would have been much sharper than what actually took place, due mainly to the countervailing role played by officially announced prices. The following table summarizes his results.

TABLE – 2

Fluctuations in Crop Production and Changes in Prices

	Wheat			*Total Cereals*		
Year	*% Change in Production over the previous Year*	*Expected Change in Prices*[1]	*Actual Change in Prices*[2]	*% Change in Production over the Previous Year*	*Expected Change in Prices*[3]	*Actual Change in Prices*[2]
1	*2*	*3*	*4*	*5*	*6*	*7*
1971-72	+10.8	-24.5	+7.0	-2.6	+6.5	+1.9
1972-73	-6.3	+14.3	+1.6	-7.4	+18.5	+13.6
1977-78	+4.4	-21.4	-1.7	+14.7	+36.8	-2.7
1979-80	-10.4	+23.6	+9.6	-15.5	+38.8	+10.1
1980-81	+14.1	-32.0	+8.7	+17.6	-44.0	+12.4
1982-83	+14.3	-32.5	+1.8	-3.4	+8.5	+9.7

Note: Price changes are for the corresponding marketing years.

1. (2) multiplied by the price flexibility coefficient.
2. Percentage change in the annual average of wholesale price indices.
3. (5) multiplied by the price flexibility coefficient.

Source: D.S. Tyagi, "Price Policy for Agricultural Development" 1986 (mimeo).

Third, the agricultural price policy, while ensuring reasonable and stable returns to producers, was also fair to the consumers. As the new technology got established and yields improved, progressively larger shares of benefits were passed on to the consumers. Thus, the minimum support prices of a quintal of wheat were nearly 110 per cent higher than the paid-out costs and family labor charges in 1970-71. By 1983-84 this margin had been reduced to 67 per cent, with the consumers taking a progressively larger share of gains in productivity. It is true that the price regime that worked well in stimulating agricultural production, particularly of wheat and rice, may not be the most appropriate one to facilitate adjustment under the new circumstances, but its role in breaking the stagnation-trap in Indian agriculture has been significant.

Land Reforms

At the time of its independence, India inherited an agrarian structure characterized by a marked skewness in the distribution of holdings, large number of functionless intermediaries, an overwhelming majority of small and marginal farmers, and a large number of tenants victim of rack renting and uncertainty of tenure. A change of this system was sought through a series of land reform legislation. Steps envisaged under such legislation included: (a) abolition of intermediary tenures; (b) tenancy reforms which included according security of tenure to the tillers of the soil, scaling down rents to one-fourth or one-sixth of the produce, and enabling tenants to acquire ownership rights; (c) ceiling on land holdings. There were several shortcomings in these legislative acts which were made worse at the time of implementation. However, over a period of time India's agrarian structure has undergone a significant change. Concentration of owned as well as operational holdings has decreased over large parts of the country. Small and medium holdings have gained in importance, while big and large holdings, relatively speaking, lost their importance.[7]

A multiplicity of factors have led to these changes. Possible explanations include: (i) legislative and administrative processes which made it difficult to enlarge further existing large holdings; (ii) demographic pressures which resulted in the division of holdings; and (iii) technological process which favored intensive rather than an extensive mode of cultivation. The net result, however, has been that hagemony of large

---

7. See V.S. Vyas "Some Aspects of Structural Change in Indian Agriculture", *Indian Journal of Agricultural Economics*, April-June 1979.

farmers in the rural areas is broken. A middle peasantry has consolidated its position. The number of small and marginal farmers as well as the area under their control have increased as their ranks have been swelled due to the absence of any remarkable increase in the alternative sources of employment.

These structural changes affected the production processes in indirect but important ways. The dominant role of a medium peasantry is the most important outcome of these changes. Fragmentation of small and marginal holdings created more non-viable farms. At the same time, access to land was denied to several landless households by a freeze in lease market. Changes in the distribution of operational holdings in different size-groups from 1973/74 to 1970/71 are depicted in Table 3.

TABLE – 3

Percentage Distribution of Household Operational Holdings, All India (rural)

Size of holding	*1953/1954*		*1960/1961*		*1970/1971*	
(ha)	*Number*	*Area*	*Number*	*Area*	*Number*	*Area*
<1	39.14	5.43	39.07	6.86	45.77	9.21
1-2	20.86	10.01	22.62	12.32	22.38	14.80
2-4	19.73	18.62	19.80	20.70	17.66	22.52
4-10	14.40	29.32	13.99	31.17	11.11	30.49
>10	5.87	36.62	4.52	28.95	3.08	22.98
Total number of households (x 10^6)	44.35		50.77		57.07	
Total area (Mha)		135.16		133.38		125.68

Sources: National Sample Survey (1968); National Sample Survey Organization (1976)

Quoted in *Agricultural Policy in India: Growth and Equity*, by J.S. Sarma, IDRC, Ottawa, 1982, p. 34.

Interaction of Institutional and Technological Factors

There are not many studies which indicate the influence of the institutional and organizational framework on farmers' decision making. It is for this reason that I quote below extensively from the findings of a study conducted at the Indian Institute of management (Ahmedabad) as a part of the Food and Agriculture Organization's global project "Agriculture Towards 2000 A.D."[8] The study *inter alia* aimed at assessing the relative role of technological and institutional variables in explaining changes in land productivity. The question posed at the outset was, "Are land productivity changes possible if each of the following factors is altered separately: (i) land ownership distribution, (ii) type of tenancy, (iii) availability of modern inputs such as fertilizers and irrigation, and (iv) availability of superior technology as embodied in high-yielding variety seeds". A simple model was conceptualized to examine cross-sectional variations in per hectare yield as a dependent outcome of the factors listed. Agricultural production data for 56 agro-climatically homogenous regions were utilized for this exercise. Because of the paucity of data at the sub-regional level, the impact of land tenure and HYV seeds could not be assessed. The study therefore, was confined to assessing the impact of the per hectare availability of fertilizers, extent of irrigable land, and inequality in ownership of land on yields.

Some of the important conclusions of the study are worth underlining.

(a) An inverse relationship between land productivity and inequality in land ownership exists, suggesting that the

---

8. Indian Institute of Management "Relative Role of Irrigation, Fertilizers and Land Inequality Changes in Land Productivity" in *Income Distribution, Poverty and Nutrition Aspects - AT2000 - An Exercise in India*, Ahmedabad, April 1979, pp. 124-134 (mimeo).

program of land redistribution in favor of small farmers would contribute to increasing per hectare yield. This would particularly be the case for rice, sorghum, rapeseed, and mustards and for aggregate agricultural output for which the indicated relationship between land productivity and inequality in land ownership is statistically significant.

(b) Changes in yield of individual crop as well as aggregate yield, however, is explained more by the variations in one or both of the two surrogate variables of technology, namely, fertilizers and irrigation, rather than by the inequality in land ownership.

(c) The per hectare availability of fertilizers in six of the ten crops was the most important factor in explaining the variations in per hectare yields. For three other crops irrigation ratio (i.e., irrigated area as a proportion of gross cropped area) emerges as the most important variable explaining per hectare yields. In the remaining crop, that is sugarcane, the regional-locational-factor was the most important variable.

These findings suggest that although a reduction in land ownership inequality would in itself contribute to an increase in land productivity, an increase in the availability of fertilizers and irrigation would make a relatively larger contribution. As access to fertilizers and irrigation - except availability of public irrigation - is positively related to the size of holdings, these findings allow a different perspective on the landholding structure. It is suggested that raising the floor of holdings is as important as lowering the ceilings.

II

POVERTY ALLEVIATION

Incidence of Poverty

There is ample literature on the norms and indicators of poverty. A number of estimates of the poor based on these norms are available. The majority of Indian scholars has defined the poverty line in terms of the level of income which would enable a person to acquire customary food equivalent to 2,250 calories per day plus leave a small amount to obtain other necessities. Generally, Rs. 180 per person per year in 1960/61 prices is accepted as the dividing line between the poor and the non-poor. Based on this norm, Ahluwalia has prepared estimates of the number of poor covering a fairly long period of time, from 1956/57 to 1977/78. According to these estimates, on the head count basis nearly 54 per cent of the rural population fall below the poverty line in 1956-57. The proportion of the poor declined to 39 per cent by the end of the fifties. It rose in the mid-sixties, reaching the level of 56.6 per cent in 1966-67. Since then it again started declining and was measured at 39.1 per cent in 1977-78, the latest year for which the estimates are available.[9] It is clear from available information that the incidence of poverty in the rural areas had declined during periods of high agricultural growth (i.e. from the mid-fifties to the early sixties and from mid-seventies to late-seventies). It is equally evident that even in the more dynamic periods of agricultural growth the poverty had not gone far below 40 per cent in rural India.

---

9. Montek S. Ahluwalia, "Rural Poverty, Agricultural Production, and Prices: A Re-examination," in *Agricultural Change and Rural Poverty Variation on a Theme by Dharam Narain,*, ed. John W. Mellor and Gunwant M. Desai, Johns Hopkins Press, Baltimore and London, 1985, pp. 59-75. Several other studies, including FAO/IIMA study cited in the text, have given much higher estimates of rural poverty.

There are two inter-related explanations for the persistent and high level of rural poverty. First, the base for agricultural growth is narrow both across regions and within the regions, and the percolation and the spread effect from prosperous to backward areas is proceeding very slowly. Second, intersectoral linkages are weak. Even in the agriculturally prosperous areas, industrial activities have remained sluggish. I will elaborate these two points in the following paragraphs.

Narrow Base of Agricultural Growth

It was mentioned earlier that much of the increment in agricultural production since the mid-sixties was constituted by wheat and rice. The heavy emphasis on HYVs of wheat and rice to increase in food production amounted to a virtual neglect of other crops, particularly coarse cereals. However, HYVs of wheat and rice could be grown mainly in the areas which had assured water supply. Over a period of time this base did expand, but mainly in the areas where irrigation could be extended. There have been no signs of progress in the country's vast unirrigated areas. Even today such areas account for more than 60 per cent of all cultivated land and constitute the backwaters of agricultural growth. A progressively larger share of incremental agricultural production is accounted for by well watered, mainly irrigated areas.

The lack of a viable technology for non-irrigated areas was compounded by the existence of a large mass of peasantry owning marginal holdings. I have maintained earlier that it is technologically quite feasible not only to sustain but to accelerate the rate of agricultural growth from the current level of 2.7 per cent per annum. Normally, one would have assumed that with the rise in agricultural production and consequently in rural incomes the poverty problem would be effectively tackled. However, that is not to be. With an accelerated rate of growth in agricultural production, the proportion of the poor in the rural population will decline, yet a hard core of the poor will still persist. It was brought out in an FAO/IIMA study cited earlier that even if the rate of growth in agricultural production is as high as 3.9 per cent per annum - a realistic upper limit - and the growth in productivity is uniformly shared by all classes of land holdings, the percentage of people below the poverty line in India will decline from nearly 62 per cent in 1971 to 32 per cent by the end of this century. Even an increase of 30 per cent in the share of the marginal holdings (i.e. those operating less than a hectare of land) will not significantly alter in this situation. The proportion of the poor households in that case will be reduced to only 30 per cent.

The situation turns out to be so difficult because of the existence of a large number of landless laborers, and marginal and small farmers. Even a significant improvement in the rate of increase in output will not provide an adequate amount, in absolute terms, to raise these households above the poverty line. The per capita incomes of the two most disadvantaged groups, namely landless laborers and marginal farmers, estimated at Rs. 21.33 and Rs. 21.07 respectively in 1971. Whereas money income required to raise a household above the poverty line was estimated at Rs. 33 per person per month. This implies that very large increases in the incomes of these disadvantaged groups would be necessary to enable them to cross the poverty line. Looking at the meager output on small and marginal holdings productivity, or the value of output, of these holdings must increase substantially to yield the minimum desirable income.

Similarly, an increase in wage-employment must be significantly larger to enable agricultural laborers and marginal farmers to cross the threshold of poverty. Agricultural growth by itself is not going to provide enough employment opportunities for all those who are available for employment. A study of the output employment relationship in Asian agriculture conducted in connection with the Second Asian Agricultural Survey suggests a figure of labor absorption in the range of 0.4 to 0.6 per cent with a 1 per cent increase in output in the more labor intensive agricultural systems of south-east Asia.[10] For a country like India, a figure of .5 per cent may be more realistic. If this relationship holds true, a growth in agricultural output in the neighborhood of 4 per cent per annum will be needed just to absorb the additional workforce from agricultural households. It will not make any dent on the existing level of unemployment or underemployment.[11]

Whatever, (realistic) assumptions one may make regarding the rise of agricultural productivity and labor absorption in agricultural sectors agricultural activity alone is not going to resolve the poverty problem in rural areas, not at least as far as the bottom one-third of households are concerned as long as a very large section of rural producers is cultivating miniscule holdings and/or depending on wage paid labor in agriculture in a major way. If these households are to be lifted above the mire of poverty, we shall have to examine carefully other available options mainly in the non-farm activities.

---

10. See *Rural Asia Challenge and Opportunities*, the Second Asian Agricultural Survey, published by Praeger, London and New York, for Asian Development Bank, 1977.

11. After an elaborate exercise, the National Commission on Agriculture came to the conclusion that by 2000 AD expansion in various agricultural programs (including those in animal husbandry, forestry and fishery) will generate employment opportunities for about 52 million persons. As against this there will be an increase of 143 million persons in rural labor force by the year 2000. See National Commission on Agriculture Report, Part XII, *Rural Employment and Special Area Programmes*, Government of India, 1976.

Weak Inter-sectoral Linkages

India's failure to diversify the rural economy and to provide opportunities for non-farm employment is reflected in the static picture of labor force disposition in different sectors over a long period of time during which the predominance of the agricultural sector has remained intact. In other words, progressively larger numbers of workers are supported by agriculture. See Table 4 below.

TABLE – 4

Labor Force Composition, 1965 and 1980 Percentage of Labor Force in Different Sectors

	1965	*1980*
Agriculture	73	70
Industry	12	13
Services	15	17

Source: World Development Report 1986

With the landholding structure characterized by a large and growing number of marginal holdings and an army of landless workers competing for on-farm jobs, the employers (i.e. medium and large farmers) were in a position to pre-empt a disproportionately larger share of the gains in agricultural productivity. A clear indicator of this unequal bargaining power is stationary or, at best, a slow rise in agricultural wages through most of the country.[12]

If non-farm activities did not increase in a remarkable measure in the rural areas, one explanation was the constraint of demand for the non-farm goods and services. According to

12. See Gustav F. Papanek, "Poverty in India", paper presented at the Conference on Indian Economy. Boston, 1986, p.6, Table 1 (mimeo).

another FAO/IIMA study for global project on "Agricultural Towards A.D. 2000", nearly 60 per cent of rural households consisting of landless laborers, submarginal and marginal cultivators accounted for 29 per cent of the total income in rural areas. This was mainly due to miniscule holdings and low value crops grown on these holdings. A large bulk of this income was in kind; the cash amounted to less than half of their total income. These groups must purchase a part of their foodgrains requirements from their meager incomes. The cash income available with these groups of households for the purchase of non-farm goods is inconsequential. In other words, a large proportion of the rural households are not only marginal as producers, they are also marginal as consumers as far as the non-farm sector is concerned.

The medium to large farmers who account for less than 25 per cent (23.4 per cent) of the rural households claimed 54 per cent of the incomes generated in rural areas. (Their share in cash incomes would be much larger). When the above figures are translated in rupee terms, it suggests a sizeable amount of over Rs. 18000 million in 1970-71. It can be safely presumed that the bulk of the income of rich farmers was available for purchase of non-farm goods and services. Why did this not boost a dynamic non-farm sector in the rural areas? The answer to this lies in the faulty industrial policies.

India's industrial strategy was based on an overwhelming emphasis on import-substitution. As a result, efficiency in the use of scarce resources was not given the importance it deserved. The emphasis on heavy industries at the cost of wage goods was, again, a reflection of faulty industrial priorities. So also was the neglect of complementary infrastructure. For example, the failure to provide adequate power plagued, and continues to plague, the progress of industrialization in several parts of the country. Although India cannot be blamed of distorting its foreign exchange rates to any significant extent, the pricing of resources, particularly capital, did not reflect their true scarcity value. The relatively low price of capital and, more importantly, the relatively easier access to capital by the large enterprises compared to the smaller ones, prevented, as if by design, a larger absorption of labor in non-farm activities.[13] Finally, inefficient management of industries by a number of public sector enterprises which preempted a significant proportion of savings in the economy, meant that the large amount of resources was dissipated. In its fears of foreign economic dominance and hegemony of domestic monopolies – the fears which were not unreasonable – India opted for short-sighted solutions. Worse still, India's policy makers became insensitive to the waste of resources and missed opportunities. The impact of all these policies was felt more seriously by the rural poor.

III

LESSONS

Agricultural Growth

India's rural development strategy contains many relevant lessons for other developing countries. The agricultural growth strategy pursued by India turned the country from a heavily food deficit economy to a country that could, at least in more favorable years, export small quantities of foodgrains. This was certainly not due to any fortuitous set of circumstances.

---

13. Reviewing past performance, the Planning Commission in the draft Fifth Plan pointed out, "Between 1961 and 1976, in the modern factory sector, investment increased by 139 per cent and output 161 per cent but employment increased only 71 per cent. Therefore, employment per unit of capital *declined* by 28 per cent." (emphasis added). *Draft Five Year Plan 1978-1983*, Planning Commission, Government of India, New Delhi, p. 82.

The goal was reached by appropriate policy interventions, organizational changes and investment decisions. The main strands of the country's agricultural production stategy and its major implications can be briefly summarized.

(a) Political support as well as bureaucratic skills and scientific talents were harnessed to achieve a well defined goal, namely food self-sufficiency. The convergence of various interests to achieve a single objective was one of the most distinguishing features of India's planning efforts.

(b) India opted for a yield augmenting, size neutral technology. In a country facing a scarcity of land and a surplus of manpower, it was a correct strategy to pursue.

(c) Along with the technological interventions, institutional support was provided to implement the strategy. Creation of institutions such as the Indian Council of Agricultural Research, state level Agricultural Universities and Integrated Agricultural Research Schemes provided the necessary organizational capability. Similarly, the establishment of Agricultural Prices Commission and the Food Corporation of India, made the management of the food economy reasonably easy. For each major policy thrust there was a corresponding institution ready to translate it into action.

(d) Producers were not only provided with incentive prices, they were also protected from sharp fluctuations in commodity prices.

(e) Land reform legislation, though failing to achieve a redistribution of land in any remarkable way, did succeed in breaking the hegemony of the large farmers and created conditions which enabled the middle peasantry to consolidate its position.

(f) Through the mechanism of administered prices, gains in agricultural productivity were shared between the producers and the consumers. Therefore, attention to agriculture did not provoke hostile reactions from the powerful urban interests.

It should be remembered that not all of these measures were thought through as elements of a "grand design." Mainly because the directions were right, and India's political system provided the necessary checks and balances, a viable strategy could be forged.

Poverty Alleviation

In a poor country characterized by a skewed distribution of resources, some form of asset creation for the poor is a pre-condition for poverty alleviation. It could be achieved through a redistribution of existing assets (e.g. redistribution of land through land reforms), or access to new assets, (e.g. livestock), or transfer of productive skills, or investment in human capital formation through health and education. Without assets and resources, people cannot respond to market signals.

India's experience shows that a democratic and pluralistic state can introduce legislative measures and support market and technological developments which can curb the dominance of large farmers, but it would find it much more difficult to ensure lasting gains to numerous small and marginal farmers or landless laborers. The power structure at the grass roots level, the bureaucratic apparatus, and the delivery systems are not sympathetic to a genuine redistribution process. It is no wonder then that the redistribution features of the land reform legislation were hardly complied with.

The government did have a much better record in the distribution of reproducible assets (e.g. livestock or credit or improved inputs). There were "leakages" even in these programmes but, as the recent experience of India's Integrated Development Programme (IRDP) has shown, such programmes have fared relatively better than the land redistribution program. However, proper implementation of these programs hinges on correct targeting of activities and involvement of the beneficiaries. Both of these conditions were largely absent. As a result, the benefits of such programs have been pre-empted by the non-poor, (not necessarily by the rich).

Equally important support to the poor can be channelled through the social sectors. India does not have a distinguished record in bringing health, nutrition or educational opportunities to the poor. In a large country like India one can always cite some glorious examples, but the general state of health, nutrition and education among the poor households suggests a bleak picture. Efforts to invest in human capital were not taken as an important plank of the government's poverty alleviation strategy.

Poverty alleviation programs presuppose public assistance to the poor in a variety of ways, yet the critical decisions (i.e. to save or to invest, the manner in which to dispose of family labour, or how to use the meager production resources) are made at the household level. The decision-making process at the micro-level in different socio-economic milieu has to be understood and strengthened by providing the right type of information. A top-down approach to rural development precluded an understanding of this nature.

An increase in productivity in agriculture will help increase gainful absorption of poor households' labour on own farm and on other farms. However, labour absorption in agriculture soon reaches the limit. One escape route for several poor small farm households is the emphasis on high value crops and/or more productive supplementary activities. In India the proportion of low value crops, such as coarse cereals, is higher on the small farms. The reverse is true when it comes to high value crops. The reason for sticking to food crops is basically self-provisioning. As long as the market does not ensure adequate food at the right prices, at the right time and at the right place to numerous small farmers, farmers will not take the additional risk entailed in switching to high value crops.

Apart from this major policy change and the need for developing marketing infrastructure for food, public support will be needed to provide credit, input supply and output marketing once high value crops are introduced on the small farms. Also, a measure of stability in prices of inputs and output is necessary to minimize the risks, and the poor farmers are ill equipped and ill prepared to face these risks.

India's record in creating non-farm job opportunities in the rural areas is worse than that of several other developing countries. The basic reasons are demand constraints and faulty industrial priorities and policies. The solution to rural poverty in a very meaningful way lies in expanding and strengthening non-farm employment opportunities which are integrated with agriculture and which capitalize on the backward, forward, and, more importantly demand induced linkages between farm and non-farm sectors.

Over a period of the last two decades India has provided important lessons in how to get agriculture moving in very difficult circumstances. It has also shown in some of the failures of its rural development strategies, that the problems associated with the distribution of gains of additional production among the poorer sections are much more difficult to handle.

11

The New Economic Policy and the Vulnerable Section

Rationale for Public Intervention

SOME of the policy measures commonly known as the New Economic Policy (NEP) were taken a few years back. However, the name NEP given to the measures initiated since the beginning of 1991 has a significance both because of the comprehensiveness of the measures and the coherence of the whole package. As is now well-known NEP envisages a stabilization phase and an adjustment programme. Both need not run strictly in a sequential order. In the present context, the stabilization programme is more urgent and to a large extent the success of the adjustment phase largely depends on the success of the former. For conceptual clarity we may discuss these separately.

The Stabilization Programme

In India the stabilization programme is aimed at restoring balance on the fiscal side as well as in the external payments. Fiscal imbalance was expressing itself in the growing budgetary deficit of the Central Government. The resultant deficit

---

An edited and enlarged version of the presentation made at the National Consultation on New Economic Policy and the Vulnerable Sections, held under the auspices of the Institute of Development Studies, Jaipur in 1992.

financing was the principal cause of the inflationary pressure in the economy. Rising prices not only seriously hit the fixed-income earners, they also made Indian products costlier and thereby non-competitive. An inflexible exchange rate further exacerbated the difficulties in securing export markets. There were periodic spurts in economic activities but underlying trend of stagnation was easy to discern.

The measures taken under stabilization programme (SP) mainly revolved around curtailing the budgetary deficits on the one hand and devaluation and partial convertibility of Indian Rupee on the other. The impact of these measures on the poor would depend on the speed and the content of these measures. For example, in the political setup of our country one would not expect any cuts in defence expenditure or on civil services, or on some of the subsidies. The expenditure cut would most probably fall on the so-called welfare programmes or on capital expenditure. These cuts can be avoided if we can raise enough resources through taxation. This route is seldom taken by the developing countries including ours, since more affluent sections have also greater political clout. In any event, raising taxes violates the spirit of Structural Adjustment Reforms as preached by the Brettonwood Institutions (who do make a possible exception of tax on agricultural incomes).

Impact on the Poor

During the period of stabilization phase attention to the poor and vulnerable sections should be all the more sharper. This is because of the acute and pervasive nature of poverty in India. More so, because, two important planks of stabilization policy, namely, curtailment of public expenditure and withdrawal of subsidies, can have important repercussions on the employment situation and welfare level of the vulnerable sections. There is an urgent need for designing proper protective measures for the poor in this context.

Curtailment in Public Expenditure

A cut back in public investment, as much as the closure of the uneconomic units, leads to retrenchment of the workers particularly those who are easily dispensable. These belong, generally, to the unskilled, unorganized and weaker sections. The impact of the cut in public expenditure may go beyond the difficulties to be faced by retrenched workers and may prove more damaging to the poor.

By cutting back on the investment in the infrastructure, prospects for employment are further jeopardised; as infrastructure creation is more labour intensive the impact on employment is also more serious. Secondly, infrastructure has strong forward linkages with several other economic activities. A curtailment of investment in infrastructure will have a multiplier effect on unemployment. A cut-back in the welfare activities will have the additional debilitating impact on the vulnerable sections. A decline in the investment in health or education or nutrition even if filled in by the private entrepreneurs will deprive the poorer section the basic avenues for self improvement.

Subsidies

The arguments for reducing subsidies are very strong at the theoretical level. Apart from their macro level implications, i.e. in generating inflationary pressures, they are counter productive as they take away incentive from the beneficiaries to become self reliant. They conceal the true social cost of an enterprise or a product. The most important argument against the subsidies is that they are difficult to target. Rarely they reach the right group for any length of time. There are, however, two powerful arguments in favour of the subsidies; one is the famous "infant industry" argument which does not need any elaboration. Another major argument is in terms of transfer of income from more affluent groups to less affluent groups.

From the perspective of the poor, two types of subsidies are more important in this context: agricultural input subsidies and the food subsidies, accounting for nearly Rs. 3444 crores and Rs.2572 crores in 1987-88, (at 1980-81 prices), respectively.

Among the input agricultural subsidies, that on fertilizers has attracted more attention. The Finance Minister has instituted a 30 per cent cut in these subsidies. There is a general view that the incidence of these cuts would be more adverse for the backward regions and the small farmers who are the "late users". These effects will be compounded if the farm prices are raised to compensate the agricultural producers for the rise in the fertilizer prices. In that case only those farmers would benefit who have marketable surplus. On the other hand the marginal farmers and the landless labourers will have to pay higher prices for an essential commodity like food. What is suggested is an orderly withdrawal of the input subsidies, by taking into account the repercussion on agricultural production, regional imbalances and incentive structure of the "late users".

In the present context of a sizeable number of people suffering from malnutrition and under-nutrition there is still less justification for any drastic cut in the food subsidies, which are in the nature of the transfer of income from more well-to-do to less well-to-do. This, of course, assumes that the food subsidies are well targeted. In any event, the implications of the removal of the inputs and the food subsidies in a country like ours are lot more complicated and do not permit a doctrinaire approach.

To protect the vulnerable sections and to compensate those affected by reforms various steps are taken. We will discuss two measures which have overriding importance in our context, i.e., compensation for and rehabilitation of the retrenched workers and, the public distribution of essential commodities.

Compensation and Rehabilitation of the Retrenched Workers

Because of the curtailment of the public expenditure and an "exit" policy for the inefficient public sector as well as private sector units, a number of employed can lose their jobs and join the ranks of 'new poor'. There is a need to provide them immediate help as well as to make arrangements for their training for more viable activities. Precisely with these objectives a National Renewal (or Reconstruction) Fund, NRF, was established in January, 1992. The initial budgetary provision for the Fund amounts to Rs. 200 crores. Substantial assistance is expected from International Development Association (IDA) and from *voluntary* contribution of industry and states. Some amount has also been earmarked from the Jawahar Rozgar Yojana for similar purposes, but in this case for rural unorganized workers.

No details seems to have been yet worked out for the *modus operandi* of the Fund. The Fund in order to be useful to the affected workers has to be related to the speed with which the reforms are to be pursued and its organizational structure has to ensure speedy and effective steps. The fact that the general policy thrust is towards curtailment of government expenditure and divestment of public sector units, one would have expected a great deal of importance attached to such a fund. But, unfortunately, expected level of seriousness is not evident. The proposal seems to have been made, at best, as a humanitarian gesture.

Public Distribution System

Since the days of the second world war, India is pursuing a policy of the Public Distribution of the essential commodities. Over the years the Public Distribution System (PDS) has been made more extensive both in terms of commodities covered and the area served. In recent years the system has been examined in detail by scholars in different parts of the country. It has come under serious criticism in terms of its objectives, costs and the impact on the poor. These criticisms have become more strident in the context of the NEP. We should review them briefly before arriving at any conclusion.

It is true that there is no clarity about the objective of PDS. Is it aimed to hold down the general price level, a sort of anti-inflationary device? If so, this task is too ambitious. A few scholars have attempted to quantify the amount of the commodities needed for such "open market operations". It is quite clear that to run a system with an objective of stabilising price level of even a few commodities, say the foodgrains, is beyond our administrative and fiscal capacity. Is the system designed to make available all the goods of daily consumption, from toilet soaps to exercise books, whenever any scarcity is experienced in their availability? Again, this is beyond the organizational capacity of a system run by the bureaucracy.

Nor will everyone agree that it is state's responsibility to procure and distribute every "essential" good the price of which shows an upward movement. Afterall price does perform a critical role in the allocation of resources by the enterprises. Besides, it is neither possible nor desirable to meet the requirements of each and every household for what it considers essential commodity. So long as there is a market for goods and services, the state need not intervene to "regulate" the prices unless there is a clear case of foul play, collusion or unfair practices. Through PDS the state's operations should be limited to provide the basic necessities to the poorest sections.

There are objections even to such a limited, well-targeted, PDS. The "leakages" in the system are pointed out as one argument against PDS; and it is asserted that the same amount invested in the employment generating schemes would yield better results for the poor. These arguments are not tenable. There are "leakages" in the employment schemes also. Besides, for a basic necessity like food a minimum of security must be assured to the vulnerable sections. A subsidised PDS for the well targeted groups is the best form of food security that we have been able to find out.

This does not mean that there is no scope for improvement in PDS. The objectives have to be well defined, the costs have to be controlled and targeting should be more effective. One of the main pre-requisites for the latter is to decentralise the operations.

Structural Adjustment Programme

It is assumed that once the decks are cleared, by correcting the fiscal imbalance and by a realistic alignment of the value of the domestic currency, other policy measures designated as Structural Adjustment (SA) can accelerate pace of economic growth. These measures can be broadly classified in two categories; (a) deregulation and privatization of the domestic economic activities i.e., debureaucratization and encouragement to competition in domestic markets, and (b) globalization of Indian economy. Several steps under these two categories were taken during the primeministership of Rajiv Gandhi. However, a logically more consistent package is being tried out only since 1991. It is not germane to the present discussion as to at whose instance these measures were initiated, we are interested in understanding their impact on the poor.

'Spread Effects' of Economic Growth

The proponents of NEP do not rule out state intervention in favour of the poor, but they consider that really effective weapon for poverty alleviation is accelerated economic growth. It is the 'trickle down' or the 'spread' of growth on which major reliance is placed. There are two implicit assumptions underlying this approach. The first assumption is that NEP will lead to accelerated growth. Historical evidence in this regard is, to put it mildly, inconclusive. The second assumption is that economic growth will lead to poverty alleviation. We are more concerned with the latter assumption.

We have in India experience of the states registering at different growth rates and their respective experience in poverty alleviation. Without going into details I will like to highlight three main lessons from Indian experience.

(i) Rate of economic growth has to be fairly high, say 6 to 8 per cent per annum or more, to have measurable "trickle-down" effect;

(ii) The composition of growth is as important as the rate of growth; an agriculture led growth is likely to have a more remarkable impact on alleviating poverty;

(iii) Spread effect of growth is likely to be faster if it is accompanied by investment in infrastructure and in human resource development.

Indian experience also suggests that faster economic growth with all these qualifications may only affect the economic aspects of poverty but if we consider the social handicaps of the poor as well, these may not be corrected even with fast economic growth. Even among those households who have crossed the economically determined poverty line one may find low level of literacy, low standards of child and mother care, discrimination against women etc. Thus, in the Indian context to have a favourable impact on the poor households i.e., to generate employment and to provide for the long term opportunity for growth, public investment in some of the sectors, especially infrastructure and agriculture, needs to be augmented, and protective measures like NRF and the Public Distribution of the essential foodgrains have to be further strengthened. On these issues we have dwelt above. There is a further need to make the markets "poor friendly". This last aspect needs some elaboration.

Markets and the Poor

The poor are handicapped in responding to the market signals at two levels. They find the entry to the markets very difficult, especially those who do not have assets or skills. Second, even when they enter the market they are not able to obtain fair returns. Latter, because of the low "reserve price" they set for themselves, and high transaction costs which the other transacting party has to incur. There is also an overarching consideration of risk which the poor have to take into account. The state has an important role in making markets "poor-friendly", by strengthening their asset base, by helping in the reduction of the transaction costs and in creating an environment for steady growth.

In our country, efforts were made to provide assets to the rural poor through land reform programme. At least this was one of the objectives of the land reforms programme, e.g. of the land ceiling legislation. However, the failure in this respect is more or less total. The extent of the failure and the reasons thereof are well researched and well documented. I will not go into these reasons. It will be unrealistic to assume that we can once again revive these measures and obtain any great success. Redistributive land reforms was a good idea, but its days are gone.

Current efforts under Integrated Rural Development Programme (IRDP) are in the same direction. There are several evaluative studies on this programme. These studies have pointed out the high costs and limited benefits of the programme, as well as large "leakages" under this effort, latter mainly because the non-poor try to pre-empt the benefits meant for the poor. At the same time these studies, or most of these studies, have also shown that the weaknesses observed under IRDP are being progressively reduced. Still there is a long way to go but the progressive improvement in the implementation of the Programme makes one more hopeful.

There is a similar but less ambitious programme for skill formation, known as TRYSEM. What has been said about IRDP applies more or less in the same measure to this programme also. However, the progress under the programme is much slower. During the Seventh Plan hardly 6 to 7 per cent of the IRDP beneficiaries were trained under TRYSEM. An indepth review of the programme done by the researchers at the IDSJ has pointed out two major weaknesses, very little interaction with the beneficiaries at the grass root level, and lack of concern for responding to the real market demand.

Under new policy dispensation both these programmes, IRDP and TRYSEM, deserve greater support if we want poor to take advantages of the market development.

Relevant Markets

There are three markets which are particularly relevant to the poor: Labour Market, Product Market and Credit Market. In all these markets the poor are handicapped. Functioning of the rural labour market can illustrate the situation faced by the poor.

Most of the poor households have only physical labour to sell. A study of the labour markets will suggest that real wages are, by and large, stagnating during last decade or so, including in areas where agricultural productivity has considerably increased. This is mainly because the growth in employment opportunities has not kept pace with the growth in the labour force. And partly because the labour market is segmented, people cannot move easily out from the areas of low wages to areas of high wages. Also, because of the dependence of the labourers on the same employers in more than one market, (a phenomenon known as inter-locked markets) i.e. same labour household dependent on the same employer not only for employment but also for credit or land, latter if it happens to be the household of share croppers their bargaining capacity is circumscribed.

It is not only the low "reserve price" of the poor that the non-poor take advantage of but as the transactions with the poor, especially in the product and credit markets are numerous but small, the transaction costs are also high. This applies as much to the public institutions which are established with the clear objective of giving support to the poor households, e.g. state run credit institutions, cooperatives etc., as to the private profit seeking establishments. In other words, there is a lack of congruence between the recipient system and the delivery system.

In all such cases action has to start at two levels. At the recipient level there is a need for the organization of the poor. Wherever the poor have been organized, whether the organization is a rural workers trade unions as in Kerala, or the cooperative societies of the small milk producers as in Gujarat, the results have been very satisfactory. At the same time the delivery system has also to adopt to the requirements of the small producers and borrowers. There are several examples of innovations in delivery arrangements to meet the requirements of the poor household without necessarily incurring high costs. The Grameen Bank in Bangladesh and SEWA in India provide good examples.

Summing Up

There are several areas where concerted action is indicated if the poor have to participate in the growth which NEP promises. Prominent among these are:

(i) Greater investment in infrastructure to facilitate the "spread effect" of economic growth and to generate productive employment;

(ii) Greater investment in human resource development to strengthen the recipient system and improve its social status;

(iii) Greater emphasis on the programmes like IRDP and TRYSEM to provide an asset and skill base to the poor;

(iv) Strengthening a well targeted PDS catering to the basic needs of the poor;

(v) Devising adequate and timely social security measures for the 'new poor'.

Even while taking these measures the basic tenets of NEP should not be lost sight of. For examples,

(a) although there are some spheres where only the state can take action, e.g., institutional reforms, there are several other areas where private initiative and social action should be given preference;

(b) the state should not embark on the programmes either with its own resources or with borrowed funds, which are likely to remain a liability in the future;

(c) as in the case of the major initiatives even individual

> projects should be subjected to the test of sustainability. Even if subsidies are involved, one should be clear on the questions, "for whom" and "for how long".

While pursuing the old economic policies it was never seriously questioned how they were likely to benefit the poorest of the poor, the DARIDRA NARAYAN. Let us not make this mistake once again.

12

The Second Round of Reforms in Agriculture

DURING the last decade there has been a major shift in economic policies in our country. It is not only because several policy measures aimed at liberalization and globalization were initiated during this period – the trends towards debreaucratisation and 'opening up' of the economy were already set in during the 1980s. The real difference between the current reform process and the earlier measures is that the former challenges the very basis of planning and policy making which guided Indian economic development since Independence. A faith in central control on the allocation of resources, "commanding heights" to the public sector, inward looking approach and, key role assigned to bureaucracy to implement development strategies were the principal features of the earlier approach to development.

These were seriously challenged with the initiation of the new reform process. We do have vestiges of the old structure, and more so the old attitudes, at different levels and in different areas of our economy and polity, but for good or bad a new chapter has been opened in our economic policies and development stategies. It something which we can not ignore whatever might be our ideological predilection.

(Prof. Dantwala memorial lecture delivered at the 83rd Conference of Indian Economic Association at Jammu in 2000).

I

ECONOMIC REFORMS — THE FIRST PHASE

Basic tenets of the current economic reforms, liberalization and globalization, are accepted by a large number of developing countries. In essence, Indian government's approach in this regard is not dissimilar to the policies pursued by a number of countries who have opted for what has come to be known as "structural adjustment". However, a distinguishing feature of our experience has been a sequential, and a cautious, approach to reforms. Accelerated, if not triggered, by the balance of payment crisis of 1991 it was natural to institute reforms in the foreign trade sector in the first place. Such reforms also became necessary with our acceptance of a world trade regime under the aegis of an international authority. Reforms in the foreign trade sector were followed by domestic reforms, i.e., doing away with a large number of centralized controls and regulations as well as different forms of restrictive trade practices; in other words, dismantling of 'permit quota raj'. These were followed by reforms in financial sector, with more autonomy being extended to the financial institutions. The entry of foreign capital was liberalized and made less discriminatory. There was also pious resolution to curtail fiscal deficit. We all understand that what I have described above is in some ways caricaturing the reform process, which was much more blurred, with overlapping measures in different areas. But the underlying sequence is clear. More importantly, the policy makers in our country have so far resisted the so-called "comprehensive approach" to reforms, engulfing all sectors in one sweep.

The second distinguishing feature of Indian reform process is the slow and halting manner in which reforms were executed. The pressure exerted by some quarters to hasten the pace of reforms was resisted. Again, as in sequencing, the slow pace of reforms was not a part of pre-planned design. Several ad-hoc decisions were taken, and as is expected in competitive politics, several compromises were made. But the dominant trends in the reform process, atleast in retrospect, seem to be on the lines I have described above. The main reasons for following such sequential and cautious approach, in my view, have to be sought in the compulsions of a democratic, multi-party, polity where a measure of consensus building is imperative before any drastic step can be taken. One fact, however, is clear, i.e., India did not suffered from major dislocations as have been faced by several other countries in the initial phase of reforms, e.g. sharp decline in GDP and employment, raging inflation and collapse of institutions. On all these counts, we have come out more or less unscathed. It is different, and a debatable, issue whether due to these reforms the rate of growth has been accelerated, and whether the plight of the vulnerable sections has become less serious. On these matters jury is still out.

Now that we are entering into the second phase of reforms, which admittedly is a much more difficult phase, we have to be careful about the future course of action. The first phase of reforms was relatively easy as the required changes in trade, finance and fiscal areas were known. In the second phase, issues of equity, regional and sectoral allocation, good governance, institutional changes etc. will become more prominent. Hard decisions on competition policy, labour policy, disinvestment and privatization will have to be taken. The sections of population who will be adversely affected are numerically important, better organized and articulate. They are capable to shift negative consequences of reforms on those who are poor, unorganized and handicapped. I will attempt in this lecture to suggest the imperatives for the next phase of reforms in agriculture, a sector with which I am slightly more familiar and in understanding its features and characteristics I learnt a lot from my guru Prof. Dantwala in whose memory this lecture is dedicated. Following him I will try to apply the touchstone of "growth with equity" while examining contemplated measures of reforms in agriculture.

Reforms in Agriculture

Even in the backdrop of the slow pace of reforms in the country, policy changes in agriculture were still slower. There were sufficient reasons to take a more cautious approach to economic reforms in this sector. In the first place, there were no serious distortions in agriculture as were evidenced in industrial sector. Aggregate measure of support calculated by various scholars, though yielding different results, did not suggest any gross distortion either in positive or in negative terms. A more sensitive indicator, the inter-sectoral terms of trade, although adverse to agriculture, was gradually improving in favour of agriculture. Reforms in non-farm sectors, and better alignment of Indian currency had a salutary impact on agriculture. Besides, it was recognized that non-price measures, such as development of technology and creation of infrastructure, were more important for agricultural growth than the market oriented measures. In any case, a large section of population in agriculture had very weak linkages with the markets both as producers and as consumers. Those who had such linkages were fairly articulate and would not yield any advantages which they might be extracting from the system. Government was also extra careful as nothing could be done that might jeopardize Food Security. Finally, agriculture being a state subject, in forging and implementing policies for this sector states had a larger say. Most of the states were dragging their feet in implementing reforms in the non-agricultural sectors. They were more than lukewarm when it came to reforms in agriculture.

Mainly for these reasons no drastic policy changes could take place during the first phase of reforms. Nevertheless, certain irritants and obvious distortions were sought to be removed. The most important among these being the abolition of zonal restrictions on the movement of agricultural commodities, especially foodgrains. Even after the abolition of zones, occasionally state governments did impose movement restrictions. But, the fact that India was a single market for agricultural commodities was by and large well established. The other direction in which economic reforms got a fillip was in the area of privatization. Private agencies were given larger scope, in the distribution of inputs, provision of some of services and in agricultural extention. Also, controls were relaxed for a few commodities, such as non-nitrogenous fertilizers. In line with general trade reforms, there was liberalization of imports as well as exports of agricultural commodities to a certain extent.

Before we think of the second round of reforms in agricultural sector, we should bring some of the measures already initiated to their logical conclusion. For example, monopsony of Cotton purchase in Maharashtra, or food rationing in Calcutta are clearly anomalous in the present context. Irrational levies on sugar or rice milling have not served any useful purpose. They have added to price discrimination, clandestine trade, risk and uncertainty. Use of Essential Commodities Act, in most of the circumstances is a panicky reaction rather than a part of a well thought-out strategy. Some of the road blocks have to be removed before we think about significant changes in the policies.

Now a time has come to make a comprehensive review of the government policies in agricultural sector. This is mainly because of the changes in the external environment, especially after our joining WTO. There are also important changes in the internal environment; the country has been transformed from a deficit country to self-sufficient, in fact, marginally surplus, in the staple foodgrains. Yet dependence of work force on agriculture has not declined in any remarkable way; nor the incidence of rural poverty is significantly reduced. Recent stagnation in agricultural productivity, in the face of rising demand, is another worrisome feature. The building up of foodgrains stocks to an unsustainable level is another indicator which puts a question mark on the validity and efficacy of our price and subsidy policies. The growing burden of subsidies contributing to mounting fiscal imbalance and crowding-out public investment in agriculture is another area of concern. These are basically symptoms of an underlying rot. A serious look at the agriculture policies is, therefore, urgently called for. In a meaningful way, success or failure of our economic reforms can be clearly judged as to what is happening in the sector on which largest number of people are dependent for their livelihood, and which still has significant impact on other sectors of the economy.

Critical Areas

Four major weaknesses plague Indian agriculture. These include: preponderance of low-value agriculture, low cost-benefit ratio, inefficient use of natural resources and, deterioration in the self-held institutions. The development strategy, therefore, should aim at

- increase in "value-added" per hectare, more so on the small and marginal holdings.
- Improvement in productivity of inputs, especially the purchased inputs, such as fertilizer and irrigation water.
- Prevention of environmental degradation, especially degradation of land and water resources.
- encouragement to farmer' self-help institutions, particularly at the grass root level.

It will be an over – simplification if we were to assume that these and other problems of growth and equity can be resolved only by policy initiatives. However, economic policies have an important role, and if used judiciously can supplement or support technological and institutional developments.

While discussing the economic policies for agriculture, I wish to state at the outset that the macro policy reforms such as attempts to curtail budgetary deficits or realign the value of domestic currency, have profound impact on agricultural sector. In this lecture, however, I shall be mainly concentrating on the sectoral policies. There too, I shall comment only on few critical issues, such as, (i) next phase in Land Reforms, (ii) policies on Prices and Subsidies and, (iii) Agricultural Trade Policies. There are several equally important areas, e.g. Research and Development Policies, Credit Policies, Policies on Agricultural Taxation, Investment Policy for Agriculture, etc., which I am not able to cover mainly because of the paucity of time.

II

NEEDED REFORMS IN AGRICULTURAL POLICIES

(a) Land Reforms

Through a series of land reforms major changes in the land relations were attempted in our country. Land reforms are a state subject. However, similar reforms were implemented all over the country, and that too more or less in the same sequence. They comprised of abolition of functionless intermediaries, protection to tenants, rationalization of different systems of land tenure, and imposition of ceiling on land holdings. A few states took the process further. Consolidation of fragmented holding was a feature of reforms in some states.

Similarly, West Bengal's move of giving protection to share croppers, well known as "Operation Barga," extended the provisions for the protection of tenants to the share croppers.

The loopholes in the legislation, tardy implementation and consequent evasion of some of the provisions, especially in the ceiling reforms are well known and well documented. However, it will be wrong to conclude that land reforms did not make any impact on our agrarian structure. Following these reforms agrarian system witnessed several important changes. Enlargement of land holdings beyond the ceiling was halted; phenomenon of absentee landlords was severely weakened; due to tenancy reforms greater convergence of ownership and management took place; more or less uniform land system (approximating to the *ryotwari system*) emerged throughout the country. Mainly due to land reforms, a middle peasantry sharing the characteristics of capitalist farmers emerged in large parts of the country. It is now well established that the Green Revolution in the sixties and the seventies was largely carried out by this section of peasantry. These are no mean achievements.

Whatever might have been the equity implications of the these reforms, they could not contribute to the overall growth in agricultural productivity. This was evident from the fact that generation of agriculture surplus was restricted to a relatively small number of medium to large holdings in well endowed regions. A large number of agricultural holdings remained deficit, at best self sufficient. The surplus generated in agriculture was not large enough to give boost to a speedy diversification from farm to non-farm sector, or transform our agriculture into a high-value agriculture.

In view of low-value agriculture on a large number of holdings, it is now suggested in some quarters that more capital needs to be injected in farming to raise productivity, and that the ceiling on farm holdings is the major bottle-neck for high capital investment in agriculture. This proposition is seriously flawed on several counts.

There is no evidence to suggest that small size of holdings *per se* have inhibited high-value agriculture. Most of our vegetable and horticulture farms, as well as those growing specialized crops are small to medium farms. Economies of scale especially in the high-value crops are availed not at the production level but at the processing stage. Such economies can be enjoyed by the small farmers through contract farming. There are the examples of East Asian countries, including China, to illustrate the point I am making. We too have large number of examples of contract farming systems in high value crops. Sugarcane farming in the areas covered by sugarcane cooperatives in Maharashtra is one such example of production on small holdings and efficient processing in large size, sophisticated, factories. Similar example in the face of even greater handicaps is provided by the dairy farming in the cooperative sector, especially in Gujarat.

Away from home, the Felda scheme of Malaysia, encouraging production of oil palms on small holdings and processing in high-tech processing plants, or for that matter small tea garden schemes in Kenya, illustrate that production and processing of high-value crops can be delinked, and that crops can be grown or animals can be raised very effectively on the small farm. Further value addition can be done in technically sophisticated, capital- intensive processing units. To the extent such processing is organised by the farmers cooperatives, not only the growers benefit, spill-over effects in the region as a whole are also quite remarkable, as is evidenced in several parts of our country.

At this stage of development there are important reasons for desisting from any move to relax ceiling on farm holdings.

The obvious danger of such a relaxation in the present circumstances is that it may lead to dislocation of large number of people from the farm lands to whom system will not be able to provide meaningful alternatives. They will be swelling the army of landless workers. Also, the motives for those asking for relaxation of ceilings, and for permitting entry of large corporate units on farm lands are not above suspicion. Could it be to use it as a safety valve to escape from income tax? Or the objectives is, at least in the areas in the vicinity of the urban centers, to indulge in land speculation?

There is some force in the argument for relaxing ceiling in case of uncultivated waste land where large and long gestating investment may be needed, provided it can be ensured that the land will be used for agricultural (including animal husbandry) purposes, and that it will not be used as a tax shelter. We should learn from the past experience when several attempts were made to defeat ceiling legislation by people who had no intention of engaging themselves in agriculture by posing as agriculturists. I wish to repeat that present is not an opportune time to relax ceilings on land holdings, which may lead to immiserisation of large number of people whom the system at the moment is not able to give alternative productive employment. Once the needed resilience is imparted to our rural economy, we can review the question of ceilings on the farm lands.

There is, however a clear and convincing case for liberalizing tenancy provisions. A time has come when we should allow the lease market to function. By putting restrictions on leasing-out the land we are forcing people, especially those owning marginal holdings, to continue with the ownership of plots without any prospect of a fair return to their asset. At the same time we are depriving other small farmers to supplement their holdings and make them viable. Relaxing tenancy law will have positive impact on both the groups. We can introduce safeguards to ensure that the investment in land by the tenant is compensated, and that land owner does not lose his/her ownership right. This single move will impart the needed flexibility in the land market. In any agenda of economic reforms for agriculture unfreezing of the lease market should be given a high priority.

(b) Agricultural Price Policy

The objectives of price policy as propounded in our country from time to time are multiple and often conflicting. There is a need to take a serious look at the scope, instruments and institutions of agricultural price policy.

Currently, agricultural price policies comprise of a minimum support price to ensure that producers of certain commodities, mainly cereals, are not put to loss should the market price fall below a certain level; a procurement price (which is now the same as the minimum support price, though earlier it was different) which entitles producers of certain commodities – again, mainly cereals – to sell all their produce at a price declared in advance by the government; a buffer stock to cushion the country from any large shortfall in foodgrains production; a public distribution system to distribute procured foodgrains at an issue price, generally, lower than the market price, to the vulnerable sections of the consumers. This policy structure had served well in the period when overarching objective was to close the gap between demand and supply of foodgrains from domestic production. The goal of food self-sufficiency was reached by the late 1980s, mainly due to the 'Green Revolution'. Price policies assured the producers that they would not be 'out of business' if they accepted new technology and production would increase to the extent that the price in the free market would drastically fall. The minimum support prices – later the procurement prices – acted as cushion against price-induced risk.

Since then situation has changed, and several distortions have crept in due to this system. The more important among these are.

- The concept of minimum support price which was originally based on the "paid-out", or variable cost of productions was enlarged to take into account full cost of production – in the farm management parlance from A2 cost to cost C.
- Principle of fixing minimum support prices mainly on the "cost-plus" basis got established.
- Due to the pressure from the vocal and organised large farmers' lobby, all types of farm expenditure, incurred or imputed, were added to the cost-of-production for the purpose of fixing the minimum support price. This escalated the minimum support price which had to be increased year after year.
- The distinction between procurement prices and minimum support prices was first blurred, and later abolished, and all quantities of foodgrains, mainly cereals, offered for sale by the farmers were procurred at the enhanced "minimum support" prices.
- Continuous rise in procurement prices on the one hand, and obligation to purchase all grains offered by the farmers at that price, led to accumulation of stocks of wheat and rice much above what is required for Public Distribution System. Today, foodgrains stocks stand at a staggering figure of 40 million tonnes and if the policies are not changed they will further accumulate.
- The operation of procurement and public distribution is handled by a top-heavy institution, namely FCI, in collaboration with similar bureaucratically managed institutions the state level. Only in a few cases

cooperative institutions are associated with these operations. As a result, cost of procuring and distributing foodgrains is very high and escalating.

– With mounting subsidies resulting from high minimum support prices and higher cost of procurement and distribution, foodgrains distributed through the public distributing system (PDS) had to be released at progressively high issue prices defeating its purpose, i.e. to issue foodgrains to the vulnerable sections below the market prices.

Today, we are in a strange situation. The surplus farmers and their spokepersons are asking for, and actually getting, progressively higher procurement prices on the plea of the rise in the cost of production, while the attempt to curtail subsidies are mainly directed to raise issue prices of the grains released through PDS. The net result is that expected offtake from public distribution system is declining and the stocks are rising at the unsustainable level. A time has come to seriously think about dismantling the "high-cost high-subsidy" regime which is eating into the vitals of our agriculture economy by diverting resources from more productive use, such as investment in research and extension and creating better rural infrastructure.

While it will need serious thinking and elaborate consultation, some considerations for forging a 'new price and subsidy policy regime' may be as follows:

– Policy of **minimum support prices** could continue till we are able to have comprehensive coverage through crop insurance and more crops are brought under forward marketing. But, support should be restricted to a few important commodities, and should be in the nature of assurance against recouping variable costs of production. To mitigate or atleast minimize price-induced risk, greater recourse should be taken to crop insurance and forward trading.

Crops which can be considered as price leaders, or the crops for which technological breakthrough is imminent, ought to be covered under the minimum price support. The other candidates for the support prices would be the crops grown in the high-risk environment where the producers of the designated crops deserved to be given an assurance of guaranteed prices. In all these cases, minimum support prices should be treated as a transient measure, i.e., till we are able to evolve a viable crop insurance and or forward trade programme.

The **procurement operations** could aim at basically two different objectives viz., (a) to purchase minimum necessary stocks from open market- or by imports- to meet the needs of truly vulnerable sections and, (b) to influence the open market prices by mopping up or releasing the grains as the situations warrant. This operation will be in the nature of "open market operation", with explicit aim of restraining foodgrains prices in a narrow band.

The decisions involving the amount of foodgrains (or any other commodity) to be procured, price at which to procure, place from where purchases may be made, etc. should be carried out on commercial considerations. Decisions on the markets and the timing of the operations should also be left to the judgement of the procurement authority. There is no compelling reason to announce all these decisions beforehand. Procurement operations are in the nature of market operations. The authorities have to pre-judge the markets and act accordingly.

- **Public Distribution System** should be made 'primarily' a responsibility of the states. In fact, states should be encouraged to give responsibility for Public Distribution to lower tiers of the Panchayati Raj System, i.e. upto the village panchayat level. Centre should be responsible for coordinating and balancing demand and supply of the state level PDS operations targetted at vulnerable sections, and that too for few essential commodities.
- There should be a greater coordination between the price policy and the trade policy which, at present, are executed in a parallel fashion. The importance of coordination between various policy instruments becomes obvious with the emphasis on export promotion on the one hand and commitment to food security on the other. The current spectacle of export of certain commodities at one point of time and import of the same commodities at a loss, to meet domestic demand only after a few months, would be repeated more often if trade and price policies are not properly matched.

To conclude, time has come to take a serious look at the scope, instruments and institutions of agricultural price policy. There is a need to recognize that the price policy is a weak instrument for income transfers; our capacity to offer minimum support prices for a large number of commodities is limited; instrument of minimum support prices has to be used sparingly; greater reliance needs to be placed on crop insurance and on forward markets; procurement operations need to be made more business like; need for dovetailing agriculture and trade policies is urgent; FCI should be decentralized and debureaucratised; states should be made major stakeholders in Public Distribution System.

(c) Input Subsidies

A disturbing feature of agricultural policy in our country is the large and growing amount of input subsidies. These subsidies are progressively losing their relevance and are becoming an unbearable fiscal burden. Input subsidies were justified on the ground that the agricultural producers, as much as consumers of the agricultural products are poor, and it is the state's obligation to subsidize the poor producers as well as poor consumers. This has come to be known as 'cheap-input cheap-output policy'. The argument of subsidies leading to increase in the use of inputs and consequently resulting in improved productivity was added to it. These, then, were the main arguments for the introduction and continuation of subsidies in agriculture.

A policy of subsidizing inputs can be justified if

- introduction of a new input warrants sharing of risks by the state;
- use of subsidized inputs ensure continuous increase in productivity which is shared both by the producers and consumers;
- subsidizing inputs is the only way to transfer income to the poor producers;
- in case of heavily traded products, the trading partners are resorting to overt of covert subsidization, and there is no other way for redressal.

A close scrutiny at the functioning of the subsidy regime in agriculture suggests that none of the arguments for input subsidization apply in the present circumstances. Neither fertilizers, nor irrigation, nor for that matter power, is an unfamiliar input. Increasing use of the subsidized inputs is not contributing to productivity at the margin. Reverse seems to be true. Marginal productivity of fertilizers and water applications is declining, largely because of weaknesses in the organization and functioning of the extension system. There are better ways of transferring incomes to the producers i.e. by improving income terms of trade. Only justification for subsidies is, and that too in the case of heavily-traded agricultural produce, when our trading partners are not playing according to the rules of game. Even in that case we have to take recourse first to WTO provisions since we and practically all our trading partners are members of the same.

A determined move needs to be made to dismantle subsidy regime in agriculture. It should be recognized, however, that our system has been addicted to subsidies. Also, in case of some major subsidies, irrigation and power in particular, while the Centre has a limited role, the states have to take initiative. Action is needed in following directions to enable use 'retreat without disarray'.:

- A cap on the subsidies should be put in the current year's budget.
- A phased programme of progressively withdrawing subsidies should be announced.
- Amount thus saved from input subsidies should be earmarked as addition to the funds for strengthening rural infrastructure, research and extension.
- Well defined measures should be taken to improve efficiency and plugging leakages in input supplies.
- States should be impressed on the need for cost recovery, particularly in irrigation and power.

None of these are likely to prove easy options. But continuing the same regime will make future tasks all the more difficult.

(d) Agricultural Trade Policies

With the establishment of the World Trade Organization (WTO) in 1994 a major change has taken place in international trade scenerio. The agreement to establish WTO which was signed by over 100 countries has by now been subscribed by virtually all the remaining countries except China, which also is likely to join the organization within a short period of time. The Uruguay Round of trade negotiations which paved the way for the establishment of WTO, for the first time brought agriculture in the discipline of GATT. These agreements (by now 20 or so) are fairly complicated; in fact, a delight for the lawyers ! The intent of these agreements is to facilitate the process of trade liberalization and provide a mechanism for arbitration. The most important feature of WTO is that the signatories abide to treat all members as "most favoured nations", without any discrimination. Agreement on Agriculture which is of immediate concern to us, covers three basic areas: (i) market access, (ii) export competition, (iii) domestic support.

There is an apprehension in the country that the WTO agreements may be against the interest of India. Initially atleast this is not so. The conditions spelled out for a free and liberal trade in WTO charter already existed in India. The country was not violating any of these initial conditions. For example, both the product specific subsidies and non-product subsidies were deem to be negative in case of India and, therefore, no major change was needed from WTO side in these regards. The stipulated process of tariffication is gradual and gives ample scope for adjustment. The ceiling on tariffs proposed by India and accepted by WTO are fairly high; for example, 100 per cent on primary products, 150 per cent on processed products, 300 per cent on edible oils. The country can also take advantage of the provisions on balance of payment exigencies and food security concerns to moderate the tariff structure to an extent. Compared to the developed countries, developing countries, more so the least developed countries, have been given ample time for adjustment. Thus, initially atleast, there are no major handicaps faced by India; on the other hand there are the possible advantages of a freer but more disciplined trade regime. Only snag is that developed countries are not playing fair.

In this context, the recent developments have to be carefully watched. These include developed countries' insistence on bringing non-trade issues, such as issues of environment and labour, as part of trade negotiations; inclusion of various types of "blue boxes", "green boxes" and "amber boxes" which provide possibilities of direct income transfer to the producers, particularly in developed countries; non-tariff restrictions in the garb of sanitary requirements. While vigilance on all these fronts has to be there, we have to be prepared also for the next round of negotiations. It needs to be stressed that till now our joining WTO has not constrained us in pursuing agricultural trade policy which is advantageous for the country in the long run. There is enough space for us to design and take appropriate measures.

One of the major issues in agricultural trade policy is our stance on food self-sufficiency. There is a pressure from several quarters to wean away from this policy which was till lately the overarching objective of agricultural policies, not only in India but also in several other medium and large countries. The widespread move towards globalization on the one hand, and secular decline in the foodgrains prices at the international level on the other, have been advanced as the arguments to forsake food self sufficiency as a national objective, and organize production on the basis of comparative costs.

This proposition is flawed on several counts. In the first

place, the notion of comparative advantage (often represented by the border prices) is, at best, a static concept. It does not take into account the dynamic role of technological and institutional measures. It also assumes ability for quick and frequent shifts in cropping pattern by domestic producers to adjust to the changes in international prices. Wide swings in inter year and intra year fluctuations in the international prices of foodgrains, greater in magnitude than the fluctuations in the domestic prices, enhance risk and uncertainty for the domestic producers as well as consumers. Advocacy of unrestricted exposure to international markets ignores the fact that a large majority of rural producers depend on foodgrains production as their main source of livelihood; and, it overestimates the resilience of the system to compensate these producers from heavy and sudden dislocations. Thus, the assumptions on the basis of which plea for abandoning the food self sufficiency is made are not borne out by the facts, not at least in a large and poor country such as India. For some time to come we have to stick to the objective of food self-sufficiency.

As I have mentioned elsewhere, food self-sufficiency is not an article of faith. Once our livelihood and consumption patterns change, with small number of workers engaged in food production and small percentage of expenditure spent on food, and more resilience is imparted to the economic factors, we can think of reviewing the policy of food self-sufficiency. To take a doctrinaire approach on 'free' trade in foodgrains would amount to jeopardizing one of the essential attributes of food security, i.e., adequate and dependable availability of foodgrains at reasonable prices, and will compromise the prospects of livelihood of those producers who themselves are inherently food insecure. At the same time, food self-sufficiency should not be interpreted as an invitation to autarky. It simply connotes a trade strategy which would not expose the vulnerable sections of producers as well as consumers to avoidable shocks from external trade.

While there is a little justification on foodgrains imports to meet the domestic requirements to any significant extent, there is no firm basis to consider the possibility of foodgrains emerging as major exports either. With the satisfactory growth in foodgrains production in the 1970s and the 1980s an euphoria has set in certain policy making quarters, and it is suggested that determined efforts should be made to register India as an important exporter of foodgrains. This euphoria is, to a large extent, unwarranted. It should be remembered that we are lagging behind our targets of foodgrains production. Even from the point of comparative advantage India loses out to other main producers of wheat as well as coarse cereals. Rice is the only cereal in which the domestic-foreign price ratio has remained in country's favour in most of the years. However, both the demand and supply aspect of rice suggest that large export of this commodity is not in the interest of the country. Marketable surplus in rice is limited, and price elasticity of rice is very high. This means that a small drawal from the domestic markets would give rise to disproportionately high prices. Rice is the staple food of the majority of the people. Even a small rise in the price will affect the living standard of large vulnerable section. Considering all these factors, I would suggest that, we should continue with the policy of self-sufficiency in foodgrains. If due to rise in productivity possibility of genuine 'surplus' becomes imminent, then the strategy should be to divert the resources to commercial crops, or even out of the agricultural sector, rather than to take a chance with basic commodities such as foodgrains. This, of course, does not preclude 'switch' trade to meet requirement for particular grains; nor it excludes international trade in foodgrains at the margin.

The criteria by which we should judge the export-potential of an agricultural commodity could be: (a) the place of the commodity in the consumption pattern of the people, especially the poorer sections; (b) supply and price elasticities; (c) the ratio of export price and the domestic price; and (d) future demand/supply prospects in the international markets. These criteria should be kept in the forefront while deciding the strategy of international trade in agricultural commodities.

Until recently, agricultural trade policy was designed to pursue twin objectives, namely food self-sufficiency and promotion of exports of the so called "commercial crops" e.g. cotton, jute, tobacco etc. Export orientation for the later group of crops is justified as they satisfy basic conditions to qualify as export crops as suggested above viz: (a) there is a genuine and growing surplus after meeting domestic requirements, (b) ratio of export to domestic prices is favourable, (c) there is a growing international demand.

There is, another area of potential growth in agricultural exports where India can exploit the international markets to its advantage mainly because of its diverse soil and climatic conditions. This is constituted by the "dynamic" commodities (i.e. commodities which are occupying progressively large space in international trade), like fruits, vegetables, flowers, herbs etc. Apart from fulfilling the criteria mentioned above, the other advantages enjoyed by these commodities are (i) a faster growing demand in the affluent parts of the world, and (ii) high value added as well as high labour content of these commodities. Needless to say that the second characteristic helps in the fulfillment of one of the main objectives of the agricultural policy, namely, introduction of high value added agriculture, especially on the small and marginal holdings.

The pre-conditions for the growth of export of these commodities would include, (i) vertical integration of the small holding with appropriate secondary and tertiary organizations for input supply, quality control, marketing and processing and, (ii) the infrastructural support in terms of communication, transport, cold storage etc. The development of economic and social infrastructure, e.g., adaptation of banking facilities, insurance facilities, pricing policies, and development of appropriate information system are equally important. The countries that are making a success in the export of these commodities have taken necessary steps in the areas mentioned above.

Thus, a review of experience in agricultural trade and an examination of future prospects would suggest that we should:

- reach effective food self-sufficiency in cereals and be prepared for diversification once a situation of food surplus arises;
- emphasize export of the commercial crops where India has comparative advantage, particularly in cotton, tea and tobacco.
- harness export potential of processed agricultural commodities, fruits, flowers, herbs etc., and ensure participation of small holdings in their production.

There is also a need for institutional reforms. Policy for canalization of exports through public sector organization, fixing arbitrary minimum base line price for exports, and "stop-go" policy based on adhoc consideration will have to be substituted by a well thought out, long term strategy, for agriculture exports in tandem with domestic economic policies.

With a determined bid to orient agricultural production to exports in commodities in which we have comparative advantage, we can make agriculture contribute substantially to foreign exchange earning and can introduce "value-added" agriculture even on the small and marginal holdings. At the same time, we have to ensure that agricultural exports may not prove counter productive by fuelling inflation within the country and adversely affecting the standard of living of the common people.

III

SUMMING UP

Let me conclude above discussion on the direction of reforms in agriculture in next round of economic reform. But, before that, I will reiterate that in two areas we need to "hasten slowly". I submit that, we should maintain ceiling on agricultural land holdings till the pace of diversification in the rural areas is accelerated, and should not abandon the policy of food-self sufficiency till livelihood and consumption patterns change remarkably.

The main ingredient of a reform agenda in agriculture should be:

(i) Acceleration of the process of liberalization in domestic markets.

(ii) Un-freezing the lease market

(iii) Throughly revising agricultural price support system by (a) curtailing the scope of minimum support prices to aim at *protecting variable costs* for a few commodities in selected regions, (b) giving greater emphasis on crop insurance and forward markets

(iv) Carrying procurement operations on commercial lines.

(v) Involving states and the lower tiers of Panchayati Raj in public distribution of foodgrains

(vi) Dovetailing price and trade policies in an effective manner.

(vii) Establishing the principle of cost-recovery in agriculture inputs, and phasing out input subsidies, by (a) placing a 'cap' on existing subsidies, (b) announcement of a time bound programme of phasing out input subsidies.

(viii) Working out a long-term export strategy for "commercial crops" and other dynamic and high value crops.

(ix) Progressive decannalisation of exports of agricultural commodities and removing other irritants.

(x) Preparing to challenge any deviation from the main objective of WTO, and take initiative in organizing other developing countries for the same purpose.

13

Agricultural Trade Policy and Export Strategy

INTRODUCTION

A stylized version of the changes in agricultural trade pattern during the course of economic development will suggest that with the growth of an economy not only the share of agriculture in GDP declines, share of agricultural exports to the total merchandise exports also declines. As the economy gets diversified the non-agricultural commodities acquire greater importance in the product mix, and also in exports. Part of the explanation for the relative decline in agricultural commodities in the developing countries also lies in the rising share of processed agricultural products. On the imports side, with larger share of purchased inputs in the input base of agriculture, quantum of imports of inputs such as fertilizers, pesticides, farm machinery, etc., rises. However, as the import intensity of agricultural production is low the earnings from exports outpace the outlay on imports. Most of the developing countries maintain a favourable trade balance in agriculture.

India is no exception to these general trends, with a few special features. During last two decades India's agricultural exports as a part of total merchandise exports have continued

(Presidential Address at 12th Annual Conference on Agricultural Marketing, Institute of Development Studies, Jaipur in 1998).

to decline from the preponderant position they occupied in the pre-Independence and in the early years of Independence. Their share in the merchandise exports of the country in recent years (1991-97) ranges between 15 to 18 per cent. But with the achievement of self-sufficiency in foodgrains and some other major agricultural commodities, which used to account for large portion of import bill, overall imports of agricultural commodities have sharply declined. The outlay on agricultural imports as a proportion of earnings from agricultural exports has progressively declined, and the overall balance has become progressively more favourable.

Contribution of agricultural exports to foreign exchange earnings is critical for a country such as India which faces a chronic balance of payment problem. With the growth in economy, specially with the growth of more import intensive sectors such as 'industry' the need for foreign exchange earnings from agricultural exports becomes increasingly more important from the national point of view. From agricultural producers point of view, expanding export opportunities mean bigger markets and higher value for their output. However, while thinking about exports of agricultural commodities in a poor country like India the implications of export growth on domestic availability of agricultural produce, especially the foodgrains, cannot be overlooked. The moot question, therefore, is: how to augment export earnings without jeopardizing the basic objective of food security. Discussion on these issues has, naturally, to take into account the new trade regime evolved after the Uruguay Rounds as the stated objective of the trading partners is to achieve economic efficiency and international competitiveness through increased reliance on market forces.

In the first part of my presentation I will briefly introduce the external economic environment obtaining in the recent years, more specifically after Uruguay Rounds. In the next part I will review agricultural trade policy as it has evolved in our country in the recent years and account for the important factors which have shaped the policy. I will also examine whether there is a need for any major shift in this policy. In the third part, I will look into the developments in agricultural trade specially the agricultural exports at the world level in the recent years and discuss the performance of Indian agriculture in this respect. In the fourth and final part, I will try to spell out the ingredients of a strategy to augment agricultural exports in the changing, and more demanding, global economy.

I

THE EXTERNAL ENVIRONMENT

The economic environment for agricultural trade is changing in a remarkable way due to changes in the domestic policies as well as in international trade arrangements. A number of scholars and practitioners have commented on the move towards the policies on liberalization and globalization and their implications for agriculture in our country (Bhalla, 1994). I will briefly touch upon the developments at the international plane and their implications for the agricultural trade. The international developments relevant to agricultural trade are taking place at two levels. One, several groupings of the countries are emerging with the objective of forming unified trade blocks, starting from EEC and ASEAN to more recent attempts at forming NAFTA (North American Free Trade Agreement) and SAFTA (South American Free Trade and Agreement) and, of course, SAARC (South Asia Association of Regional Cooperation). Second, and probably more important, development is the signing of various agreements as a result of the Uruguay Round of trade negotiations. I shall comment on the latter of these two developments mainly because the Uruguay Round has now more or less universal coverage in terms of the countries agreeing to its covenants. Also, because various trade blocks would, hopefully, converge on a global trading system initiated by the Uruguay Round.

The significance of the Uruguay Round agreements could be well appreciated once it is recognized that for the first time agriculture is brought under the General Agreement on Trade and Tariff (GATT) discipline. Until the present round of trade negotiations, the contracting parties to GATT had reconciled to a waiver on agricultural trade obtained by USA, which was also used by all other countries. The situation has changed, ironically, at the instance of USA which, in fact, pleaded for complete removal of all interventions in agriculture (the so-called "zero-option"). The proposal to bring agriculture under GATT discipline evoked a responsive chord in several countries which were concerned with the rising burden of subsidies in their budgets.

After lengthy and tortuous negotiations under the Uruguay Round, agreements have been reached on several important areas. These include:

(a) reduction in the farm subsidies;

(b) enhanced market access;

(c) limits on public stock holdings of grains for food security;

(d) sparing use of sanitary and phytosanitary import barriers; and

(e) introduction of intellectual property rights[1].

1. I have discussed these agreements in somewhat greater details in a paper I had prepared for the Asian Productivity Organisation's Study Meeting on Agricultural Trade Policy in Asia Pacific. (Vyas, 1996).

It is relevant to note here that the industrially developed countries made commitments in regard to all these provisions, and gave an assurance that concrete steps will be taken between the years 1995 and 2000 to redeem their obligations. For the developing countries the implementation period is longer and the extent of reforms is less demanding. Special provisions have been made in favour of the least developed countries. Provisions have also been made to assist heavily importing countries to tide over the difficulties during the transitory period and to reduce possible negative effects of trade liberalization on these countries.

The Uruguay Round agreements are a milestone in the development of the international trade in agricultural commodities. The very fact that agriculture has been brought under international discipline is of great significance. However, exact outcome of various provisions of the agreements on the developing countries is difficult to foresee; partly, because of great complexities of provisions and instrumentalities in the agreements which could subject it to a variety of interpretations. Even the highly simplified version which I have presented will not permit one to arrive at a definite conclusion on the net outcome of the agreements. This is mainly because a lot depends on the developed countries subjecting themselves to the implicit discipline of such agreements. Taking a more optimistic view, and making some heroic efforts, a few scholars have tried to foresee the results of these agreements on *a priori* grounds (Anderson and Tyres, 1990; Goldin *et al.,* 1993; Brandao and Martin, 1993). Not surprisingly, they have not come up with a unanimous conclusion !

One may speculate, again on *a priori* grounds, on the likely effects of the agreements on the agriculture of the developing countries. In spite of all the loopholes, it is quite likely that the agreements will help in reducing the amount of subsidies enjoyed by the agricultural producers in the developed world.

This would mean that the price of agricultural commodities produced and traded by the developed countries will rise in the international market place. Since bulk of agricultural production in these countries is accounted for by the (temperate) foodgrains, especially cereals (and there too, mainly, wheat and corn), prices of cereals are likely to rise. If we were to continue as wheat importers this could result in an inflation-induced demand for wage rise, and would have deleterious effect on the pace of industrialization. On the other hand, this would also act as an incentive for the domestic food producers to embark on production raising efforts. The net outcome will depend on the supply elasticity of foodgrains production. The latter is high in the situation of developed infrastructure, stock of relevant technology, and efficient market institutions. Developments in these areas, even in the best of the circumstances, will take some time. In the interim, the developing countries, particularly the food importing ones, will face an economic bind. The steps which are necessary not only for the short-term relief, but also for equipping the developing countries, including ours, to take long-term advantage of a liberal international trade regime in agricultural commodities should, in my view, include the following :

(i) Macro economic reforms which discourage high tariffs and overvalued exchange rates are beneficial to agricultural trade and need to be continued.

(ii) Adjustment of agriculture to a more liberal and global economy should be attempted carefully. A firm beginning could be made by domestic economic reforms, especially by encouraging liberalization, deregulation and de-bureaucratization within the country.

(iii) Implicit taxation of agriculture through price discrimination should be avoided. International prices could be used as referral for this purpose, although no sanctity need to be attached to the border prices.

(iv) Nothing should be done to impair food security and poverty alleviation efforts in the process of economic reforms. Adjustment in the food sector should be gradual and non-doctrinaire.

India together with other developing countries should develop GATT consistent instruments to protect our interests. This is important because the next round of trade negotiations are on anvil, and we should not be caught unprepared (Vyas, 1994).

II

AGRICULTURAL TRADE POLICY

India like several other large countries is not an export-oriented economy. This is particularly true of agriculture. In recent years the ratio of agricultural exports to agriculture GDP has seldom exceeded 3 per cent. This in itself is not a disqualification. Nor, if the example of the African countries is an indication, a high export to GDP ratio is a blessing in itself. The importance of exports as an economic activity has to be judged by the objectives it serves.

India's foreign trade regime till the reforms initiated in 1991 was primarily dictated by two important considerations, a quest for import substituting industrialization and concern for dwindling foreign exchange resources. The major instruments used to implement these policy goals comprised of quantitative restrictions, heightened tariffs, surcharge on imports, rebate on exports and severe restrictions on foreign exchange transactions. There were phases in which these provisions were relaxed. Yet the basic characteristics of an inward looking import substituting policy frame remained more or less intact (Srinivasan, 1998). The instrumentality of canalizing large part of exports and imports reflected the other element of the developmental thinking, i.e., an implicit distrust of private sector and an implicit faith in bureaucracy to achieve the stated goals of development.

All these ingredients of overall trade policy applied to agricultural trade, especially till 1966-67, i.e., the second year of serious draughts of the mid-sixties. Till then the agricultural trade was also subjected to a regime of quantitative controls and other State interventions to conserve foreign exchange. However, while in industry the policy of import substitution was clearly manifest, in agriculture the trade policy was designed to pursue twin objectives of food self-sufficiency and promotion of exports of the so called "commercial crops". In regard to the regulation and control, agricultural trade was no exception. The role of State Trading Corporation (STC) and the Cooperative Federations was emphasized as canalizing agencies for agricultural exports. The public sector agencies were given equally important role in the imports of inputs, particularly fertilizers and chemicals.

In the second phase, starting from the mid-sixties this policy was pursued more rigorously, and Food Self Sufficiency became the corner stone of the development strategies in agriculture. Two severe droughts, in 1965-66 and 1966-67, and the difficulties in importing foodgrains from food surplus countries — mainly the western countries — forced the policy makers to opt for a policy of food self-sufficiency. Normally, an import substitution policy leads to high unit cost of production. However, mainly because of the availability of a high yielding technology in cereals, not only the task of food self-sufficiency was accomplished, the country could fill-in the gap between the demand and supply of foodgrains without raising the real cost of production, a fact which is generally not appreciated. In fact, along with higher yields the unit cost of production of superior cereals came down and benefits of growth in productivity could be shared by the producers (in terms of higher income) and consumers (in terms of stable prices) in an equitable manner (Vyas, 1990).

This policy continued till 1991. Since then some questions are being raised about pursuing the policy of food self-sufficiency, partly due to the euphoria generated by the satisfactory performance in agricultural production in the previous decade, and also because of the governing paradigm of economic liberalization and globalization. It is now suggested in some quarters that there are enough justifications for opening up food sector to international trade based mainly on the considerations of comparative costs as reflected in the border prices.

Continuation of the strategy of food self-sufficiency is challenged mainly on three grounds. Firstly, it is suggested that with the new economic regime brought in by the Uruguay Round of agreements, the developed countries will also have to withdraw subsidies for agricultural products and, therefore, there will be a level playing field, and existing distortions in agricultural trade will be removed. Secondly, it is now generally accepted that food security means entitlement to food and, therefore, if the country can earn foreign exchange, import comparatively cheaper foodgrains and distribute it equitably, the country as a whole as well as the poor will benefit more. Thirdly, it is suggested that unlike in the 1950s and the 1960s when the foodgrains surplus was mainly concentrated in USA and few other developed countries there is much more widespread distribution of tradable quantities of foodgrains. There is hardly any country which is in a monopolistic position. In any case, it is argued, with big players in the foodgrain marketing, i.e., the large multi-national companies, governments' capacity to dictate trade pattern on political considerations has considerably weakened.

While there is a compelling case for instituting a liberal trade regime in agricultural commodities, there are certain key considerations which cannot be assumed away. The agricultural commodities can be broadly divided into two categories. The food crops and the non-food crops. The distinction between two is not firm but understandable. There is an established policy of encouraging exports in commercial crops, and it has to continue. There are, however, several reasons why the policy of food self-sufficiency which largely applies to self-sufficiency in principal cereals, i.e., wheat and rice, has to continue. The major considerations justifying self-sufficiency in principal foodgrains are the following. Expenditure on foodgrains, mainly cereals, account for over 40 per cent of the expenditure of the bottom one-third of India's population. Any fluctuations in foodgrains prices will result in undue hardship for this section of population. Price elasticities with respect to prices of cereals were estimated at –0.493 for the very poor and –0.409 for the poor in the rural areas. Corresponding figures for urban areas for the two groups of the poor population are –0.313 and –0.166 (Radhakrishna and Ravi, 1992). It is now well established that the international prices are far more volatile than the domestic prices (Nayyar and Sen, 1994; Bhalla 1994). Therefore, an opening up of the economy for foodgrains imports to any sizable extent will tantamount to importing price instability, the main victims of that would be the poor in the rural and the urban areas.

It is not only as the consumers, also as producers the poor have a stake in maximizing foodgrains production. Bulk of the poor are in the rural areas. Their livelihood depends on the growth of agriculture. At present foodgrains occupy nearly 68 per cent of cropped area and account for the same weight in output. There is a gradual shift in production from foodgrains to non-foodgrains in which, presumably, poor cultivators are also participating. However, the agricultural economy, particularly the economy of the small and marginal farmers is not resilient enough to enable poor farmers to make drastic switch over from food crops to non-food crops within a short period. The switch over from agriculture to non-agricultural production will be even more slow and gradual.

On the supply side, it has to be recognized that the foodgrain surpluses in food exporting surplus countries are not adequate to meet the demands of the large countries like India and China to any measurable extent. India's food requirements by year 2000 are expected to be of the order of 210 (209.4) million metric tonnes (Kumar and Mathur, 1997). In this, the wheat requirement is estimated at 71 million tonnes and rice requirements are estimated at 88 million tonnes. Production of wheat in 1995 was estimated at 60.8 million tonnes and that of rice 78 million tonnes. If production of wheat and rice were to be frozen at 1995 level, and rest were to be imported, we will have to import not less than 10 million tonnes of rice and wheat each by the year 2000. On the other hand, global cereal stocks had slipped to 14 per cent of the estimated consumption requirements in 1995-96. FAO considers 17 per cent of stocks as critical minimum, i.e., a safety-margin for world food security. In last year or so world stock of cereals has improved, but still remains below the safety level of 17 per cent (Pinstrup-Anderson, *et al.*, 1997). With progressively larger demand from China[2], and disruption in cereal production in former Soviet Union, any rise in India's demand for cereals would result in rapid increase in the cereal prices. Thus there is no escape from encouraging foodgrains

2. An IFPRI study concludes that by 2000, China's imports of foodgrains are expected to reach 24 million tonnes. Increasing imports arise mainly from the accelerated demand for meat and feedgrains and continued slowing of supply (Huang, *et al.*, 1997).

production in the country, at least for the coming few years. The imports of more than a marginal quantity do not provide a viable solution.

A question which is not frontly addressed is whether the food surplus developed countries have capacity, and economic rationale, to go on increasing their exportable surpluses in foodgrains. More so, once the props of subsidies are progressively withdrawn under the new international trade regime. Unfortunately, we do not have any systematic study on the supply response of foodgrains in the developed countries. Unless one assumes that agriculture has, and will continue to have, comparative advantages over, say, industry, in these countries, it is unrealistic to assume that developed countries can be relied upon to meet progressively enlarging demand for foodgrains of a country such as India by putting more resouces in their agriculture, and without seriously escalating the prices.

Other major consideration is the availability of foreign exchange to meet foodgrains imports. Exportable surplus of foodgrains, particularly wheat is still concentrated in five developed countries, USA, France, Canada, Australia and Germany, who accounted for nearly 73 per cent of total exports of wheat in the triennium ending 1995. Situation is better in the case of rice as all major exporting countries, except USA are from developing world. The country will have to augment its foreign exchange earnings many fold to enable it to import foodgrains, especially wheat. Even if foreign exchange resources are available, there are much better uses of these resources, e.g., in the imports of industrial raw materials, etc. So long as the other "commercial crops" do not generate measurable foreign exchanges surplus, over and above the cost of imports of agricultural inputs the country cannot afford to divert foreign exchange resources to import large quantities of foodgrains. Lastly, the political implications of dependence on imports of foodgrains, most of which have to be brought from the developed countries, should not be under-estimated. The post-Pokhran sanctions have once again reminded us that we are living in a unipolar world in which one country has a decisive voice.

There is no escape from enlarging foodgrains production to meet the basic requirements for food from domestic production. Marginal imports of food, say, one to two million tonnes in the total requirement of 200 million tonnes does not vitiate above arguments. Nor a "switch over" trade of a few hundred thousand tonnes goes against the tenets of food self-sufficiency.

However, food self-sufficiency is not a matter of faith. We can review the policy when the following conditions are met:

(i) When expenditure on food becomes a minor part of the consumers budget, especially the budget of the poor,

(ii) When food production does not remain the main source of livelihood for the small and marginal farmers,

(iii) When non-food exports become sufficiently buoyant to generate enough foreign exchange surplus,

(iv) When country has enough buffer stocks to ward off any significant price fluctuations imported from external sources, and

(v) When there are numerous and assured sources of supply to cope with any sizeable shortfall in domestic foodgrains production (Vyas, 1994).

III

PROSPECTS FOR AGRICULTURAL EXPORTS

What I have said above does not minimize the need for augmenting exports. One is advocating a more cautious and discriminatory approach, especially when it comes to food security. Traditionally plantation and the fibre crops occupied primary position in the agricultural exports of our country. Cereals, and in the later years, oilseeds occupied a dominant position in the imports. From the beginning of the planning era a two-pronged approach to the international trade in the agricultural commodities became evident. As far as foodgrains were concerned, the major thrust of the policy was towards imports substitution. As against this, non-food commodities, which in common parlance are referred to as "commercial crops" were identified for export promotion. As I have mentioned earlier, there were justifications for two different norms in relation to these two commodity groups.

Important changes are taking place in the demand and supply of foodgrains in our country which has prompted some people, who are willing to accept the strategy of food self-sufficiency in the time of foodgrains deficit, to question the same strategy once we have foodgrains surplus. They advocate, why India should not aspire to become a major foodgrains exporter. This position also needs to be examined carefully. It is suggested that for following reasons, we may have exportable surplus in foodgrains :

- Although the rate of growth in foodgrains production in the 1990s is slower compared to the rate of growth in the 1980s it is still ahead of population and income induced demand for foodgrains.
- The intake of foodgrains in general and cereals in particular is at a much slower pace than was

anticipated by the planners. As a result, margin between the availability of cereals in relation to demand, year to year fluctuations notwithstanding, is widening with foodgrains supply outpacing the demand.

- The real cost of buying a kilogram of foodgrains, say, wheat, is lower today than it was earlier. This suggests that slackening of demand is not due to higher prices but due to a change in the structure of demand; latter induced by the growth in income as well as by non-economic factors, such as urbanization.
- Surplus of supply over demand is particularly noticeable in the superior cereals, i.e., wheat and more particularly in rice, mainly because of the availability of high yielding technology in these crops. This technology is not yet fully exploited and one can expect a further increase in the output of these crops.

If the exports of cereals is considered as "residual" after meeting the domestic demand on the grounds I have argued earlier, then the case for an export initiative in foodgrains will hinge upon the emergence of genuine surplus in the grains. Without dependable 'surpluses', at this stage of development, it will be premature to give a go-bye to the policy of food self-sufficiency. Thus, in order to launch a strategy for exports of foodgrains first, we must ensure that there would be distinct possibility of surplus emerging in the foodgrains sector. Assuming that growth in foodgrains production will continue at the rate of 3 per cent per year or so, which given the nature of domestic demand will be adequate to meet our foodgrains requirements, what should be our strategy for the disposal of surpluses in the foodgrains sector? For this purpose, we need to look into the possibilities for each of the major cereals separately.

A carefully done study has shown that we do not have any comparative advantage as wheat exporters (Reddy and Badri Narayanan, 1992). Besides, as I have mentioned earlier, the competition for this crop will be provided by the traditional wheat exporters, i.e., by the developed countries such as USA, Canada and Australia. True, compliance to WTO conditionalities may blunt their competitive edge with progressive withdrawal of subsidies, there are various ways in which they could support their wheat producers and make it difficult for us to compete[3]. In case of wheat if we have genuine 'surplus' after meeting our domestic demand, we should encourage diversion of resources to other competing crops, or out of agricultural sector, rather than to embark on a quest for becoming a major wheat exporter.

We have distinct advantages in rice, and can emerge as moderate exporters of rice. It is one of the few agricultural commodities where the domestic and foreign price ratio has remained in country's favour in recent years (Reddy and Badri Narayanan, 1992). At the same time, we should recognize that marketable surplus in rice is limited, and the price elasticity of rice is very high (Kahlon and Tyagi, 1983). In the major rice growing States, the existing inverse relationship between size of farms and area under rice does not promise a substantial marketable surplus. This means that a small drawal from the domestic markets would give rise to disproportionately high prices. Rice is the staple food of the majority of the people. Even a small rise in the price will affect the living standard of the large, vulnerable sections (Chellaraj, *et al.,* 1992).

---

3. Ways to defeat the purpose and objective of the Uruguay Round of agreements could include resort to anti-dumping and similar provisions just to defer the agreed tariff reduction; mix up environmental protection and wages and labour standard issues with trade policy; object to the use of several chemicals which are not used in temperate countries but may be useful, and harmless, in tropical countries; undermine the global convent by unduly emphasizing regional trade agreements, such as NAFTA.

In order to establish ourselves as rice exporters and at the same time to safeguard food security of the rice consuming population in the country, we need to develop a different strategy. While continuing the export of basmati rice targeted mostly to Middle East, and to NRIs in Europe and USA we should recognize that there is a limit beyond which we will not be able to export basmati and other fragrant varieties. The real market for rice is in South-East Asian countries, e.g., in Indonesia, Malaysia and Philippines and in East Asian countries, i.e., Japan and South Korea, where rice is the staple cereal. It seems that the principal rice exporter to these countries, i.e., Thailand has reached a plateau in rice exports (Chaowagul, 1996), while the demand for rice in the countries listed above is slowly but steadily rising[4]. Further, the rice markets in Japan and South Korea which were till recently virtually 'locked up' are bound to be opened. If we want to be a major player in the rice market, we should develop varieties which are preferred by the consumers in these countries and then market them vigorously. Even with inadequate preparations, we could market more than three million tonnes of rice in 1995-96, admittedly due to fortuitous circumstances. There are distinct possibilities of raising the exports by a couple of million tonnes, if we look into the problems and issues in rice exports in a systemic perspective (Datta, 1997).

The other cereals, i.e., barley, maize and millet are used mainly as cattle feed in the developed countries. Barley and maize are also demanded as industrial raw materials. Demand for these cereals is increasing much more rapidly than for rice or wheat with increasing share of animal products in human diet in the developed as well as in developing countries. However, with low productivity we do not have any

4. However, the position of Vietnam and Myanmar as important rice exporters should not be underestimated.

competitive edge in these cereals. If we wish to tap the expanding cattle feed market in the world, we will have to raise productivity in these cereals and also change to varieties to suit international demand. In India these cereals are grown mainly as food crops by small farmers and mostly on infertile lands. Progressively more and more area under these crops should be brought under varieties which are suitable as cattle feed. Technical possibilities of raising productivity level in these so-called 'inferior cereals' are very high. High yielding varieties are being developed in maize in collaboration with CIMMYT. We have developed our own high yielding varieties in millets. These varieties need to be given as much importance in our extension efforts as high yielding varieties of wheat and rice received in the hey-days of green revolution. There is an added advantage in increasing productivity in these crops in terms of equity, as these crops are, generally, grown by the poorer sections of cultivators and in backward regions. An increase in their productivity, and in value, will benefit disadvantaged sections. Already, due to the prospects of good market and higher prices, large areas are being diverted to high yielding irrigated maize. This tendency should be encouraged with an eye on generating surpluses for exports.

The second group of commodities to be considered as thrust area are our traditional export commodities, namely, tea, coffee, cotton, oilseeds and cakes, tobacco and sugar. Among these commodities both tobacco and coffee have a dynamic demand. We have not been able to make full use of this surge in demand because of low productivity. There is need to earmark these crops, especially tobacco, as special crops for exports. Tea which is still one of our important export commodities is stagnating in the international markets, both in terms of prices and quantities. This is partly due to the demand factors — international demand for tea is lagging behind the demand for other beverages, especially coffee, at the same time domestic demand for tea is rapidly increasing — but mainly because we have not been able to impart efficiency in production and marketing of tea as much as some of our competitors have been able to do (Chiranjeevi, 1994). India should continue to aspire and work for a leadership position in this crop.

Among our traditional agricultural exports two commodities, namely, cotton and sugar are problem ridden. This is mainly because of uncertainty and fluctuations in the production. The uncertainty is further exacerbated because of adhocism, if not due to the pressure from powerful vested interests, in designing the export policies. Without stabilizing the domestic supply base, there is no point in emphasizing sugar as an export commodity. Unless a base of assured supply is created it will be difficult to compete in the international market. In case of cotton, possibility does exist to keep our presence in the international markets (Acharya, 1996). However, in order to exploit our comparative advantage in this commodity, we have to minimize wide year to year fluctuations which are induced as much by natural phenomena as by the inept export policies.

In refining our export strategy, more important considerations should be given to what we may call the "dynamic commodities" in international trade. To identify such commodities, I have looked into the growth of world exports in different commodities during the period 1989 to 1995. Among the major agricultural commodities which have shown high rate of growth, the following are notable : Tobacco unmanufactured, milk and milk products, rice, fruits and vegetables, coffee, soyabean and soyabean oil, oilseeds, cakes and meals.

India's share in these commodities is very small except in two commodities, namely, tea and rice. Besides, India accounts for nearly 8 per cent of world exports in oilseed cakes. In rest of these "dynamic commodities" our share is negligible, in many cases non-existent. On the other hand, most of our traditional exports, except rice (which, in any case, is a new entrant in agricultural exports), are stagnating, if not declining.

If we want to make our agriculture exports a major plank of export strategy, it is important to concentrate on the commodities which constitute the dynamic group, especially those such as milk and milk products where we have distinct comparative advantages. India is the second largest producer of milk. In terms of resource use efficiency, its cost of production is the lowest among the major dairy producers except New Zealand. However, as I will try to indicate later, the low cost of production is only one of the factors to impart a competitive edge. There are equally important questions of quality and reliability.

Export operations are essentially private sector operations. Traders in agricultural commodities will always seek opportunities to make profitable deals. So long as their interests do not conflict with wider national objectives, they should have freedom to do so. It was not my intention to narrow down the list of exportable commodities. My purpose was to illustrate some of the key considerations which Government should keep in view while developing an export strategy. To summarize, following could be used as guidelines :

(i) Commodities, such as cereals deserve an export thrust only after the domestic demand is satisfied.

(ii) Commodities with large fluctuations in the supply or in prices (cotton, sugar) should be traded with caution, unless compensatory mechanisms are put in place, such as forward trading to compensate for the risk and uncertainty.

(iii) Commodities where we have dynamic comparative

advantage, such as fruits and vegetables (because of diverse climate and soil conditions), and dairy products (because of large cattle herd and low cost of production) should receive special attention.

(iv) The varieties which have expanding world markets (rice for the East Asian markets, millets for cattle feed, and maize and barley as industrial raw materials) should be given high priority in our export strategy.

(v) There should be some consistency, and long-term thinking, while designing the export policy. An adhocism or surrender to vested interests (sugar and cotton export policies illustrate) can do severe damage to our export prospect.

In the next part, I will outline the needed changes in policies and indicate priorities in investment in infrastructure and in organizational developments in order to strengthen our competitive position in agriculture exports.

IV

ELEMENTS OF A STRATEGY

India's export efforts have to be made in an environment which is characterized by progressively more openness and competition. Corollary to that is the need for customer orientation, quality consciousness, timeliness and reliability, and, of course, competitive prices. Indian exporters of agricultural products have to go a long way to establish their superiority on these counts. Some of the important aspects which deserve special attention are as follows :

Timeliness and Thoroughness of Information

One of the major handicaps faced by Indian exporters is the lack of information on the key aspects of exportable commodities and relevant developments in the export markets. The exporters may be able to gather partial, and not necessarily accurate, information on prices, supplies and demand for the commodities they are dealing with, and may have some general idea about the cost of ancillary operations in transport and handling. Such partial and inaccurate information is not a substitute to timely, comprehensive and systematic information. As far as the agricultural producers are concerned their information on these matters is minimal. Even the policy makers are not fully aware of the developments in our client countries where we may have interest either as exporters or as importers. We do not have a systematic collection of relevant data; most of our information is based on the newspaper reports or on routine dispatches from the concerned sections of the embassies. There is a need to have a nodal point both at the Centre and in the States for collecting and collating all relevant information for the commodities in which we wish to play a role. Equally important is the dissemination of this information. In this respect the agricultural marketing boards and committees, which many of you are representing here, have a significant role. The linkage between the nodal agencies at the Centre and the States and the marketing committees at decentralized levels has to be firmly established.

Research Support for Agricultural Exports

The agriculture is becoming progressively more knowledge and skill based activity, which also gets reflected in agricultural trade. If we want to make a dent in agricultural exports, we should ensure a firm support from agricultural research and technology. Part of the reason of our losing grounds in our conventional export crops, say, tea, is the stagnation in productivity. When it comes to the newer products, apart from a high level of productivity the need for encouraging specific qualities in the products becomes important. As I have mentioned earlier, if we want to be a major exporter in rice, we have to think in terms of developing varieties which are preferred by the South-East Asian and East Asian countries. Similarly, we have to develop the maize and barley varieties which can be used profitably as industrial raw material. There is an equally urgent need to develop varieties in millets which can serve as good cattle feed. Without a proper research base, it will not be possible for us to play a significant role in the emerging markets. But with proper research support, the possibilities are immense.

Organizational Imperatives

Generally, it is proposed that if we want to have a competitive position in agricultural exports, we will have to revise our norms of land ceiling. It is contended that only large farms will be able to give the output of desired quality, uniformity, etc. This is a false notion. Nowhere in the world, the large farmers enjoy superiority as primary producers. In most of the circumstances, there is an adverse relationship between size and productivity; in some very special circumstances, the primary production may be neutral to scale. It is true that most of primary products need proper handling, sorting, grading and initial processing, particularly when they have to be exported, and these operations have scale economy. The solution is not the large farms but the specialized agencies to do precisely these tasks. In a very large number of countries, where such products as fruits and vegetables or dairy products are exported in bulk, the primary production is left to the small producers, but there are organizations at the secondary level which bring-in the required degree of expertise and specialization.

Through various arrangements ranging from cooperatives to contract farming, the small farmers can contribute to agricultural surplus without being dispossessed of their meagre land base. Along with Prof. Kruse-Rodenacker I had examined these possibilities at the instance of FAO, by looking into the cooperative arrangements for processing in a large number of countries in Asia, Europe and America. We found that with proper organizational support at the secondary level, size of operational holding was not a handicap even for the sophisticated products (Vyas and Kruse-Rodenacker, 1974). Within our own country, the success of the dairy industry as well as the sugar industry illustrates this point. What is required, therefore, is to organize appropriate secondary organizations and equip them with adequate resources and expertise. At the same time, the arrangements which these agencies make — be they public, private or cooperative organizations — with the primary producers have to be open, transparent and mutually beneficial. A two-tier organization for production and processing of exportable agricultural commodities is practical solution which will prove economically viable, and will not jeopardize the interests of the small producers.

Need for Capital Infusion

Exports of, what I have described as "dynamic commodities", e.g., fruits, vegetables, dairy products, flowers, fish products, etc., while present an exciting possibility is not going to be a cheap proposition. Substantial investment in infrastructure, starting from roads and communications to the warehouses and cold storage facilities, together with the investment in human resource development, has to be made to get a competitive edge. Export-oriented agriculture is going to be fairly capital intensive. The encouragement to private sector for investment in infrastructure facilities, particularly in warehouses and cold storages, etc., is needed, and the handicaps faced by the private sector in these areas have to be removed. However, the Government cannot abdicate its responsibilities. The investment in infrastructure creation should be considered as a part of export strategy.

Emphasis on Quality

With the signing of WTO agreements, it will become progressively more difficult for the developed countries to impose quantitative restrictions or place high tariff. They, however, can take recourse to non-tariff measures, mainly on the ground of quality. It is important, therefore, that the Indian exporters must be fully aware of the standards accepted by the international importers and should have mechanisms to introduce these standards right at the primary level. Our record in this respect has not been always inspiring (Acharya, 1996). Again, there is a role for agricultural marketing organizations to contribute to the establishment, and compliance, of the rigorous quality standards on which the prospects for exports are vitally dependent. The Uruguay Round agreements have sanitary and phytosanitary provisions which the exporters are supposed to comply with. Steps should be taken to make producers, traders and exporters aware of the health and safety standards imposed by different countries.

Let me conclude: Because of the diverse climatic and soil conditions and an enterprising peasantry as well as a trading class, India has the necessary qualifications to emerge as a leading exporter of agricultural commodities. The external climate is favourable. It is important now to design a strategy which should give us the benefit of external trade without jeopardizing the basic goals of food security and poverty alleviation. Some of the points I have raised will probably help in that direction.

14

Globalisation

Hopes, Realities and Coping Strategy

THERE is a 'great divide' in our country on the issue of Globalisation. Enthusiasts on globalisation consider this the only path for accelerating economic development and reducing poverty. They are rather impatient with the slow pace of reforms in this direction. There are others who are equally vehement in condemning the moves towards Globalisation, and consider it a sure recipe for economic subjugation and a process leading to further exploitation of the poor and the defenceless. Both sides can quote scriptures in their favour, refer to history to support their position and cite examples from contemporary developments. Part of the problem is due to different concepts of Globalisation. One can take a wider stand and equate it with the notion of *Vashudhewa kutumbcam* (Whole world is my family), or subscribe to a narrow economic interpretation, i.e. increasing ratio of foreign trade and investment in a country's output.

Whatever definition one adopts, Globalisation implies weakening of the restrictions imposed by or inherent in nation state. These restrictions had become more severe in the first half of the twentieth century. Earlier, nineteenth century had seen weakening of the national barriers as the movement of

---

(C.N. Vakil Memorial Lecture, delivered at South Gujarat University, Surat in 2001).

goods and services and of capital, even of labour, was lot more easier. Harbinger of globalisation then were the imperial powers. The twentieth century saw progressive liquidation of the colonialism and corresponding rise in the powers of the nation state. The pendulum started to swing in the opposite directions since second world war, and the move towards Globalisation started gaining strength. In this period mainspring of Globalisation was the developments in the Information Technology which contributed more than any thing else to the emergence of the 'Global Village.'

Characteristics of Globalisation as it is now unfolding are multifarious. It is influencing culture as much as the economies of the nation states. Our attention on this occasion is focussed on economic integration but we should also note that the objection to the current developments is as much on the cultural grounds. It is felt that Globalisation is leading to cultural hegemony – in effect in the sway of the 'Coca Cola – MacDonald' culture. Such homogenisation of diverse cultures certainly makes the humanity poorer. However, there is also another, and a positive side of the present trends, and that is the emergence of universal values. Societies which are not noted for their concern for environment, or gender sensitivity, or human rights, have to face opposition not only from within but from different quarters of the globe as well. Global concern is being expressed, admittedly only by a small section, on poverty and exploitation. It will be cynicism of first order if the large gatherings of protesters in Seattle or Geneva are dismissed either as hooligans or as sleep-walkers. Tentatively, haltingly, a universal conscience is emerging.

How the trends towards integration of world economies are going to affect economies of the poor countries, and livelihood of the poorer sections in these countries, is a moot question? Let us discuss this in the context of our own country.

Hopes from Globalisation

Theoretical case for free movement of goods, services, capital and labour across the borders is fairly strong. Take for example free trade in goods and services. Benefits of free trade are reflected in specialisation, expansion of the market, and economies of scale. International trade, governed by comparative advantages, benefits producers by allowing them to specialise in those products for which the local market is restricted and or can be soon saturated. Free trade also encourages competition leading to efficiency in production and eventually benefiting the consumers. However, even at the theoretical plane, several caveats have to be introduced. Border prices are not firm guides to demarcate comparative advantages, there is a difference between static comparative advantages and the dynamic comparative advantages, competition can also be wasteful, economies of scale may favour oligopolies and eventually negate competition. Even while granting all these limitations, free trade comes out as a superior alternative to autarky.

Similarly, a strong case can be built for free movement of capital, especially if the objective is to have infusion of outside capital in the capital starved countries. And more so, if new capital comes with superior technologies. Generating technologies has now become a capital intensive, long gestating, proposition where the poor countries are handicapped. In any event, there is no point in reinventing the wheel. Again, the utility of infusing capital will depend on the investment portfolio. If the capital is invested in speculative ventures, in takeovers and mergers, or is extremely mobile it may do more harm than good. Practically every country therefore regulates entry and allocation of foreign capital, and the developing countries are not particularly enamoured by universally applied investment rules. The resistance of the developing countries to a universal protocol for foreign capital investment in WTO negotiations in Doha has to be understood in this context.

Free movement of labour has all the advantages, at least in the long run, for the 'importing' as well as 'exporting' countries. The arguments advanced generally by the developed countries resisting free flow of labour on cultural ground, or on short term destabilising impact on certain sections of their labour force, are precisely the arguments used by developing countries in restraining unbridled trade or capital inflows. The encouragement to selective immigration of skilled persons, e.g. software engineers, by the developed countries, and hurdles put in the immigration of unskilled labour are in the same class of discriminating measures as the restrictive clauses in the trade regimes. If one is illogical and indefensible, so is the other. In essence, all that the votaries of Globalisation are talking about is a partial and selective integration of the world economies. Its sequencing and prioritisation are decided upon not by the theoretical justification but by exigencies of circumstances as perceived by the developed countries.

The Realities

Growth of World Trade

One of the indicators of a nation's integration with the world economy is the participation in the world trade. There has been remarkable increase in international trade in recent years. Percentage of trade in goods to the PPP GDP (i.e., GDP measured in purchasing price parity) has increased from 22.5 per cent to 27.4 per cent during the period 1989 and 1999[1]. The expansion was much faster in the high income countries, 28.5 per cent to 37.4 per cent. Increase in the low income and lower middle income countries was minuscule, less than

1. All figures, unless otherwise stated, are from World Development Indicators, 2001.

one percent. India did not fare better in this regard. Generally, large countries have a smaller proportion of trade to GDP. It is true for India also. Over the period of time not much change has taken place in this situation. Share of trade in GDP (PPP) increased from 3.2 to 3.6 percent. It was lower than the increase in the low and medium income countries, and far below the rate of growth in the high income countries. As late as 1999 India's share in the world trade was insignificant, at 0.7 per cent. This is despite several reforms in the trade sector, the most important being progressive tariffication and overall reduction in tariffs. For example, simple mean tariff has been reduced from 79.1 per cent in 1990 to 32.2 per cent in 1999, and move for further reduction is afoot.

There has been, however, a remarkable change in the structure of trade. Share of exports of manufactures increased from 71 per cent in 1990 to 76 per cent in 1999. As there was a downward slide in the international prices of agricultural commodities a larger share of manufactures helped in raising net barter terms of trade for India, from 79 in 1990 to 104 in 1999 (with 1995=100). As an interesting sideline one may note that the share of developed countries in India's agriculture trade has, in proportionate terms, declined; WTO agreements have done precious little in expanding markets for our agricultural goods in the developed countries. It is quite clear that the developed countries are not adhering to the rules of the game. Under the guise of various "boxes" the subsidies extended to their agricultural producers have increased, and on the plea of sanitary and phytosanitary considerations entry of agricultural goods from the developing countries is resisted. I have more to say on this later.

Two facts are clear from above. One, the maximum advantage of the expanding trade regime in the world has accrued to the rich countries. Low and medium income developing countries have to rest content with insignificant gains[2]. Second, judged from the criterion of international trade, Indian economy is only marginally integrated with the world economy. Importance of the domestic market in our case is overarching. But the directions, as suggested by progressively increasing ratio of trade to GDP as well as changing composition of trade, are clear. We have to take these as *datum* and devise our strategies accordingly.

Financial Integration

Another important facet of Globalisation is the financial integration. In the earlier post second world war years developing countries had to place greater reliance on development aid and financial debts on public accounts. In recent years more and more reliance is placed on foreign capital from private sources. Apart from direct foreign investment (FDI), private borrowings and banks and trade related transfers are becoming progressively more important. As a part of development strategy developing countries, including India, are keen to attract FDI. Several measures are taken to attract foreign capital, latest being the removal of cap on foreign ownership in several industries. These measures have resulted in the increase in Foreign Direct Investment. FDI increased from 162 million U.S.$ in 1990 to nearly 2.2 billion U.S.$ in 1999. According to the Centre for Monitoring Indian Economy (CMIE), during this fiscal year the FDI is likely to be around 2.3 billion U.S.$. However, this pales into insignificance when compared to FDI received by China (approximately 40 billion U.S. $). More importantly, this is hardly 2 per cent of the gross domestic savings. *As in trade, in capital formation also we have to rely basically on our domestic resources.*

---

2. It should be recognised, however, that the domestic policies play an equally important part in determining the ratio of international trade to GDP.

A worrisome feature is the nature of deployment of these foreign resources. A lion's share of these resources is not going into fresh capital formation but in the takeovers and mergers. According to CMIE about 50 per cent of the FDI inflow went into either foreign partners buying out Indian partners or even public holdings in the joint sector. Another feature to be careful about is the growing proportion of portfolio investment in equities. Such investment was of the order of 105 million U.S.$ in 1990, it increased to 1302 million U.S.$ in 1999. There is little new capital formation in the economy with foreign financial resources. Besides, deployment of foreign private resources is largely in 'white goods' sector, in automobiles and, other luxury items catering to the needs of rising middle and upper middle class. Share of investment in strategically important high-tech sectors, or in consumer goods industries catering to the needs of the poor is not significant.

Apart from FDI, portfolio investment and private borrowings are playing a crucial role in financial integration. Private foreign investments are very mobile. Advances in the Information Technology has facilitated transfer of resources with an unimaginable speed. The high mobility has also lead to what has come to be known as 'contagion effect'. Higher the role of private foreign financial investments, generally, more vulnerable the country becomes. Even the fast growing Asian Tigers could not escape from this impact and had to face financial crisis of severe magnitude a few years back, from which they have not yet fully recovered. In India since our regulatory mechanisms are fairly strong so far we have been able to weather these shocks more satisfactorily. However in our case also exchange rate of Rupee, our interest rate structure and prices in the stock markets are significantly affected by the short term, in most of the cases speculative, movements in the financial inflows. The degree of volatility imparted by such flows has so far been manageable, partly because of the appropriateness of our regulatory institutions but mainly because in the Indian context such inflows are not sizeable, at least from international standards. Once their share in the short and long term investment increases we will also be exposed to the vagaries of sharp international fluctuations.

Impact of Globalization

International trade and foreign investment can potentially affect economic growth and income distribution. In this respect global economic integration of the type we are witnessing today, i.e. corporate led globalisation, can be faulted on two counts. It has imparted more volatility in economic transactions thereby increasing the risk and uncertainty, and it has aggravated economic inequality among the nations and within the nations. I have already commented on the first, let me say a few words on the second.

In a recent article (Economist, April 28th, 2001) Prof. Robert Wade of the London School of Economics has brought out some startling facts based on well researched papers. Covering admittedly short period, from 1988 to 1993, Wade draws following conclusions: during this period gini coefficient of the world income increased by 6 per cent; share of world income going to the poorest 10 per cent of the world's population fell by over a quarter, where as the share of the richest 10 per cent rose by 8 per cent; the richest 10 per cent pulled away from the median, while poorer 10 per cent fell away from the median. In other words, poorer countries and the poor in these countries were left behind in the process of growth. In recent years world has become much more unequal. While analysing these trends Wade has offered explanation too. I cannot do better than quote him from the same article, "Technological change and financial liberalisation results in the disproportionately fast increase in the number of households at the extreme rich end, without shrinking the distribution at the poor end." These conclusions should impart a degree of sobreity among those who are impatient with the slow extent of integration of Indian Economy with global economy.

Coping Strategy

Where do we go from here? One thing is clear we cannot go back to the old days. On none of the criteria of development or welfare the old regime, identified as 'quota permit raj' was a desirable one. Economic growth was sluggish, sarcastically described as "Hindu rate of growth", hovering around 3 per cent per year. With population growth of nearly same order there was hardly any improvement in the standard of living. Poverty was rampant, reaching, according to some measures, a level of 50 per cent or more. Human deprivation in terms of access to health, education, nutrition was extremely serious. Under a highly protectionist regime competition was effectively thwarted with the consumers paying high prices for goods of shoddy quality. A dependency syndrome took hold of the whole country. Only silver lining was the improvement in agricultural productivity, mainly because of the small farm dominated agrarian structure. We are still paying the price of an inefficient and oligarcic industrial structure and inadequate investment in social and physical infrastructure. The earlier system was both unjust and inefficient. If we compare *like with like*, things as they existed in the pre-Reform days with what obtains since then, the current situation with all its imperfections is better than the bad old days. Of course, if we have an ideal notion of *Swadeshi*, for example, what Gandhi would have liked, we are in a different, and non comparable, realm.

There is another fact to be reckoned with. Thanks mainly to information technology, penetration of ideas and images have become all pervasive. Whether one likes it or not people's aspirations have changed and it is a common desire to reach the standard, at least the content, of western style of living. Most of the advocates of Swadeshi in their own life style are no exception to this general trend. Nor is it possible, and much less desirable, to shun all western communications and immunise the society from these influences. It was tried by Mao Tse Tung in the 'cultural revolution' days, and by Talibans in more recent times. The disastrous results are for all to see. I hasten to add that apeing western styles without any discrimination, and ignoring brighter aspects of our own heritage will put us in double jeopardy. What is true for general approach to life style is also true for economic activities. We should take advantage of the emerging, integrating, world economy without sacrificing our own priorities to build a just and caring society.

Till date the experience of Globalisation for the developing countries, including India, is not happy. If we wish to make Globalisation to contribute to the objectives of equity and growth we will have to take action at two levels: to strive for changing the rules of Globalisation, and to equip the country to face the challenges of, rather take advantages from, the emerging world economy.

The rules governing world level economic institutions, particularly International Monetary Fund and the World Bank are biased against the developing countries. The international agreements, particularly the agreements under World Trade Organisation have not helped the developing countries as was professed at the time of the establishment of WTO. On the former, many knowledgeable persons in our country and abroad have made valuable suggestions. I am slightly more familiar with the working of WTO. Let me take this as an example for elaborating what I mean by "changing rules of the global institutions".

Changing Rules of Global Institutions: Lessons from WTO

There is a serious on-going debate in the country on the gains we have realised and price we have paid due to our joining World Trade Organization [WTO], and implications of this association for different sectors of our economy. It is important in this context to understand the historical background of WTO. It was only after 1980 when the United States agriculture exports faced a steep decline and a view emerged that the decline in the agricultural exports was due to protectionist policies of EEC and Japan, that USA started supporting an agreement which would enable free trade in agricultural commodities. The GATT provisions for agricultural trade were found weak, and need for a stronger trade regime was keenly felt. Cairns Group of countries headed by Australia and other important agriculture exporting countries also found the progress in the GATT negotiations inadequate and unsatisfactory. The final decision on establishment of WTO was facilitated by the agreement between USA and EEC, so called "Blair House Agreement". Thus, it is important to remember that WTO came into existence because of the need for such an organization perceived by the developed countries which were important exporters of agricultural commodities.

Several agreements have been made or negotiated under the auspices of WTO. One of the most important being the Agreement on Agriculture [AoA]. The main features of AoA are the market access without discrimination, and discouragement to domestic support and export subsidies with a view to provide a level playing field to the traders in agriculture commodities. The other provisions of AoA address some of the non-trade concerns, such as multi functionality of agriculture, food security, etc.

The signing of AoA in 1995 created a euphoria in some

quarters. It was suggested that if implemented properly it will result in a rise of agricultural trade to the extent of US $ 450 billion. It was also maintained that the developing countries will have a fair share in the increased agriculture trade. These hopes proved to be exaggerated as neither the rise in the volume of agriculture trade nor the share of developing countries in the trade measured up to these highly optimistic expectations.

Part of the shortfall in the expected gains is due to loopholes in the Agreement itself, such as inadequate time for adjustment for the developing countries, tariff picking, tariff escalation etc. The main reason however is the non-trade barriers (e.g., rules for origin, product standardization, quality assurance etc) by the developed countries. The overall support to agriculture, under the so-called "*blue boxes*" and "*amber boxes*", puts agriculture in these countries to an advantageous position. Stringent sanitary and phytosanitary standards on agricultural imports are used to inhibit imports of these commodities. The increasingly powerful MNCs and the emerging Trading Blocks have also weakened AoA. Finally, the organizational strength and capabilities of the staff is far below the requirements for a body with as wide a mandate as WTO.

Inspite of these failures there are certain positive features of WTO which need to be recognized. The provision of "one member, one vote" distinguishes this organization from the Brettenwoods institutions. In this respect, as we found in the last Doha meeting, it is much more democratic then several other international institutions. With all its limitations, WTO could exercise greater discipline in agricultural trade, especially due to its dispute settling mechanism. It has also contributed in opening up the markets in some of the highly "protected" countries, e.g. South Korea, Japan, EEC. The WTO agreement also gives recognition to the non-trading concerns of the developing countries; for example, it mentions in its Preamble the need for and importance of "sustainable living standard"

India is favourably placed with regards to the main conditionalities of AoA, namely market access, domestic support and export subsidies. In all these respects the India fulfills the basic provisions of AoA. Most importantly, the Aggregate Measure of Support (AMS) for agriculture in the country is well below the minimum conditions laid down by WTO. Yet India, like other developing countries, has to face difficulties in expanding its trade in agricultural commodities with developed countries, mainly due to sanitary and phytosanitary standards, and also due to covert subsidies (under various types of "boxes", e.g. "Green Box", "Amber Box"), and the discrimination in the guise of quality assurance etc., in these countries.

More than the current provisions, some of the imminent developments are likely to put countries like India in a disadvantageous position. For instance, there is a clamour on the part of some of the developed countries to bring in new issues in the next round of trade negotiations; the issues which are not strictly relevant for trading purposes, and for which other, more relevant, international organizations already exist. The labour and environment clauses (and also a clause on animal welfare!) proposed by some of the developed countries are pointers in this direction. These handicaps are likely to be enhanced with the emphasis on, what has been called "market-plus" agenda, i.e., the provisions on competition policies, investment policies etc. Due to superior bargaining power of the developed countries these may further tilt the balance against the developing countries.

In view of the above, we have to ask ourselves, what should be our stand. I would submit that India's stand in the next round of negotiations should encompass the following:

- take a proactive role – not a responsive one;
- insist on giving priority to food self - sufficiency, as long as fifty percent or more of workers depend on food production for their livelihood;
- ask for better market access for tropical products;
- ask for internationally determined norms on sanitary and phytosanitary safeguards;.
- resist introduction of hidden subsidies;
- insist on closer scrutiny of the non-product specific subsidies in developed countries.
- as a countervailing strategy bring issues such as 'sustainable living standards' 'rural development' etc., on the agenda of WTO.

We will be able to improve upon the existing conditions and face the likely pressures only if we are well prepared. This would be possible with:

- involvement of all stakeholders, especially the states, at the stage of formulating strategies;
- clear understanding of the pace and pattern of agriculture development of our trading partners, especially the developed countries;
- a sound technical research base;
- preparedness to bring down the "binding" rates at somewhat more reasonable level, to be used as a bargaining device[3].

Finally, India should take a leadership role among the developing countries, and seek alliances to protect not only

---

3. The "binding" rates on some of the commodities at the level of 300 per cent or more do not serve any purpose but are treated as irritants by other countries.

its own interests but also the interests of the other countries which are in more or less similar situation, in terms of level of development and the pattern of agricultural trade. It is heartening to note that India's stand in Doha meeting was more or less on these lines. Our stand in Doha serves as an example of what I have mentioned as "striving to change rules of globalisation".

Domestic Reforms

For a country of India's size and diversity development of domestic market will simultaneously strengthen its competitive position in the international arena. We have already started a process of economic reforms with the objective of correcting distortions in the economy and clearing grounds for further development. By and large these reforms are in right direction, with right sequence and pace. In particular, emphasis provided on the macro stability, especially on containing the rate of inflation is the most welcome feature. There are still areas in macro economic reforms, most importantly in the fiscal arena which need our attention. A singular failure in this regard has been the expanding budgetary gap, especially on the revenue side. The Central Government deficits are accounting for more than 6 per cent of GDP, and if Centre and States' budgetary deficits are put together the fiscal gap amounts to 11 per cent of GDP which, obviously, is unsustainable. There are also difficulties in moving the tax reforms in right directions, more so in the states. However, substantial progress has been made in monetary and banking fields. Our objective has been to introduce a regime of autonomy in the banking institutions, and simultaneously strengthen regulatory mechanism. There are still problems in the credit delivery systems, reflected in a number of weak institutions in public, private and co-operative sector. In particular there are serious problems in the rural credit area which need to be looked into urgently. Along with other colleagues, I have recently reviewed the performance and problems of the rural credit system, and the needed reforms to strengthen it, in a report submitted to the National Bank of Agriculture and Rural Development. [Report of the Expert Committee on Rural Credit, 2001].

We have an unfinished agenda in the industrial, agriculture, domestic trade, energy and labour sectors. More difficult among these are the reforms to be undertaken in the labour and agriculture sector. I feel that there is a strong need for reforms in these two areas, but not necessarily in the directions which many of our colleagues are advocating, who would give priority to measures such as introduction of "hiring and firing" regime in labour relations, and discontinuation of "ceiling" on land holdings in agriculture as the next steps. In my view these are not the essential reforms for these sectors, and are likely to seriously jeopardize a broad national consensus on reforms which has been built over the years. Generally, we give negative connotation to reforms, i.e. emphasizing "what should not be done". But there are positive contents of reforms, specially in the area of labour and agriculture, on which not much thought is given. However, this is not the occasion to dwell on these aspects of domestic economic reforms in any great details.

In the context of globalisation the paramount consideration guiding all our actions should to make our products competitive in international markets. To achieve this objective there are certain critical areas in the domestic economy which need to be given greater attention. I will like to emphasize three of these areas:

1. Improving labour productivity
2. Infrastructure development, and
3. Strengthening supportive institutions.

A few words on each may be in order.

Improving Labour Productivity

By all standards, productivity in our country is very low, more particularly when it comes to labour productivity. If we compare our performance with a country like China, and that will be the correct comparison to make, we will find that not only at the aggregate level but practically in each sector our labour productivity is lower. If today China is able to flood the world markets with whole variety of things it is mainly because of the higher level of productivity in that economy.

For enhancing capabilities and skills of labour, illiteracy is one of the important inhibiting factors. We have made substantial progress in removing illiteracy but much remains to be done in this direction. It should be recognized at the outset that importance of eradicating illiteracy, or improving health conditions for that matter, is not only as a contributing factor in raising labour productivity in economic activities, it is an end in itself. Going beyond the removal of illiteracy we have next to think in terms of skill enhancement, a largely neglected area in our country. Strangely enough there is hardly any programme of skill enhancement in the sector which accounts for the largest proportion of our labour force, i.e. agriculture. The same is true of the large labour force engaged in arts, crafts and cottage industries. We have never looked at the skill enhancement of agricultural producers and workers in the unorganized sectors as a priority. However, these are the sectors where we can have a niche in the international markets, apart from the fact the skill enhancement of workers in these sectors is likely to contribute to raising level of living of some of the most deprived sections.

Going beyond agriculture and the unorganized sectors, even in the corporate sector our concept of productivity is narrow and inadequate on two counts. First, we interpret improvement in productivity only in output terms. In the competitive world we are living in, quality improvement and customer satisfaction are as much a part of raising productivity as the growth in output. Secondly, we interpret productivity only in terms of productivity of floor labour while the real bottleneck may be the inefficiency at managerial level. A more forward looking view in interpreting productivity and appreciation of the role of different sections in improving productivity is necessary.

If such a broad view is taken, there would be specific role of the government, (in organizing training), of social organizations (in inculcating a sense of responsibility), of corporate sector (in creating a conducive work ethos at the firm level) and of course, of the individuals worker (to have motivation to improve his/her living conditions). The countries which have registered high productivity have worked simultaneously at all these levels.

Infrastructure development

The next important item on our agenda should be the development of infrastructure, both economic and social. India lags behind some of the other developing economies of Asia in terms of infrastructure facilities not only in roads, power and communication but more importantly in the area of education and health. As I have mentioned earlier, improvements in education and health should be considered as ends in themselves. Our low position in these areas is too well known to need elaborate description.

As regards physical infrastructure, though starting late we are making satisfactory progress in building roads and developing communication sector. Power sector is still an Achelles heal. For a variety of reasons private sector, both foreign as well as indegenous, has so far not been able to play a significant role in developing power sector. We have to recognize that in developing countries provision of infrastructure is primarily the responsibility of state. Apart from the over all paucity of resources, and "crowding out" the funds for infrastructural development by huge expenditure on public administration and subsidies, the basic handicap in finding resources for infrastructure is the absence of proper "user prices" i.e. the prices which could generate adequate income to sustain maintenance, if not the growth, of these sectors. It is important to note that unrealistically subsidized prices of water and energy, for example, are acting as a "block" against expansion of these facilities. Economic reforms aimed at recovering user prices need to be accorded a high priority.

Strengthening supportive institutions

The third area requiring strong action is to strengthen the supportive institutions of credit and marketing. Chinese example will tell us that with this type of support even small firms can achieve wonders. There are major lacunae in our marketing structure and so also in credit delivery systems. For example, if we wish to compete in the international markets for high value, perishable, products such as fruits, flowers, fish products etc, we have to think in terms of a marketing chain which supports producers at all intermediate stages, right upto the level of importers of these products. Similarly, in credit also we need to have more flexible and pro active approach, and appropriate institutions, e.g. institutions of venture capital, to assist the entrepreneurs who are coming out with innovative products. Because of the defects in the credit delivery system many of high- tech enterprises in our country are languishing, although prima facie we have distinct advantage in such enterprises.

I would like to maintain that with appropriate measures in these three directions we can make our firms competitive without necessarily increasing their scale or changing the nature of ownership. There is now universal appreciation of the fact that competition in most of the circumstances generates efficiency. In our country major emphasis in this regard has been on controlling mergers and takeovers by large firms. Such an emphasis to discourage monopolistic tendencies is, of course, desirable, but a more positive aspect of a competitive policy i.e., making small enterprises more competitive is not given due attention. In this respect, again, we can learn lessons from China. Most of the Chinese exports of consumer goods are produced in the tiny, household, sector. However, with proper skill enhancement, adequate support from advance technology (through a programme such as Spark Programme under which technocretes team up with small enterpreneurs), and the provision of the needed infrastructure, these enterprises have become competitive even at the international level. In our own country, in fact in the very state where I have the privilege of addressing you an organization such as AMUL has been able to raise productivity and incomes of the small dairy farmers. Neither the public enterprises nor the small industries per se are incapable of improving efficiency, or are inherently non-competitive, as is assumed in some quarters. They can be efficient and competitive as several examples in our country and in a number of other developing countries have shown.

Summing Up

To sum up, we will not be able to isolate ourselves from the world economy. Neither it would be to our interest to by-pass globalization. We should face the forces of globalization with a sense of confidence, and with full realisation that the developing countries, including India, are the "engines of growth" for the developed countries, as the providers of markets and raw materials. Without our markets and our raw materials, developed countries will not be able to achieve progressively higher level of living, or even sustain their present standards. Therefore, developing countries need not have a sense of diffidence. Also a country such as India, because of its size and institutional framework, is in a position to develop a vibrant domestic market if proper reforms are introduced, in right sequence and at right pace. This would enable not only a very large number of people to participate effectively in, and benefit from, international trade but a strong domestic base will also immunize the country to a large extent from the volatility of the international economic fluctuations.

We can achieve this and more provided two pre-conditions are met. One, that there is a national consensus on broad issues of reforms and not a dogmatic posturing at all times. And second, that we do not dilute our basic concern benefiting a caring society while striving to inject efficiency in our economic activities. To meet these preconditions is the challenge that the country is facing.

15

Our Agrarian Future

A Medium Term Perspective on Asian Agriculture

ON the basis of certain commonly agreed indicators agriculture is considered the world over a declining industry. The share of agriculture in GDP, share of workforce engaged in agricultural production, and share of agricultural exports in the total exports progressively declines. Perception of agriculture as a 'declining industry' has led, consciously or unconsciously, to neglect of agriculture in the development discourse as much as in development strategies. Many countries in this region and elsewhere have learnt to their regret that such neglect entails high costs in terms of economic growth as well as human welfare. The sequencing and speed of decline in sectoral GDP, workforce and agricultural exports impacts in a profound manner on the overall economic growth and wellbeing of large sections of society, particularly in the early phases of a country's development. Another role of agriculture, especially in the medium income countries which is only now being appreciated is that in turbulent times agriculture acts as a stabilizing factor in the economy. The other aspect, which

---

Presidential Address to 4th Conference of Asian Society of Agricultural Economists, Malaysia in 2002.

Author is grateful to Dr. Vidya Sagar and Dr. Sunil Ray for helpful comments. Usual disclaimers apply. Research support by Shri Kamal Swami is thankfully acknowledged.

was largely neglected till recently but has now come to the fore with the emphasis on environmental and ecological safety is the fact that agriculture is one of the largest user of land, and the largest user of water. Even with increasing use of these resources for non agricultural purposes, agriculture has a pivotal role in the protection of (or damage to) these natural resources, and as a consequence for ecologically sustainable development.

In the following presentation, I would like to highlight the extant and the emerging role of agriculture in our region by reviewing the past performance and postulating the conditions for sustainable growth. The discussion is based on the review of the agricultural development of a few selected countries of Asia during the last decade or two and the portents for the coming decade. The selected countries, wherever necessary, are grouped as south Asian countries, south-east Asian countries and east Asian countries. The south Asian group comprises the five larger countries of the region, i.e. Bangladesh, India, Nepal, Pakistan and Sri Lanka. South-east Asia group includes Indonesia, Malaysia, Philippines, Thailand and Vietnam. In the third group we have included China, and Republic of Korea. The experience of Japan is referred to wherever relevant. I am aware that this leaves out several important countries of the region, in fact a few sub-regions. Partly, paucity of time, but mainly my own limitations have prompted me to be selective.

In the first section, we draw attention to the initial conditions impacting on the pace and pattern of economic growth. In the second section, we review the performance of agriculture on well established parameters, bring out the pattern of growth witnessed during the last two decades or so, and discuss the exogenous and endogenous factors responsible for changes in this sector. The third section takes medium term view of the likely changes in the demand and supply conditions affecting Asian agriculture and the economic environment it is likely to face. In the fourth and final section we try to outline key issues which have ramifications for achieving a sustainable and humane development in our region.

I

INITIAL CONDITIONS

Asian economies are characterised by several distinctive features, some of which are common to a large number of the countries in the region and some others more specific to certain countries. In terms of land surface as well as in terms of population, the selected countries can be categorised as 'medium-to-large' countries. This gives them a real – at least potential – advantage of large domestic markets and a diversified production base. But it also handicaps them as the regional heterogeneity is likely to be more pronounced, and would led to regional inequalities. Most of the selected countries witnessed moderate to high rate of growth in GDP during the last two decades. They have a fairly well developed institutional framework and human resource base. In these and several other respects, the adjoining countries of south Asia, south-east Asia and east Asia have much in common, not only in terms of economic features but also political and social institutions. The latter may have had, and continue to have, a profound influence on the pace and pattern of development. There is a pronounced 'contagion' effect within these three sub-regions. Some of the notable features of each of the sub-regions are outlined below. (See Tables 1, 2, 3)

South Asia: Due to geographical contiguity the social and cultural features in the countries of this sub-region have acquired a certain degree of similarity. Apart from geographical

TABLE – 1

Size of Economy in 1999

Regions & Countries	*Surface Area 000 Sq. Km.*	*Population (Million)*	*Population Density per Sq. Km.*	*Gross National Income*		*Gross National Income per Capita*	
				$ Billions	*Rank*	*$ 1999*[a]	*Rank*
South Asian Countries							
Bangladesh	144	128	981	47.1	50	370	170
India	3288	998	336	441.8	11	440	163
Nepal	147	23	164	5.2	108	220	195
Pakistan	796	135	175	62.9	44	470	160
Sri Lanka	66	19	294	15.6	76	820	139
South East Asian Countries							
Indonesia	1905	207	114	125	31	600	150
Malaysia	330	23	69	7609	42	3390	84
Philippines	300	74	249	78	41	1050	133
Thailand	513	60	118	121.1	32	2010	103
Vietnam	332	78	238	28.7	60	370	170
East Asian Countries							
China	9598[a]	1254	134	979.9	7	780	142
Japan	378	127	336	4054.5	2	32030	7
Korea, Rep	99	47	475	397.9	13	8490	54

a : Includes Taiwan, China; Macao, China, and Hongkong, China.
Source : World Development Indicators, 2001.

TABLE – 2

Average Annual Growth in GDP, Population and Per Capita GDP (1965-1999)

Regions & Countries	*GDP Average Annual Growth*	*Population Average Annual Growth*	*Per Capita Growth in GDP*
South Asian Countries			
Bangladesh	3.8	2.3	1.3
India	4.6	2.1	2.4
Nepal	3.7	2.4	1.2
Pakistan	5.6	2.8	2.7
Sri Lanka	4.6	1.6	3.0
South East Asian Countries			
Indonesia	6.9	2.0	4.8
Malaysia	7.0	2.6	4.3
Philippines	3.4	2.5	0.9
Thailand	7.3	2.0	5.1
Vietnam		2.1	
East Asian Countries			
China	8.1	1.7	6.4
Japan	4.1	0.7	3.4
Korea, REP	8.1	1.5	6.6

Source: World Development Indicators, 2001.

TABLE – 3

Poverty and Human Development Index

Region & Country	Poverty According to National Poverty Line				Poverty According to International Poverty Line			Human Development Index [HDI] Value 1999
	Survey year	% of Population below Poverty Line	Survey year	% of Population below Poverty Line	Survey year	Population on below $ 1 a day	Population below $ 2 a day	
South Asia								
Bangladesh	1991-92	42.7	1995-96	35.6	1996	29.1	77.8	0.470
India	1992	40.9	1994	35.0	1997	44.2	86.2	0.571
Nepal	1995-96	42.0			1995	37.7	82.5	0.480
Pakistan	1991	34.0			1996	31.0	84.7	0.498
Sri Lanka	1990-91	20.0			1995	6.6	45.4	0.735
South East Asia								
Indonesia	1996	15.7	1999	27.1	1999	7.7	55.3	0.677
Malaysia	1989	15.5						0.774
Thailand	1992	18.0	1992	13.1	1998	<2	28.2	0.757
Philippines	1994	40.6	1997	36.8				0.749
Vietnam	1993	50.9						0.682
East Asia								
China	1996	6.0	1998	4.6	1998	18.5	53.7	0.718
Japan								0.928
Korea, REP					1993	<2	<2	0.875

Source: World Development Indicators 2001, and Human Development Report 2001.

proximity, they have undergone a common historical experience i.e. the hegemony of the British colonial power for nearly two centuries. The influence of British rule has been direct on Bangladesh, India, Pakistan and Sri Lanka. The impact was indirect but powerful in the remaining countries of this sub-region. British rule has left an indelible mark on the social, economic and political institutions.

In terms of area and population, the selected countries of south Asia fall in the category of 'large to medium'. Within the countries, there are pronouncedly distinct and diverse parts. Another feature which has an important bearing on development is the fact that large areas in several of these countries are disaster-prone.

This is one of the poorest regions of the world. In terms of per capita GDP all the selected countries are placed in the last quartile, among the 200 and odd countries for which data have been compiled by the World Bank[1]. Two of the countries of the region, Bangladesh and Nepal, are designated as the 'least developed countries'. A large part of the world's poor – approximately 40 per cent of the total number - live in this part of Asia. Poverty as reflected in low incomes is further compounded by deprivations in other aspects of wellbeing. The Human Development Index compiled by UNDP places these countries at the bottom of the list with the solitary exception of Sri Lanka, which is closer to the medium income countries in this regard. The more disaggregated indicators of health, education and nutrition tell the same story. Invariably the rural population is worse off on all these counts. Incidence of related deprivations is more serious for certain groups, particularly women, and for certain regions within these countries. The social structures are divisive and internal strife

1. Figures quoted in the text unless otherwise specified are from *World Development Indicators, 2001*. The World Bank Washington, D.C.

and conflicts are widespread.

However, it needs to be appreciated that these are large economies. In terms of Gross Domestic Product, India ranks 11th in the world. The other selected countries of this region, except Nepal and Sri Lanka, are placed in the first quartile on the same criterion. The second remarkable feature of this sub-region is the relatively faster rate of economic growth, particularly in the last couple of decades. As the countries have started with a very low base, the impact of growth has not yet fully manifested itself in reducing poverty. Besides, the rapid growth of population in these countries which, though declining, is still among the highest in the world (with the exception of Sri Lanka), has negated the benefits of the fast growth in GDP to a significant extent. Per capita income per year in these countries again, is less than U.S. $ 500, with the exception of Sri Lanka, which has a per capita per annum income of U.S. $ 820. The picture improves, if one takes per capita income in terms of Purchasing Power Parity into account. However, even then the facts of low incomes and widespread poverty are quite evident.

These countries are going through structural changes manifested in demographic transition and changes in occupational pattern, social institutions and, systems of governance. They have had the advantage of a developed institutional base. With recent moves towards decentralisation, transparency and accountability, the quality of governance has been enhanced. The same, however, cannot be said about the efficiency of public institutions.

Agriculture occupies an important place in all these economies. On three indicators, viz., contribution to GDP, share in the work force and place in international trade, agriculture's role, though declining, is still of considerable importance, particularly so as far as workforce disposition is concerned. Agriculture in all these countries accounts for the lion's share in the total workforce. Large areas of land resources are devoted to agriculture, and its share in water use is overwhelmingly large. We would review the status and changes in agriculture in greater details in subsequent sections.

South-east Asia: The five selected countries of the south-east Asia can be considered medium sized in terms of surface area, except for Indonesia which in the context of this sub-region is a large country. Three of the selected countries have populations in the range of 60 to 80 million (in 1999). Indonesia has the largest population in the region at 207 million, while Malaysia's population is the smallest, i.e., 23 million. The countries in this region are also more densely populated, with the exception of Malaysia which has the lowest population density, at 69 people per square km. Philippines and Vietnam could be compared with the more densely populated countries of South Asia. (Of course, nothing comparable to the high population density of Bangladesh!). The rate of population growth, though declining is fairly high.

Most of these countries have social and ethnic problems arising from relatively small but affluent minorities. With the exception of Thailand, all these countries have a colonial legacy. Many of them, particularly Indonesia and Vietnam have fought bitter wars of liberation. Poverty and food insecurity are concentrated mainly in the rural areas, and there too in the small peasant sector. Large regional inequalities persist within the countries. This can be partly explained by geographical factors; the economically backward regions have poor natural resource base and are more disaster-prone. Urban bias in policies has exacerbated the handicaps faced by remote and backward regions. Political institutions are in transition. A more representative democratic system is evolving. Economic institutions are well developed but the attributes of transparency and accountability are emerging only gradually.

The size of the economies, in terms of Gross National Income, places these countries in the first quartile among 200 countries, ranking between 31 (Indonesia) to 42 (Malaysia), the one exception being Vietnam, which ranks much lower (60). However, in terms of per capita income these countries are in the bottom half of the league, with the exception of Malaysia which ranks 84th in the same table. The distinguishing feature of this region is a respectable rate of economic growth – 6 to 7 per cent per year-, over a long period of time, with the exception of Philippines where the rate of growth in GDP approximated more to that in south Asia. However, once we take into account the growth in population, the per capita growth in income, between 4 to 5 per cent even in the faster growing economies, is not that impressive. Besides, for the last five years, i.e. since 1997 the countries in this sub-region are facing economic slow-down at a varying pace and of varying severity.

Another distinguishing feature of this region is high investment in human resources, resulting in high levels of literacy, and reasonable standards of health and nutrition. Poverty is present at a disturbing level in some countries, e.g. Philippines and Indonesia. In the remaining countries too, certain sections and regions are deprived of decent human existence. However, compared to south Asia, the situation in this region in this regard is much better.

East Asia: The world's most highly populated country, and one of the largest in surface area, i.e. China, is located in this region; so also economically the most developed country of Asia i.e. Japan. The other country selected by us in this sub-region Republic of Korea, has recorded one of the highest rates of growth in Asia. In terms of gross GDP Japan ranks second in the world and China, 7th. Korea also claims a respectable 13th place. A distinguishing feature of this region is high rate of growth. Even a mature economy like Japan registered till recently a long term (1965-1999) growth rate of above 4 per cent per year. The figures for China and Republic of Korea are above 8 per cent per year during the same period. As the rate of population growth is barely above the replacement rate in China and Republic of Korea, and is lower than that in Japan, the growth in GDP is adequately reflected in the progressively rising per capita income. Yet because of the late start China with a per capita income of U.S.$ 780 has to go quite far to catch up with the developed countries.

Both the advantages and disadvantages of large economies are exhibited by these countries, particularly China. The large population bestows the benefits of a large domestic market and the potential of a diversified economy. At the same time the large land mass invariably gives rise to inequalities between central and peripheral regions. A political oligarchy is much in evidence, though its nature and roots are different in the different countries of this sub-region. Economic institutions and delivery systems are generally well developed. The societies are more cohesive and share, what has come to be known as 'Asian Values', i.e. entreprenuership, discipline and loyalty to family, clan and country.

As in south-east Asia, in fact even more than in that sub-region, there is a strong tradition of investment in human resources. This is evident from the very high level of literacy, much better health facilities – even in a 'poor' country like China– and a relatively better record in nutrition. Sharp regional differences, however, persist in Republic of Korea, and more pronouncedly in China. Poverty, measured on the 'U.S.$ 1 per person per day' norm, is low and is largely concentrated in a few disadvantaged regions.

To sum up, the initial conditions obtaining in these countries played an important role in shaping the subsequent developments[2]. The location and the size of the country, its demographic profile, social structure, nature of governance and initial economic conditions have profoundly affected the course of economic development. True, some countries have overcome their initial handicaps more rapidly than others, but they too had to face an uphill task.

II

AGRICULTURE IN ASIAN ECONOMIES

The place of agriculture in an economy, as well as the changes in its role over a period of time, generally follows a uniform pattern. In the less developed economies, agriculture occupies an important place in terms of its share in the GDP, work force and foreign trade. On all these counts, the share of agriculture declines with the growth in the economy. Asian economies are no exception to these general tendencies. However, the pace of such decline varies from country to country, largely depending on the pace and pattern of economic growth, the production base, and activity mix of agriculture. This can be best illustrated in the context of the selected countries.

Share in GDP and Workforce

Countries of the Asian region have had a good record of growth in GDP over a long period of time. The annual rate of growth for the period 1965-1999 was higher than 8 per

---

2. For a detailed description of the region's economies in the mid seventies, see Second Asian Agricultural Survey. (Team leader V.S. Vyas). Asian Development Bank, Manila, 1976, published as *Rural Asia – Challenges and Opportunity*, Praeger Publishers, New York, (1977).

cent for Republic of Korea and China, about 7 per cent for Thailand, Malaysia and Indonesia, above 5 per cent for Pakistan, nearly 5 per cent for India and Sri Lanka, and slightly below 4 per cent for Nepal and Bangladesh. In some of these countries, most notably in Pakistan and also in Malaysia, per capita income got subdued to some extent because of high population growth. However, compared to all the other developing regions, the performance of Asian countries in this regard was superior.

The rate of growth in 'value added' in agriculture was equally impressive. It was above, or near, 4 per cent per year in China, Pakistan, Thailand and Indonesia, and around 3 per cent per year in Malaysia, India and Sri Lanka. The countries which could be considered as laggard in this respect were, Nepal (with 2.3 per cent per year), Philippines (2.3 per cent) and Bangladesh (2.1 per cent). The rate of growth in agriculture in Republic of Korea was also rather low, at 2.1 per cent per annum. But for a rapidly industrializing country this in itself did not pose a serious problem.

The feature that should interest us is the rate at which the share of agriculture declines in the total GDP. In 1980, in most of the selected countries in south Asia and China value added by agriculture in the GDP was around 30 per cent or more, it was around 25 per cent in the countries of south-east Asia. By 1998 in none of the countries of south Asia was the share of value added by agriculture more than 30 per cent, except in Nepal. In the case of the latter too the share had come down from 62 per cent to 40 per cent. There was a drastic fall in the share of agriculture in the GDP in the south-east Asian countries also. In Republic of Korea it was already 5 per cent, and in Japan 2 per cent. Generally, there was rapid decline in the share of agricultural GDP in total GDP in the countries that started with a large agricultural sector. The decline got slower as the share of agriculture got reduced. This tendency can be clearly observed in the countries of south Asia.

A positive impact of agricultural growth on overall growth, especially in the poorer countries is also clearly evident. Out of the eleven countries for which data are readily available only three countries, – Pakistan, Malaysia and South Korea - emerged as outliers in this respect. The reason for this lack of symmetry between agricultural growth and overall growth varies from country to country. In case of Pakistan, it was mainly weak intersectoral linkages. Such linkages are stronger when growth is equitably shared, and weaker when there is large inequity in asset holdings and income generation in the rural sector (Mellor, 1995). In the case of Republic of Korea, and to an extent Malaysia, the agricultural sector has already become a minor partner in the economy. Industry and services were propelling the growth in these economies.

Even in the medium income countries, agriculture had a critical, stabilizing role as was evidenced in the turbulent period of 1997 to 2001. Not only in Malaysia and Republic of South Korea, but also in two other relatively larger economies of this region, Indonesia and Thailand which also suffered recession during this period, fluctuations in agricultural growth were more muted. Agriculture emerged as one of the stabilizing factors in these economies. (See charts).

Another remarkable, though not universal, feature of these economies is the slow diversion of the workforce from agriculture to non-agricultural sectors. This is true, to a larger or smaller extent, for all the countries in South Asia, in the agriculturally fast growing countries as much as in the slow growing countries. Thus, the performance of Pakistan with its annual growth in value added by agriculture for the period 1980 to 1998 at 4 per cent per year – the highest in the south

Asia region – was not much different in this respect from that of Bangladesh with the lowest rate of growth in agriculture during the same period (2.1 per cent per year).

Surprisingly, some of the selected countries in south-east Asia i.e. Indonesia and Vietnam, the pace of labour force diversification from agriculture to non-agricultural sectors was not much different from that of the countries of south Asia, even with relatively higher rates of growth in agriculture. Malaysia and Thailand could be considered as exceptions, as the percentage of the labour force in agriculture in these countries came down by nearly 20 per cent during the period 1980 to 1998. In east Asia, China and Republic of Korea registered impressive shifts of the workforce from agriculture to non-agricultural sectors. The experience of Malaysia and the Republic of Korea is all the more remarkable as the proportion of the workforce in agriculture was already low, i.e., less than 40 per cent in 1980. In the remaining countries of these regions, as in the south Asia, the share of the workforce in agriculture in the total workforce, though declining, was still fairly high. (See Tables 4, 5).

Stickiness in the diversion of the workforce from agriculture to the non-agriculture sectors was clearly evident in south Asia, but less so in south-east Asia. The selected countries of east Asia, China and Republic of Korea, showed much greater resilience in this respect. Two clear patterns are observable in this regard. In the poorer countries, say the countries in south Asia, labour force diversification from agriculture to non-agricultural sectors depends on the strength of inter-sectoral linkages. In other words, the role of agriculture has to be judged in terms of how it triggers growth in the non-farm sector. In relatively more developed countries, in the south-east Asia and east Asia, trade plays an important part in stimulating industrial growth, which in turn "pulls" labour from

TABLE – 4

Growth of Output (Average Annual % Growth 1965-99)

Region & Country	Gross Domestic Product		Population		Value Added By		
	Total	Per Capita	Total	Labour Force	Agriculture	Industry	Services
South Asia							
Bangladesh	3.8	1.3	2.3	2.3	2.1	4.4	4.3
India	4.6	2.4	2.1	2.1	2.8	5.5	5.8
Nepal	3.7	1.2	2.4	2.0	2.3	7.9	4.6
Pakistan	5.6	2.7	2.8	2.9	4.1	6.5	6.1
Sri Lanka	4.6	3.0	1.6	2.2	2.7	5.1	5.3
South East Asia							
Indonesia	6.9	4.8	2.0	2.7	3.8	8.7	7.5
Malaysia	7.0	4.3	2.6	3.1	2.9	8.1	7.7
Thailand	7.3	5.1	2.0	2.6	3.9	9.4	7.2
Philippines	3.4	0.9	2.5	2.8	2.3	3.5	4.0
Vietnam	-	-	2.1	2.1	-	-	-
East Asia							
China	8.1	6.4	1.7	2.1	4.1	10.9	9.3
Japan	4.1	3.4	0.7	1.0	-0.2	4.3	4.6
Korea, Rep.	8.1	6.6	1.5	2.6	2.1	10.8	7.6

Source: World Development Indicators 2001.

TABLE – 5

Share of Agricultural GDP in Total GDP and Share of Agricultural Labour Force in Total Labour Force During 1980 and 1998

Region & Country	Gross Domestic Product ($ Millions)		Agriculture Value Added % of GDP		Decline in Agricultural GDP in % Points	Total Labour Force (Million)		Agricultural Labour Force as % of Total Labour Force		Decline in Agriculture Labour Force % Points
	1980	1998	1980	1998		1980	1998	1980	1998	
South Asia										
Bangladesh	17430	42702	38	22	16	41	64	73	63	10
India	186392	430024	38	29	11	302	431	56	45	11
Nepal	1946	4783	62	40	22	7	11	94	-	-
Pakistan	23690	63369	30	26	4	29	49	53	44	9
Srilanka	4024	15707	28	21	7	5	8	72	-	-
South East Asia										
Indonesia	78013	94156	24	20	4	58	98	56	45	9
Malaysia	24488	72489	22	13	11	5	9	37	19	18
Thailand	32354	111327	23	11	12	24	37	71	51	20
Philippines	32500	65107	25	17	8	19	32	52	40	12
Vietnam		27184	-	26		26	39	73	71	2
East Asia										
China	201687	959030	30	18	12	540	743	69	47	22
Japan	1059254	3782964	4	2	2	57	68	10	5	5
Korea, Rep	62543	320748	14	5	9	16	23	34	12	22

Source: World Development Indicators, 2000, World Development Indicators 2001

the agricultural sector. As we move from south Asia to south-east Asia to east Asia the latter clearly becomes more evident.

Production Base: Land and Water

Asian countries are, by and large, densely populated countries, with a high proportion of useable land under cultivation. Density of rural population per square kilometer (sq. km.) of arable land was more than 1000 in Sri Lanka, Bangladesh and Vietnam. It was around 700 per sq. km in Nepal, Indonesia and China; between 400 to 600 in Japan, Philippines, Malaysia, South Korea and India and around 400 in Pakistan. Only Thailand had a low density of rural population, 281 per sq. km. Paucity of cultivable land area coupled with a high proportion of workforce in agriculture resulted in the high density of rural population in several of these countries.

The proportion of arable area to total surface area is largely determined by the natural and physical features, although demographic factors and non-farm uses of land also have a part to play. In respect of arable land, Asian economies are not favourably placed. Except for Bangladesh and India, which had more than 50 per cent of the land area as arable area, and Philippines and Pakistan, where arable area was around one-third (33 per cent) and one-fourth (28 per cent) of the surface area, in most of the other selected countries it was between 10 to 20 per cent of surface area. As the limits to "extensive" farming had already been reached in most of the selected countries, in very few countries did any significant expansion in arable area take place in the last two decades. Only in Nepal, arable area increased by nearly 4 per cent between 1980 and 1998. It expanded by 3 per cent in China and by 2 to 3 per cent in Pakistan and Malaysia. There was a contraction of arable area in Japan and Republic of Korea.

The real worrisome feature was soil erosion and soil deterioration over large areas by wind and water. This resulted in heavy loss in productivity. The problem is more serious in south and south-east Asia. According to one estimate, human induced soil degradation in these sub-regions has led to degradation of 27 per cent of all land, and deforestation to the extent of 11 per cent (Sherr, 1999). The situation is not likely to be much better in east Asia.

Apart from its claim on land, agriculture everywhere makes a preponderant claim on water. Asian countries are no exception, as reflected in the heavy withdrawal of fresh water for crop production. More than two-thirds and in several instances more than 90 per cent of fresh water withdrawal was for agricultural use. Even in highly industrialized countries such as Japan and Republic of Korea, agriculture claimed 64 per cent and 63 per cent of the total withdrawal of fresh water.

In the dry areas of south and east Asia growth and stability in agricultural production are largely dependent on irrigation. The proportion of irrigated land to total arable land is as high as 81 per cent in Pakistan, a country which also had the highest rate of growth in agriculture in south Asia. In the remaining countries of south Asia the proportion varies between 32 per cent (in Sri Lanka) and 45 per cent (in Bangladesh). In east-Asian countries also, the proportion of irrigated land to arable areas is as high as 61 per cent in Republic of Korea, and 55 per cent in Japan. China has the lowest area, i.e. 38 per cent, under irrigation in this sub-region.

Two major problems have surfaced in this regard. In the first place, withdrawal of water is much more than its recharge. This has led to the lowering of the water tables on the one hand and water logging and soil salinity on the other. These phenomena are well documented for some of the countries, e.g. India (GOI, 1996). The second problem is the rising cost of irrigation. In countries where irrigation is important for crop production, the costs have risen 2 to 3 times during the last few decades (Rosegrant and Svendsen, 1993). High cost of irrigation results in low rate of return from new irrigation projects and this acts as a disincentive for investment in irrigation.

In sum, irrespective of the stage of development, agriculture claims a large proportion of useable land and even an larger proportion of useable water. Apart from its implications for improving crop production and productivity, the ecological significance of this feature of Asian agriculture has to be fully appreciated (Table 6).

Agrarian Structure

Asian agriculture is characterised by small holdings structure, the exception being the plantations in some of the south and south-east asian countries. Even in these countries, staple crops are raised on small holdings. Over a period of time two opposite developments have taken place in this regard. In the slow developing countries of south Asia, there has been a downward slide in the land holding structure with the number of the small and marginal farmers increasing and the average size of landholdings becoming smaller. Rapid population growth, coupled with lack of opportunities in the non-farm sector, exacerbated the process of sub-division of cultivated holdings. Institutional reforms initiated in the fifties and sixties also contributed, directly or indirectly, to the breaking up the large holdings and emergence of small farms. As the land and lease markets were restricted – due to legal provisions as well as institutional constraints – acquisition of the small holdings by larger and more resourceful farmers was discouraged. India provides a typical example of such developments, where holdings below 2 ha. already claimed 36 per cent of the cultivated area by the mid-nineties, and

TABLE – 6

Arable Land, Water Withdrawal (For Agricultural Use) And Proportion of Irrigated Area to Total Arable Land

Regions and Countries	*Arable Land as % of Land Area*		*% of Water Withdrawals*[a]	*% of Irrigated Area to Total Crop Land (1968-98)*
	1980	*1998*		
South Asia				
Bangladesh	68.3	61.4	86	44.8
India	54.8	54.3	92	33.6
Nepal	16.0	20.3	99	38.2
Pakistan	25.9	27.8	97	81.2
Sri Lanka	13.2	13.4	96	32.1
South East Asia				
Indonesia	9.9	9.9	93	15.5
Malaysia	3.0	5.5	76	4.8
Thailand	17.5	18.4	88	15.6
Philippines	32.3	32.9	91	23.1
Vietnam	18.2	17.5	86	42.0
East Asia				
China	10.4	13.3	77	38.3
Japan	12.9	12.0	64	54.6
Korea, Rep	20.9	17.3	63	60.5

a: Unless otherwise noted, sectoral withdrawal are estimated for 1987.

Source: World Development Indicators, 2001.

their share was continuously increasing (Vyas, 2002).

On the other hand, in the fast developing countries, such as Japan, and the Republic of Korea – which had undergone far reaching redistributive type of land reforms in the late forties and the early fifties – the market led forces as well as technological developments are influencing the post land reform agricultural holding pattern in favour of larger holdings, the most important factor being the dearth of farm labour, and hence the need for introduction of labour-saving, capital intensive mechanization. Increasingly pressure is being exercised in these countries to abolish the existing ceiling on land holdings and allow the emergence of large corporate farms. Japan provides a typical example of progressive increase in the size of holdings, particularly in the last decade (Shimoji, 1999). Similar pressures are being exerted in other relatively faster developing countries. Moves are already afoot in these countries to relax, if not revoke, existing provisions of the ceiling legislation. Surprisingly, such demands are also voiced in the over-populated, slow-developing countries although the objective conditions in the latter are vastly different.

Normally, in traditional agriculture, there is an inverse relationship between size and productivity. The factors explaining this relationship have been carefully analyzed and reported in the literature (Berry and Cline, 1979, Correa, 1985). Basically, the outcome in traditional agriculture hinges on the larger availability and more intensive use of family labour and other family owned resources. The situation changes once the purchased inputs start claiming a higher share in the input structure. The role of supportive institutions of extension, credit and marketing becomes progressively more important. In the South Asian countries, in general, these institutions were not attuned to small farm agriculture. As a result, growth of productivity on small farms was stunted. The fault lies, therefore, with the supportive institutions rather than the holding pattern.

Production Pattern

In all the selected countries, growth in agricultural production improved over the last decade, with 1981-91 as base, except in Japan where it was negative (-0.86 per cent), and in the Republic of South Korea where it stagnated (per year growth being 0.07 per cent). The growth in production was less than 2 per cent per year in Indonesia, Thailand, Bangladesh and Sri Lanka. Slow growth in these countries, especially in Bangladesh and Sri Lanka, is certainly a cause for concern, as agriculture is still a dominant sector in these countries.

Within the agriculture sector, livestock production outpaced crop production in all the selected countries with the solitary exception of Japan. The most rapid growth in livestock production was registered by China, Philippines and Vietnam. Two of these countries, China and Vietnam had the highest growth in agricultural production also. The Republic of South Korea which was a laggard in total agricultural production showed a buoyancy in livestock production. At the other extreme, Nepal showed the slowest, though positive, growth in livestock production.

The rate of growth in production of food crops was generally higher than the growth in crop production as a whole with the exception of Vietnam and the Republic of Korea. This suggests slower growth of non-food crops, although many countries of the region should have comparative advantage in these crops because of their location. Overall lack of buoyancy in the non-food crops popularly called 'commercial crops', is partly due to the greater attention and resources devoted to food crops in comparison to the non-food crops. Added to that are the much larger price fluctuations in the non-food crops.

Among food crops, cereals comprise the most important group. However, during the last decade the area under cereals declined, or remained stagnant in most of the countries, except those where land frontiers were not yet reached, e.g. Indonesia, Nepal and Malaysia, or where extension of irrigation had made it possible to use arable land to raise more than one crop a year, e.g. in Vietnam and Pakistan. Diversification from cereals to non-cereal crops seems to have started in a modest way in India, Sri Lanka and Thailand, and more pronouncedly in Philippines (where the area under cereals had declined by nearly 12 per cent between the late eighties and the late nineties) and in the two industrialised countries of the region, Republic of Korea (18.2 per cent) and Japan (15 per cent). At the same time, yield per hectare had increased significantly, over 10 per cent during the period under review, in all those countries where the area under cereals had declined, the only exception being Japan, where the increase in the yield was around 5 per cent over the decade. As a result, the production of cereals increased in all the selected countries with the exception of the two industrialised countries, Japan and Republic of Korea, and all these countries reached a higher level of food self sufficiency.

The production of and the area under pulses, which are the major source of protein in this region, declined in a number of countries. A significant increase in their production took place only in Indonesia, Philippines and Pakistan. However, in these countries also, the increase in production was mainly because of the increase in the area rather than in the yields. A similar disappointing performance is reported for oilseeds, the principal source of fat for the poor and an important ingredient in cattle feed. Production performance of pulses and oilseeds in the Asian economies needs careful review and remedial action.

To sum up, several interesting developments have taken place in the pattern of agricultural production in Asia in recent years. There is a marked shift towards high value enterprises, especially livestock; within agriculture, food crops; and within food crops, production of cereals have shown greater dynamism. Increase in cereals output is largely accounted for by improvements in the yields. While these are positive developments, certain negative features can also be discerned. Production of pulses and oilseeds, poor people's sources of protein and fat respectively, is declining. Production of non-food crops, the so-called commercial crops, is fluctuating widely around a declining trend. This is worrisome as many of the tropical and sub-tropical countries have, or ought to have 'natural' advantages in growing these crops. (Tables 7 and 8)

Agricultural Trade

Four broad trends could be observed in agricultural trade during the last decade. In the first place, agricultural trade as a proportion of total trade declined in practically every selected country. The decline was very pronounced in the countries where agricultural trade claimed a high proportion in the total trade at the beginning of the period (i.e. in 1991). For example, agricultural trade as a proportion of total trade was 27.1 per cent in Sri Lanka, and 22.1 per cent in Nepal. Near the end of the decade (in 1998) in none of the selected countries did agricultural trade account for more than 18 per cent (Sri Lanka) of the total trade. In the fast industrializing countries i.e., China and the Republic of Korea the share of agricultural trade in total foreign trade came down to 5 per cent or less. This development was basically the result of rapid diversification of economic activities in these countries.

TABLE – 7

Growth in Agricultural Production 1990-1999 (Base 1989-91)

(Percent per Annum)

Regions & Countries	***Agricultural***	*Crop*	*Food*	*Cereals*	*Vegetables*	*Fruits*	*Livestock*
South Asia							
Bangladesh	1.57	1.24	1.65	1.39	1.86	0.62	3.49
India	2.61	2.34	2.65	1.93	2.17	3.98	3.45
Nepal	2.20	2.12	2.23	1.43	4.66	-1.07	2.49
Pakistan	3.31	1.90	4.05	2.80	3.78	4.00	4.94
Sri Lanka	1.51	1.26	1.40	2.61	0.52	1.28	3.23
South East Asia							
Indonesia	1.78	1.60	1.79	1.40	1.70	3.88	2.56
Malaysia	2.81	1.79	3.90	-0.20	5.89	-0.52	4.88
Thailand	1.65	1.44	1.48	2.02	1.10	1.82	2.84
Philippines	2.85	1.55	3.02	1.45	2.01	2.10	6.50
Vietnam	5.48	5.43	2.97	5.71	3.24	2.81	6.20
East Asia							
China	5.36	3.94	5.74	1.66	7.72	11.84	8.31
Japan	-0.86	-1.15	-0.80	-1.31	-1.10	-1.64	-0.71
Korea, Rep	0.07	0.83	0.12	-0.84	1.20	2.21	3.17

Source: Based on Index Numbers of Agricultural Production, FAO Production Year Books.

TABLE – 8

Percentage Increase/Decrease in Area, Yield and Production of Cereals, Pulses and Oilseeds in T.E. 1999, Over T.E. 1991

Regions & Countries	Cereals			Pulses			Oilseeds		
	Area	Production	Yield	Area	Production	Yield	Area	Production	Yield
South Asia									
Bangladesh	1.03	6.80	5.46	-8.88	1.12	11.03	213.20	0.00	-13.36
India	-2.18	15.64	18.23	0.49	7.27	6.72	242.07	36.95	13.54
Nepal	7.72	9.56	1.72	-16.49	-1.27	18.07		0.00	27.13
Pakistan	5.26	25.48	19.17	15.69	48.82	-13.72	13.12	-0.64	15.10
Sri Lanka	-2.27	8.55	10.88	52.69	-60.28	-17.66	-11.28	0.00	-11.54
South East Asia									
Indonesia	11.91	14.75	2.60	61.88	95.90	-2.09	28.76	-24.99	37.03
Malaysia	7.12	21.41	13.28				0.00	0.00	-4.06
Philippines	-12.03	7.56	22.53	-94.88	67.59	-0.17	-43.78	-7.83	-79.96
Thailand	-3.04	20.99	22.75	-35.19	-24.84	11.23	-45.93	-35.12	10.53
Vietnam	22.55	55.56	26.77	19.46	22.66	2.81	24.00	22.74	30.21
East Asia									
China	0.60	16.91	16.25	-36.10	-19.35	-71.43	7.33	-24.99	19.43
Japan	-15.06	-10.49	5.34	-34.40	-31.21	6.02	-33.07	-34.02	-16.36
Korea, Rep	-18.24	-9.75	10.45	-24.35	-26.36	-24.82	-28.89	-37.03	-61.58

Source: FAO Production Year Books

TABLE – 9

Growth and Composition of Agricultural Trade (in 1991 and 1998)

Regions & Countries	Agri. Trade as % of Total Trade		Index of Agri. Trade T.E. 1991=100	Proportion of Agri. Export in Agri. Trade		Proportion of Agri. Import to Agri. Trade		Net Surplus/Deficit in Agricultural Trade	
	1991	1998		1991	1998	1991	1998	1991	1998
South Asia									
Bangladesh	19.21	13.26	161.90	17.57	90.58	9.42	82.43	-578.33	-1171.67
India	9.67	12.07	234.20	74.68	36.25	63.75	25.32	1879.00	2451.00
Nepal	22.07	13.65	139.66	31.00	72.79	27.21	69.00	-68.67	-115.00
Pakistan	19.82	16.39	125.23	46.87	63.89	36.11	53.13	-156.33	-868.00
Sri Lanka	27.07	18.21	148.50	57.09	43.18	56.82	42.91	170.00	-985.34
South East Asia									
Indonesia	10.03	11.64	217.26	62.82	44.71	55.29	37.20	1207.66	1084.33
Malaysia	11.39	7.74	174.17	67.15	34.93	65.07	32.85	2308.00	3533.00
Thailand	13.10	9.21	148.13	78.51	24.48	70.19	21.49	4183.34	5547.00
Vietnam	19.13	15.48	331.76	75.03	30.88	69.12	24.97	449.67	1139.67
Philippines	11.79	7.86	183.66	51.02	60.64	39.6	48.98	49.66	-950.00
East Asia									
China	8.43	5.37	140.36	51.61	54.52	45.48	48.39	673.33	-2646.34
Japan	5.82	5.46	131.55	3.88	96.00	4.00	96.12	-27940.3	-36657.7
Korea, Rep	5.60	4.12	140.47	14.62	83.88	85.38	16.12	-5446.00	-7327.00

Source: FAO Trade Year Books.

The second notable feature is that agricultural trade in absolute terms increased significantly during this period. It more than doubled in India and Indonesia, and was more than three times in Vietnam. The important fact is that in most of the countries the increase in agricultural trade was an outcome of increase in imports, as the use of fertilizers, chemicals and machinery increased in agricultural production, and the countries had to import bulk of these inputs in bulk. There was no commensurate increase in exports. On the other hand, adverse terms of trade for agriculture further depressed the value of agricultural exports. Only five out of the thirteen selected countries – India, Indonesia, Malaysia, Thailand and Vietnam - had a positive balance on their agricultural trade accounts.

The third important feature is that while the importance of agricultural trade in total trade declined, the composition of agricultural trade changed significantly. The food component in the imports declined due to the drive towards food self sufficiency which was a policy objective in a large number of countries. As was shown earlier, cereal production increased in all the selected countries. Apart from Thailand and Vietnam which are traditional exporters of food grains and continued to remain so, India also emerged as an exporter of cereals, although a marginal one. The countries which were net importers, such as Nepal and Indonesia, achieved self-sufficiency in food grains. The net imports of China, the largest food importer, remained at 3 to 4 per cent of its domestic requirements. Only the fast developing countries such as the Republic of Korea and Malaysia continued to depend on imports of food grains to a significant extent. At the same time, agricultural exports were diversified in all the countries. The share of the dominant commodities, generally cereals or plantation crops, declined. Products such as fruits and vegetables and dairy and meat products and food stuffs gained in importance.

Fourthly, the expectation that the WTO agreements, particularly the Agreement on Agriculture, would result in increased access for agricultural exports in the markets of developed countries did not materialize. In fact, in the post Uruguay period exports to Japan and the European Union from the developing countries of the region declined, or at best remained at the same level.

Economic Environment

In recent years, the countries of the region are pursuing macro-policies to make their economies more open and more integrated with the global economy. These measures have gathered momentum since the mid-eighties. Policy packages comprise fiscal policies, monetary policies, trade policies, investment policies, etc. The basic aim of all these policy measures, in fact of the economic reforms as such, is to improve the allocative efficiency, and thereby contribute to economic growth. In the following discussion, special emphasis is given to reforms as they have affected agriculture.

Domestic Agricultural Policies

In all the countries of this region, governments intervened in agriculture markets to a smaller or greater extent through administered prices for agricultural output as well as inputs. This was mainly because agricultural production and prices were used to subserve the objective of food security. Border prices as a measure of the competitiveness of domestic agriculture were given only secondary importance. The extent of the distortions caused by the administered prices, (understood broadly as the difference between the border prices and the domestic prices) and the subsequent impact of the correction of these distortions should not be exaggerated. This is because, except for China in the pre-reform period, agriculture in these countries was not as heavily discriminated against as in several other developing regions. And in practically all the countries of the region, taxation on agriculture was progressively reduced, especially since the mid-eighties (Rosegrant and Hazell, 2000). As a result correction of price discrimination could not yield as much result in terms of output growth, as was expected earlier. The non-price, – i.e. institutional and technological – factors were the prime movers of agricultural growth and rural incomes.

Another motivation in reforming agricultural prices was correcting the adverse domestic terms of trade of agriculture, which was mainly an outcome of the urban bias in government policies. This bias was gradually corrected in most of the countries in the region. There was a two-pronged attack on "disprotecting" industries. In the first place overvalued exchange rates were realigned at more realistic levels. Secondly, the 'quota-permit' regime was gradually dismantled. The net result was progressive improvement in agriculture's terms of trade. In countries where the governments had taken the responsibility of supplying foodgrains to poor consumers at below the market prices through some form of public distribution system, producer prices were protected. The difference between the purchase prices paid to the producers and the issue prices charged by the public distribution system was met by food subsidies. This, of course, meant that with rise in the procurement prices paid to the producers, the food subsidy bill of the government would rise. Besides, in order to encourage the use of modern inputs, in most of the countries subsidies were extended to agricultural inputs, i.e. fertilizers, irrigation and power. In recent years there is a move to reduce these subsidies partly for fiscal reasons, but also on consideration of allocative efficiency. So far the results have not been particularly encouraging.

The worst effect of the policy of subsidized inputs (for producers) and subsidized output (for consumers) was the 'crowding out' of resources from more productive use, e.g. public investment in infrastructure or research. The political fallout of the policy of subsidisation, i.e. emergence in terms of a strong lobby of the surplus generating larger farmers, had a pernicious effect beyond their impact on public fisc. Combination of an urban bias and a big land owner bias, as witnessed in a number of countries, places the rural poor in double jeopardy.

A major achievement of the agricultural price policy pursued by a number of countries was to impart intra-year stability to prices and, thus, reduce uncertainty. Removal of such uncertainty contributes to better resource allocation. In many countries, i.e. Bangladesh, India and Indonesia, the governments assured minimum support prices for staple food crops and, to that extent, removed part of the uncertainty. However, it was becoming clear that for achieving the same objective other measures such as crop insurance and forward trading had to be introduced to a much larger extent.

There is still an unfinished agenda in agricultural price policies. Major achievements in this area have been a reduction in the gap between the domestic prices and border prices, an improvement in the domestic terms of trade for agriculture, and reduction in the price-induced uncertainty. At the same time, the problem of unsustainable subsidies could not be resolved, and the tendency to use administered prices as a vehicle for income transfers is emerging. The latter clouds the main, i.e. allocative, function of prices.

Trade Liberalization

The 1990s witnessed a phenomenal growth in international trade. This was basically a reflection of the growing environment of liberalization. Several international initiatives, the most notable being the Uruguay Round of trade negotiations, contributed to this growth. The other supportive factor was a tendency towards regional trade blocks, with liberal trade regimes within these blocks. A large number of countries in Asia are signatories of the Uruguay Round and are members of the World Trade Organization. Recently the only major remaining country, China, also joined WTO. The countries have undertaken major trade reforms in bringing down the tariff rates, providing market access and removing quantitative restrictions. Fiscal and monetary policies and tax regimes are adapted to encourage participation in international trade.

The countries of this region, by taking advantage of the expanding world trade in the eighties and the nineties, could avail themselves of the economies of scale, greater allocative efficiency, wider access to productive resources, etc. These countries have also reaped long-term benefits in terms of enhancement of technology and access to international markets. To the extent international financial flows are attracted to the countries with extensive trading activities, they also benefited from the larger resource flow. Not only the relatively more developed economies of the region, but the poorer countries also benefited by their participation in international trade.

However, there are certain areas where the developing countries of the region found themselves severely handicapped. Larger incidence of risk, with greater exposure to international trade, is one such handicap, which is felt more seriously by the countries which do not have a diversified export base. Besides, participation in the external trade may conflict with the basic national policy objectives, say, food security, especially so if the conditions imposed by the trading partners or trade regulating international bodies are detrimental to reaching such a goal. There are, also, certain unresolved issues, i.e. 'infant industries', where different positions are taken by the developed countries (also, by different developed countries amongst themselves). However, the major handicap faced by the agricultural exporting countries of the region is the large subsidization of their agriculture by the developed countries, which has increased rather than decreased in the more recent years. U.S.A's latest Farm Act is an example. Besides, provisions of the Trade Related Intellectual Property Rights, as well as those pertaining to bio-diversity, have been contested by a few countries of the region.

The countries of this region have, by and large, followed a more pragmatic approach, while adhering to the norms set by the trade regulating organizations. Two lessons relevant to our discussion stand out. One, the countries that gave equal attention to the development of domestic markets took better advantage of expanding world trade (e.g. countries of the South-east Asia region). Secondly, countries with a diversified production base were distinct gainers (e.g. India and China).

Salient Features of Agricultural Development

With dissimilar initial conditions, differences in size and location and, differences in socio-political institutions, it may not be very meaningful to try to identify a uniform pattern of growth in the agricultural sectors of the selected economies. There are, however, certain similarities in the countries of the three distinct sub-regions of Asia. There too, a few countries can be identified as outliers, in regard to specific aspects of development. There are, however, common experiences in critical areas to justify broad generalisations. With all the necessary caveats, certain conclusions can be drawn from the above discussion.

– At low levels of income agriculture is the driving force for the overall economic growth. The impact is diluted if the linkages between the various sectors are weak, which happens with gross inequality in asset holding and income share in rural areas. Even in the relatively higher income countries of South-east and East Asia, agriculture may not have the importance of a leading sector, but it provides a stabilising effect at times of economic turbulence and overall recession.

- In general, there is a marked stickiness in the agricultural workforce, which may be a policy-induced phenomenon, i.e. an urban bias in social investment, or inappropriate technological choices.
- The natural production base of agriculture, in terms of land and water, is limited and deteriorating. It will have long term deleterious effects on productivity as well as in quality of life. In this respect there is hardly any remarkable difference in the countries at different levels of economic growth, except that the pace of degradation of the natural resources is accelerated in those countries which have higher rates of population growth.
- The experience of Asian countries clearly suggests that an agrarian structure dominated by small holdings is no handicap for high productive agriculture, provided requisite institutional support is available to the small farmers. The need for consolidation of holdings and enlargement of farms arises once labour shortage becomes a handicap for agricultural growth.
- Over all rate of growth in agricultural output was satisfactory in all the major countries. Diversification from cereal crops to non-cereal crops had started to a greater or smaller extent in all these countries, but because of rise in productivity, the food self-sufficiency ratio was hardly affected. Stagnation in production of

pulses and oilseeds among the food crops was a cause for concern, more so the stagnation in the productivity of the so-called 'commercial' crops, for which most of these countries should have a 'natural' comparative advantage. An important route to product diversification which most of the countries are taking, is higher emphasis on and faster growth of vegetable and horticultural crops, and also the dairying and animal husbandry sub-sectors.

Asian economies participated in the international trade in agricultural commodities on a progressively higher scale, although the proportion of their agricultural trade was declining in total international trade. Composition of agricultural trade restricted adverse terms of trade in these countries. The policies of the developed countries inhibited exports to their markets from developing countries.

The Domestic economic environment was characterised by macro economic reforms leading to a reduction in the bias against agriculture as industries were disprotected, and exchange rates were brought closer to the purchasing power of the respective currencies. Distortion in the domestic terms of trade was reduced, but the growth in input subsidies was "crowding out" investment in research, extension and infrastructure creation in the rural areas.

All major countries of the region had joined the World Trade Organisation and complied with the WTO discipline in reducing over all subsidies, tarrification, open trade, etc. However, due to the sluggish response to the spirit of these agreements by the developed countries, the gains to the developing countries were not substantial.

III

EMERGING SCENARIO

In the time perspective of a decade or so, certain developments seem to be imminent. The incidence and severity of these changes may differ from country to country, but they are likely to be fairly pervasive and relevant for the region as a whole. The changes which are germane to our discussion could be grouped as demand-side changes, supply side changes and, the likely policy environment. Such division, especially between demand-side changes and supply side changes is more for the convenience of discussion. In the countries where the agricultural sector accounts for a substantial portion of the GDP, and a large part of the workforce, the demand is also conditioned by the output and income of the agricultural producers.

Demand for Agricultural Products

Individual scholars and institutions have made several estimates of future demand for food and non-food agricultural produce. The demand and supply estimates for agricultural products by FAO and IFPRI are among the better known ones. Demand and supply projections for foodgrains are relatively more robust than those for the non-foodgrains crops. Food (and feed) grains occupy major part of the agricultural land and account for the bulk of the agricultural incomes. Factors determining demand for food are also better understood and analysed. The non-food crops are mostly produced in the developing countries, but have their principal markets in the developed countries. Basically, it is the demand generated in the latter that determines the prices of these commodities and the income of their producers. In the following discussion, the main attention is on the factors determining demand for food, including livestock products.

As is well known, important factors which influence the demand for food are, the pace and pattern of population growth, level and growth of income and tastes and habits. All these are dynamic variables and need to be looked into carefully in the changing context. We consider here two prime movers of demand for food, i.e. population and income.

Population

Countries of Asia are going through a demographic transition at an unprecedented pace. The rate of growth of population has drastically come down, and the prospects of further fall are imminent. During 1980-99 all the major countries of South Asia, except Sri Lanka, had annual population growth rates of 2 per cent and above. Current estimates cited by the World Bank suggest that during the next fifteen years, i.e., 2000-2015, only Nepal and Pakistan will have an annual population growth of more than 2 per cent - 2.1 per cent in case of Nepal and 2.2 per cent in case of Pakistan. Three major countries of South-east Asia had a population growth of over 2 per cent per year in the first period; none will have a growth rate of population above 1.6 per cent per year in the second period. The major countries of East Asia will have a population growth of less than 1 per cent per year in the second period.

Two factors have impacted on the population growth rates and are likely to become even more effective over time. First, the unwanted children could be avoided because of rapid increase in the knowledge as well as facilities for family planning. Second, the desire to have fewer children is strengthened with lowering of infant mortality, higher female literacy and large number of women joining the work force. Now, the only factor contributing to high birth rates in some of the Asian countries is what is known as 'population momentum', due to the relatively larger proportion of the population in the child-bearing age group. This factor is also progressively weakening. Deceleration in the rate of population growth will have, among other implications (i.e. for social security), a remarkable effect on the future demand for food.

Income

Each of these countries, poor and rich alike, shows very low overall income elasticity for foodgrains. This could be an outcome of two factors. In the first place, because of low physical exertion, partly because of growing proportion of the work force in sedentary occupations, and partly because of easier access to sources of potable water and cooking fuel – due to which the drudgery of availing oneself of these necessities in an arduous manner is reduced – the calorie requirements have become lower. The second reason is the diversification in the food basket and the decline in the proportion of food grains in the food intake. With increase in income the proportion of fruits, vegetables, fish, milk and dairy products and meat becomes higher in the consumption pattern. Demand for foodgrains as the major source of calorie supply becomes progressively less important. This is quite evident in the cross sectional context, the higher the per capita income, the less important are foodgrains as a source of calories. Current estimates of income elasticity for foodgrains, even in a poor country like India is placed at 0.2 to 0.3 or below. Thus, even if the income in the poorer countries grows at a relatively high rate of growth, say 4 per cent per capita per year, during the next 10 to 15 years, the income induced growth in demand for staple foodgrains is likely to be less than 1 per cent per year.

However, an increasing share of dairy products and meat in the diet will naturally increase the demand for food grains. This has led several analysts to conclude that Asia as a region will be a net importer of food because of the burgeoning demand for foodgrains from the animal husbandry sector. These estimates are based mainly on the analysis of demand for meat in East Asia, especially China, as the meat consumption in these countries has increased phenomenally in recent years. I have serious doubts on these estimates when applied to other countries of Asia. Firstly, the world over, diversification of food has resulted in larger share of fruits, vegetables, eggs and fish products on health as well as cultural grounds. In the coming decade, the movement toward vegetarianism is likely to gather steam. Secondly, even among the meat eaters, there is a shift away from red meat towards poultry and other white meat. Energy conversion from feedstock to meat is less inefficient in case of poultry than in the larger animals. The demand for meat in general and for red meat in particular is likely to increase more slowly. And, for this reason, the increase in the demand for feedgrains seems to be exaggerated. It is important to settle this point because conversion from a self-sufficiency status to a net importer status for India, and from a marginal importer status to a heavy importer status in case of China postulated in various projections is based mainly on the assumption of a huge increase in the demand for foodgrains as feed stuff in these countries.

A major source of demand for food, including cereals, is likely to be the demand from *food insecure* households, as their income or entitlement for food increases. A very large number of people in South Asia, in parts of South-east Asia, (e.g. Indonesia and Philippines) and in China are malnourished. So long as a large number of people are poor and food insecure, an increase in their income is likely to add to the demand for food in a measurable way. The number of the undernourished, in the years 1996-98 is estimated to be 208 million in India, 140 million in China, and 167 million in other countries of Asia and the Pacific (FAO, 2001). Depth of hunger, measured by the average dietary energy deficit of undernourished people – not of the population as a whole – expressed in kilocalories per person per day is disturbingly high in most of the selected countries with the exception of Malaysia and the Republic of Korea. (Table 10)

TABLE – 10

Average Dietary Energy Deficit of Undernourished People - Expressed in Kilocalories per Person Per Day

Region and Countries	*KCAL*
SOUTH ASIA	
Bangladesh	340
India	290
Nepal	260
Pakistan	270
Sri Lanka	260
SOUTH EAST ASIA	
Indonesia	200
Malaysia	140
Thailand	260
Philippines	270
Vietnam	280
EAST ASIA	
China	250
Japan	N.A.
Korea, REP	130

Source: The State of Food Security in the World 2000, FAO.

If the governments in these countries take their obligation to ensure food security for their citizens seriously and act accordingly, the demand for foodgrains is likely to increase before it peaks out. Thus, overall demand for foodgrains may not increase to the extent currently estimated, but the composition of the food basket is likely to change significantly. With greater concern for nutrition, the demand for pulses, oilseeds, fruits and vegetables as also milk and animal husbandry products is likely to increase much faster while the demand for starchy staples is likely to creep up much more slowly.

Supply Response

The deceleration in the rate of growth of demand for foodgrains and other agricultural products is of little comfort as the forces propelling supplies are also weakening. This is mainly due to the following reasons: (i) weakening of production base, (ii) weaker linkages between agricultural and non-agricultural growth, (iii) growing incongruence between the agrarian structure and the supply systems, (iv) weak research base, and, (v) confusion about the role of the state.

The production base of agriculture, comprising land and water, is weakening. The factors which have contributed to the degradation of the productive resources are, pressure on land resources resulting in deforestation, overgrazing, and extension of agriculture to marginal land, coupled with mismanagement of arable land. The process of deterioration is exacerbated due to lack of appropriate technologies for the proper use of land and water, and absence of proper land use policies. Similar forces have led to degradation and depletion of water resources. Lack of capital, appropriate research support and effective institutional mechanisms are making the task of land and water improvement progressively more difficult.

Agriculture's linkages with non-agricultural activities are not getting strengthened. It is not only in the developed countries that such linkages are weak. A disturbing phenomenon is the weakening of the agricultural – non-agricultural linkages, even in the poorer countries. This denies the benefits of growth in one sector percolating to other sectors. The primary reason for the weak linkages in the poor countries is weak infrastructure support and low investment in human resource development in the rural areas. In the absence of a determined public policy, such rural-urban inequalities will continue to weaken inter-sectoral relations. I have more to say on this in a latter section on public policies.

There is a growing incongruence between the agrarian structure and the supportive institutions. In a number of countries, especially the poorer ones, the agrarian structure is tilting progressively towards smaller holdings, while the supportive institutions of extension, credit, input supplies and product marketing are geared to serve the medium to large farmers. To give just one example, while agricultural production is becoming more resource-intensive, the credit institutions serving the rural sectors are in disarray at least in two larger countries of the region, China and India. In effect, a credit rationing takes place, and the farmers with little collateral are deprived of credit. A similar bias in other supportive institutions is fairly widespread.

There is no path-breaking, easily adaptable, technology in sight. The green Revolution, which had its sway over large parts of Asia in the sixties and the seventies, and carried the momentum till the eighties has peaked out. The new advances in agricultural technologies are largely incremental, and to that extent require much greater inputs of extension and supportive services. The only possibility of a dramatic breakthrough is through bio-technology and genetic engineering. It has started showing results in certain crops, e.g. cotton and soyabean, and influencing certain traits in other crops, e.g., pest and disease resistance. But its large scale application in the production of major foodgrains is still in the realm of the future. Besides, a few worrisome features have already surfaced. These include, (i) concentration of biotechnology research in a few large private sector firms in developed countries, (ii) emphasis of research on a few crops in developed countries which may pose a threat to the major exports from this region, e.g. cotton and oilseeds, and (iii) weak regulatory arrangements in the developing countries to spot and minimise potential risks. The International Research System (CGIAR) has a role to orient bio-technology research towards small farmers' and backward regions' agriculture, and to work with National Agricultural Research Systems to help them to extend the technology to disadvantaged groups and areas.

More than these handicaps, the major supply inhibiting factors are in the realm of policy – in domestic policies as well as in the external economic environment.

Domestic Policies

There is a large degree of consensus on the goal of domestic policies among the countries of the region. In practice, much remains to be done. In a number of countries domestic economic policies discriminating against rural sector in general and agriculture in particular are continuing. Not only are some minor irritants yet to be removed, but the major issues of agricultural taxation and of agricultural subsidies are to be faced in a bold manner. With the emphasis on fiscal restraint on one hand, and withdrawal of the state from economic activities on the other, public investment in creating agricultural infrastructure, e.g. irrigation, is declining. Expenditure on health, education, transport and communications in the rural areas is grossly inadequate. The urban bias in the public policies and in public investment continues. It is further compounded by a 'big land owner bias' where the small number of large farmers are able to preempt whatever facilities are accorded to the rural areas.

There is a more fundamental lacuna which has escaped the attention of the policy makers as well as the academics. Economic policies are generally directed, and analysed, to attain the objective of economic growth and stability at the macro level. Seldom are the micro level implications of the macro policies taken into account. It is assumed that (a) corrections of the so-called "macro fundamental" will result in economic growth, (b) growth will trickle down to all levels, and (c) growth will enable public authorities to expend more resources on poverty alleviation measures. A major research programme located in nine Asian countries, *Micro Implications of Macro Economic and Adjustment Policies (MIMAP),* has pointed out several instances where the reforms did not prove to be beneficial to the poor. It has been shown, for example, that in India liberalization of trade in agriculture, desirable in itself, imposes constraints on the level of private expenditure on education and health for poor households with limited income and inelastic demand for food. If the public provision on these services is inadequate or inefficient, it will increase morbidity and mortality among the poor households (MIMAP, 2001).

In any case, it needs to be emphasised that the canvas for policy intervention is much wider than implicit in the narrowly defined macro policies. This is particularly true if the objective is to ensure sustainable and equitable growth. Policies on human resource development, institutional development, asset distribution, labour market reforms, regional growth, etc., become equally, if not more, important. In agriculture itself, proper management of land and water resources, agricultural growth in backward regions, and improving the pace of agricultural technology for the disadvantaged sections and regions need much greater attention. There is a feeling among the knowledgeable circles that in the anxiety to usher in macro economic reforms, these other interventions are not getting due recognition.

Finally, a policy is as good as the implementation capability of the policy makers. Countries which took into account their social and cultural melieu and their institutional strengths, and were careful in determining the sequencing and speed of reforms, have been more successful than those which were guided, on their own or by external agencies, by mere ideological considerations.

Globalisation

As in the case of domestic policies, success from the moves towards integrating the national economy with the global economy has been conditioned by the initial conditions in the countries concerned on the one hand and the speed of reforms on the other. As the moves towards globalisation impinge more seriously on agriculture, especially after the Uruguay Round and the establishment of WTO, we have to be more careful in understanding the implications. I have dealt with this topic in detail on another occasion (Vyas, 2001). I will summarise my main contentions.

Globalisation had raised high hopes in the developing countries with large agricultural sectors. These hopes could only be partially realised, because of internal and external reasons. The countries which had given proper attention to market reforms in the domestic sphere were relatively more successful in reaping the benefits of globalisation. Even then, they had to face an unfair competition from developed countries who subsidised their agriculture under one garb or another, and placed tariff and non-tariff barriers to protect their agriculture. Opening of the agricultural sector to international competition, without reforms in the agricultural sector of the *developed countries* has led to greater risks without the commensurate advantages of a wide market and a level playing field.

The present arrangements for Special and Differential Treatment which are supposed to benefit the developing countries are grossly inadequate. The developed countries had already granted a level of protection to their agriculture before the Uruguay Round, so that even after the Agreement of Agriculture [AoA] their agriculture continues to receive higher protection in absolute terms. There are several loopholes in the AoA which the developed countries have exploited to their advantage, e.g. mandatory reduction of tariff on unweighted basis, which allowed them to reduce tariff on items which were not of much consequence to the developing countries, but retain high tariff on commodities which developing countries would have liked to export to a larger extent. Provisions of 'green, blue and amber boxes' gives legitimacy to what is outright protection of agriculture. Restriction on sanitary and phyto-sanitary grounds is another instrument which is being used in discriminating ways in the absence of international standards or internationally acceptable risk assessment.

Only a more determined international regulatory authority and the collective strength of the developing countries can enable them to reap the advantages of a large, and fair, global economy. This is not a plea for reversing the trends towards globalisation, or for that matter domestic macro economic reforms. What is suggested is that a proper assessment from the point of view of a country's own development needs and strategy is important rather than uncritical acceptance of whatever is doled out by the developed countries or the agencies dominated by them.

IV

ATTUNING AGRICULTURE FOR SUSTAINABLE DEVELOPMENT

While discussing our agrarian future we should remind ourselves about the differences in the initial conditions among different Asian countries. The countries in this region can broadly be divided into two categories: the first group comprises those where agriculture accounts for the largest proportion of the workforce, say from one-third to one-half or above, where agriculture's contribution to the GDP is nearly one-fourth or above, and where agricultural produce claims the largest chunk of a consumer's expenditure, and one-fourth to one-third of total expenditure. A large number of Asian countries fall in this category. The second group comprises only a few countries e.g. Japan, the Republic of Korea and possibly Malaysia, where agriculture as a sector of economic activity has lost its predominant position. Obviously, in this latter category impulses from other sectors, viz. industry and services, are more important. Even in these countries, agriculture is important for social and cultural reasons. It also comes out as a more stable economic activity in times of turbulence which these countries periodically face. Our focus is more on the first category.

Agriculture in these countries will have to face the following inter-related challenges in the coming years.

- Preserving the ecological balance, especially stopping the degradation of land and water resources;
- Improving the income and living standard of the rural producers, and
- Ensuring food and nutrition security for the population.

It needs to be emphasised at the outset that a large

proportion of agricultural production units in these countries are small, a large bulk of them in the range of one to two hectares. They will have to play a pivotal role in meeting all the three objectives.

Strengthening the Production Base

There is general agreement that the production base of agriculture in our part of the world is weakening. Threats of desertification, depletion of aquifer and heavy losses of topsoil are reaching alarming proportions. There is a consensus that in protecting the production base of agriculture technologies and institutions will have to play the critical role. The 'seed-fertilisers-chemicals' based technology, which gave us the Green Revolution cannot be replicated. There is a need now for resource conserving technologies. The scientists in the national and international systems will have to play a crucial role in designing such technologies. I would only add that while pursuing this goal of material-saving technology we should take cognisance of the innate wisdom of the producers themselves. We are a continent of 'farmers of forty centuries'. The accumulated wisdom of the men, and women, behind the plough should be mainstreamed. There is no substitute for this 'dying wisdom' in addressing the issues at micro level.

On institutional aspects, much needs to be done. At the moment the main emphasis seems to be on 'ensuring property rights'. It may be the right approach in several situations. However, going beyond generalisations we will have to think of proper distribution of the "bundle of property rights" in different situations, especially in those where common property rights have to be strengthened to optimise the returns even to individuals. I wish to end this part of the discussion by giving my views on one aspect of the problem of resource conservation, regarding which I have some reservations on the received wisdom, i.e. on the role played by the small farmers in damaging the natural resource base.

There is a widespread belief that small farmers, not out of cussedness but because of the nature of their economy, inflict greater damage on the natural resources. The Bruntland Commission (1989) articulated this concern precisely. As the poor have a small resource base they have to exploit it more intensively to eke out a living. Poor households have higher growth of population, and, they heavily discount the future stream of income. I examined these arguments in greater detail in my Elmhurst Memorial Lecture at the 21st Conference of the International Association of Agricultural Economists in 1991 (Vyas, 1992). To recapitulate, I maintain that, because of their small asset base, the poor have to husband their resources more carefully; although the fertility rate is higher in the poor households, so also is the mortality rate, and as a consequence the poor have smaller, mostly nuclear families, with higher work participation; because of the small asset base they have to engage in multiple enterprises, some of the short gestation type and some of longer gestation – what is known as mixed farming system – a typical example being crop production and dairying – which is generally environmental friendly.

Given a proper technology of resource conservation and institutional support, e.g. credit, the small farm dominated agriculture is more likely to conserve the natural resources. A sane zoning and land use policy will inhibit poaching on their land by non-farm enterprises and pushing them to more marginalised lands. In most circumstances, poor farmers are the victims rather than the perpetrators of resource depletion. Technology and institutional changes designed to preserve the natural resources will have to keep the small farmer at the centre.

Income and Living Standard of Rural Producers

There is enough information to indicate that a) in the developing countries poverty is concentrated in rural areas, b) within agriculture poverty is related to access to land, and c) agricultural growth has a positive impact on poverty alleviation (IFAD, 2001). In a situation where the bulk of agricultural producers are small, growth in their productivity and income will have a salutary impact on eliminating poverty, a goal which is shared by all the countries of the region.

The world over, income and living standards of the rural producers in general and agricultural producers in particular, remain subdued, or in any case remain lower than those of the urban producers as a group. There are three basic reasons for this phenomenon. First, the rate of technical progress is slower in agriculture than in the non-agricultural sector, a Ricardian handicap made familiar since our undergraduate days. Second, the nature of demand for agricultural products is such that it cannot increase in proportion to the income of the consumers, thanks to Engel's Law. Third, there is much greater uncertainty and risk involved in agricultural production due to the much larger dependence on nature, and as a consequence, allocation of resources being invariably sub-optimal. To compound all these handicaps, most of the countries' policies, more so those of the developing countries, discriminate against agriculture in particular and the rural sector in general. This is reflected in their domestic price policies, investment policies and trade and foreign exchange policies. Incidence of all these handicaps is more serious among producers with a small asset base and weak linkages with the support systems of extension, credit and marketing.

Most of the developed countries have tried to raise agricultural incomes by domestic price subsidies and overt and covert protection policies in international trade. In the developing countries also, with the growing strength of large farmers' lobby, their interests are sought to be protected by subsidising and accommodating those who have marketable surplus. This naturally precludes the small farmers who suffer from all the handicaps which agricultural production entails and they do not get even partial succour. Vested interests in both types of economies, the advanced and the poor, would like to perpetuate the existing regime, although it has become amply clear that these approaches have not been able to resolve the basic problems of the sector.

The future policy should have two main and inter-related thrusts. On the one hand, it should aim at raising productivity at the farm level. The emphasis should be on raising income terms of trade of agriculture rather than, what we call in our economic jargon, the barter terms of trade. Secondly, there should be opportunities to invest these surpluses in labour-intensive non-farm enterprises, a precondition for which would be the development of rural infrastructure. One of the policy objectives for increasing agricultural income would be to reduce concentration of labour in agriculture. Keeping in view the nature of the development strategy implicit in this presentation, the shift of labour from agriculture should not be by the 'push' factor, by a process of immiseration. The surplus labour should leave agriculture because of the 'pull' factor, i.e. better and more attractive opportunities.

In the circumstances of the countries of Asia, one should aim at a 'ladder' working in the agricultural sector. Put schematically it would involve landless agricultural workers becoming tenants, the latter graduating to small owner-operators, who should be able to expand their holdings to a surplus generating level, while the surplus farmers are facilitated to diversify to non-agricultural occupations. It would be facilitated with market-lead land reforms. It would involve an unfettered lease market, fair to the lessor as well as the leesee on the one hand and purchase and redistribution of the surplus land of those who have better opportunities in the non-farm sector and its distribution among small farmers to make their holdings viable. These reforms are possible to implement even in the present circumstances, whereas redistributive land reforms, by state fiat, are no more a practical proposition. Structural reforms of the type are only one of the policy measures to usher in a bright future for our agriculture and agricultural producers. A whole package of policies on research and extension, pricing, marketing, credit, trade and exchange rate regimes has to be evolved to reach our preferred alternative. The task will be facilitated if the international community, especially the developed countries and the aid agencies realise their responsibility. But the main responsibility will devolve on the countries of the region and their domestic institutions.

Ensuring Food and Nutritional Security

As was mentioned earlier, the major unfinished task is that of ensuring food and nutritional security to people. The World Food Summit of 1996 had set the target of reducing the number of the food insecure, then estimated at 800 millions to half by 2015. The United Nations Summit in 2000 which set the 'Millennium Development Goals' endorsed this target. However, the recently concluded Food and Agricultural Summit convened by FAO noted that instead of a target of reducing the number of the hungry by 20 million every year, implicit in the World Food Summit's recommendations in 1996, the actual progress was a reduction in the number of hungry people by less than 6 million per year. The record of Asian countries in this regard is not particularly bright. And, this is happening at a time when world food stocks are adequate to provide enough food to every one.

With the concern for food security being shared by the policy makers and policy analysts, we have learnt a lot on the concept and its ramifications. There are four common elements in various definitions of Food Security now in vogue. The first element is *Availability* of adequate quantities of food within a country, which is either produced domestically or the country has the needed foreign exchange to purchase food in the international markets. The second feature is *Stability* of supplies over the years and within the year ensured by efficient marketing and storage functions. The third, and probably the most critical, is *Entitlement* which in most circumstances is a function of livelihood. Finally, as the prevailing concept of food security goes beyond avoidance of hunger or starvation, a concept of *Nutritional Adequacy* has been added to the concept of food security. All these elements are included in a definition advanced by the World Bank. "Access by all people at all times to enough food for an active healthy life" (World Bank, 1986).

In this context, the countries of the region, once again, can be divided into two broad categories. In the first group are the countries where agriculture is a major source of employment, and where food products occupy a high position in the consumer's budget. There is a strong case for achieving food self-sufficiency, at least near food self-sufficiency, in these countries. Higher production of food would also mean the higher income, and purchasing power, for the substantial part of the population dependent on agriculture. The only exception to this would be the countries which have a comparative advantage in non-food crops. The emphasis on food self-sufficiency means, in this context, not subsidisation of agricultural produce but larger investment in technology, supportive institutions and rural infrastructure to augment food production. In this formulation, food self-sufficiency is not an article of faith. It is based on the sound economic logic of maximising the dynamic comparative advantages, which in the case of the medium to large poor countries of this region is agricultural production in general and food production in particular. The situation changes once agriculture loses its importance as a principal source of earning to a large number of people and the consumers do not spend a large part of their income on food.

To ensure food security to the poor, two more qualifications have to be added. First, in augmenting food production non-price factors, principally technological advances, have to be given higher weight. In other words, we have to see to it that the real prices of food grains do not increase. That it is possible to meet this requirement was proved by the extension of high yielding varieties, popularly known by the generic name of Green Revolution, when countries, especially the south Asian countries could reach food self-sufficiency by augmenting yield per hectare and ensuring stable, in fact, lower prices in real terms. The next technological thrust may not be in the nature of the technology identified with the Green Revolution, though its objective should be the same, i.e. augmenting production while keeping the unit cost low.

The second qualification is that, even at the initial stage progressive diversification to high value crops with higher income elasticity should be encouraged. A large proportion of the population, as we have seen above are suffering from malnutrition. Improving nutritional security should form part of this strategy. As it happens, many of these enterprises, - e.g. pulses, oilseeds, fruits and vegetables and animal husbandry - are more labour-intensive, and fetch higher prices. Their contribution in augmenting food security, by simultaneously improving income entitlement and nutritional enhancement, makes such a diversification all the more attractive.

V

CONCLUDING REMARKS

To conclude, I submit that the medium term future of agriculture in Asia, – I am mainly concentrating on the poorer countries of Asia, – is predicated upon two interrelated challenges: to what extent are we able to stop the deterioration of the natural base of agriculture, i.e. land and water, and how are we able to improve the living standard of the workers dependent on agriculture. If these twin objectives are met, the role of agriculture in providing food security to the vast numbers of the food insecure people will be easier to achieve. The latter because of the bulk of the food insecure in the poor countries of Asia are directly or indirectly dependent on agriculture.

In designing the strategy to cope with the future much greater reliance will have to be placed on technology and institutions, which I consider the two key variables. Technology will have to contribute to the enhancement of productivity on small farms, and the supportive institutions of extension, credit and marketing will have to be congruent with the prevailing agrarian structures. Economic policies, domestic as well as external, will have to be subservient to the principal goals of protection of the environment and poverty elimination in rural areas. These policies will have to be rooted in the economic, social and historical context of the country concerned, and evolved in tandem with the development of institutional strength and implementation capability. And in all these endeavour the central figures would be the small farmers and agricultural workers.

Saints and saviours in all our cultures have enjoined upon us to judge our action on the criterion of their effect on the welfare of the disadvantaged and marginalised sections. The challenge before us is to prove that their approach, which can be succinctly put as 'unto the last' is not only good ethics, but it also makes eminent economic sense.

Growth Rate of GDP and Value Added in Agriculture (% Per Year) in Korea, REP

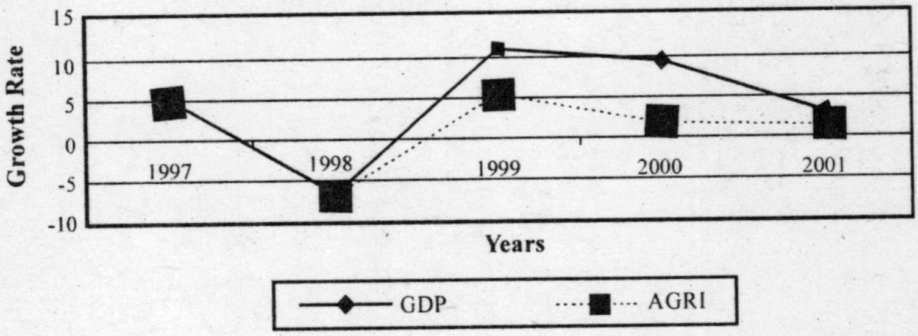

Growth Rate of GDP and Value Added in Agriculture (% Per Year) in Indonesia

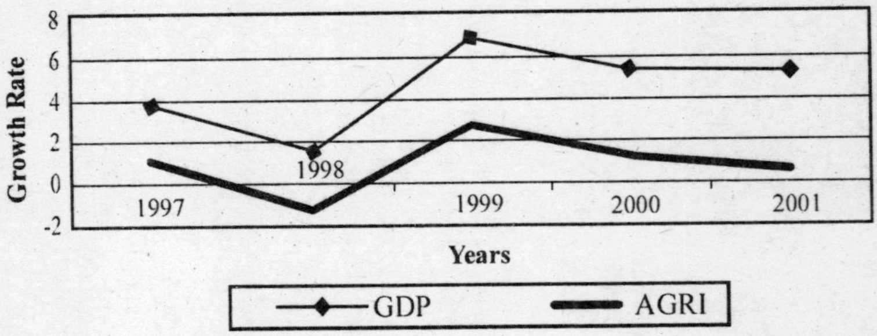

Growth Rate of GDP and Value Added in Agriculture (% Per Year) in Malaysia

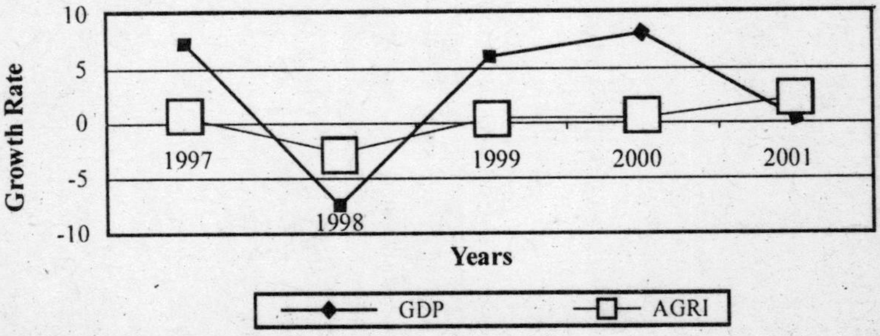

Growth Rate of GDP and Value Added in Agriculture (% Per Year) in Thailand

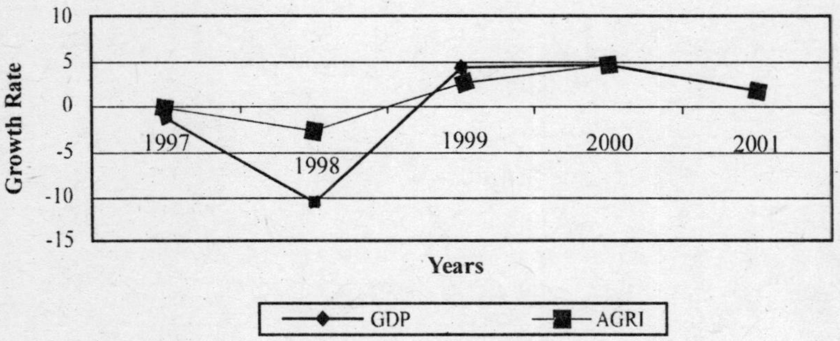

Growth Rate of GDP and Value Added in Agriculture (% Per Year) in Philippines

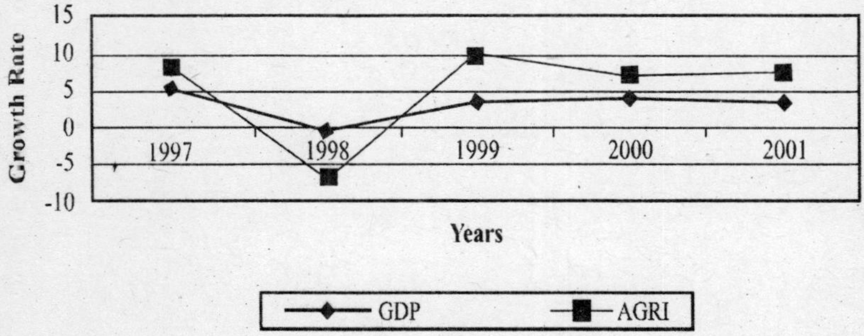

Bibliography

Acharya, S.S. (1996), "Marketing Environment for Farm Products: Emerging Issues and Challenges", *Vistas in Agricultural Marketing (1987-96)*, Vol. 1, pp. 147-188, Indian Society of Agricultural Marketing.

——— (1997), "Agricultural Price Policy and Development - Some Facts and Emerging Issues", Presidential Address, 56th Annual Conference of Indian Society of Agricultural Economics, (Thrissur, Kerala).

Ahluwalia, Montek S. (1978), "Agricultural Performance and Rural Poverty in India", *Occassional Papers,* The World Bank, (Washington, D.C).

——— (1985), "Rural Poverty, Agricultural Production and Prices: A re-examination", in John D. Mellor and Gunwant M. Desai (ed.), *Agricultural Change and Rural Poverty,* Johns Hopkins University Press, Baltimore and London.

Alagh, Y.K. (1994), "Macro Policies for Indian Agriculture", in G.S. Bhalla (ed.), *Economic Liberalization and Indian Agriculture*, Institute of Development Studies, (Delhi).

Alexandratos, Nikos (ed.) (1995), *World Agriculture: Towards 2010*, FAO & John Wiely & Sons, (Rome).

Anderson, K. and Tyres, Rod (1990), "How Developing Countries Could Gain From Agricultural Trade in the Uruguay Round?", in Golding and Odin Knudssen (ed.), *Agricultural Trade Liberalization: Implications for the Developing Countries*, OECD, Paris and the World Bank, (Washington D.C.).

As an Development Bank (1976), *Report of the Second Asian Agricultural Survey* (Team Leader V.S. Vyas), Manila also published as Rural Asia: Challenges and Opportunities, *Report of the Second Asian Agricultural Survey,* Preeger, (New York).

Asian Productivity Organization (1997), *Marketing Systems for Agricultural Products,* APO, (Tokyo).

Bardhan Pranab, K. (1974), "Green Revolution and Agricultural Labourers" in *Seminar on Rural Development for Weaker Sections*, The Indian Society of Agricultural Economics, (Bombay).

——— (1977), "Rural Employment, Wages and Labour Market in India: A

Survey of Research-III," *Economic and Political Weekly*, Vol. XII, No. 28, (July 9).

Berry, Albert and Cline, W.R. (1979), *Agrarian Structure and Productivity in Developing Countries*, University of California, Riverside, USA.

Bhalla, G.S. *et al* (1990), *Agricultural Growth and Structural Changes in the Punjab Economy: An Input-Output Analysis*, IFPRI, (Washington D.C.), (Aug).

Bhalla, G.S. (1994), "Policy for Food Security in India" *in* G.S. Bhalla (ed.), *Economic Liberalization and Indian Agriculture,* Institute for Studies in Industrial Development, (New Delhi).

Bhatty, I.Z. (1974), "Inequality and Poverty in Rural India", in T.N. Srinivasan and P.K. Bardhan (ed.), *Poverty and Income Distribution in India*, Indian Statistical Institute, (Calcutta).

Blyn George (1973), "Price Series Correlations As Measure of Market Integration", *Indian Journal of Agricultural Economics,* XXVIII (3).

Brandao, A. and Martin, W. (1993), "Implications of Agricultural Trade Liberalization for the Developing Countries", *World Bank Working Paper*, WPS 1116.

Central Water Commission (1996), *Water and Related Statistics*, Government of India, (New Delhi).

Chiranjeevi, T. (1994), *Tea Economy of India,* Rawat Publications, (Jaipur, New Delhi).

CMIE: *India's Agricultural Sector, Income Statistics,* Monthly Review of Indian Economy and India's Social Sectors, various issues.

Correa, G.A. (1985), *Farm Size, Land Yield and the Agricultural Production Function: An Analysis for fifteen Developing Countries*: World Development, Vol. 13, No. 4.

Cummings, Jr, R.W. (1967), *Pricing Efficiency in the Indian Wheat Market,* Impex, (New Delhi).

Dantwala, M.L. and Shah, C.H. (1971), *Evaluation of Land Reforms: General Report*, University of Bombay, (Bombay).

Dantwala, M.L. (1967), "Incentives and Disincentives in Indian Agriculture," *Indian Journal of Agricultural Economics*, Vol. XXII, No. 2, (April-June).

——— (1976), "Agricultural Policy in India Since Independence," in *Indian Journal of Agricultural Economics"*, Vol. XXXI, No. 4, (October-December).

Desai, M.B. (1974), *Changing Farm Production and Organization in Surat*, M.S. University of Baroda, mimeo.

Desai, B.M. (ed.) (1997), "Agricultural Paradigm: A Synthesis", *Agricultural Development Paradigm for the Ninth Plan Under New Economic Environment*, (Oxford and IBH Publishers, Delhi).

Datt, Gaurav and Martin, Ravallion (1997), *Farm Productivity and Rural Poverty in India.* (mimeo.)

Datta, Samar, K. (1997), "Why Does India Need a Total Perspective on Rice Exports?", in Bhupat M. Desai (ed.), *Agricultural Development Paradigm for the Ninth Plan Under New Economic Environment*, pp. 888-909, Oxford and IBH Publishing Co. Pvt. Ltd., (New Delhi, Calcutta).

Dhawan, B.D. (1997), "Latent Threats to Irrigated Agriculture", in B.M. Desai (ed.), *Agricultural Development Paradigm for the Ninth Plan Under New Economic Environment.*

Dreze, Jean, and Sen, Amartya (1989), *Hunger and Public Action,* Clarendon Press, (Oxford).

FAO (1991), FAO Year Book, Production.

——— (1993), Trade Yearbook.

——— (1993), Production Yearbook.

——— (1994), Trade Yearbook.

——— (1994), Production Yearbook.

——— (1995), FAOSTAT, State of Food and Agriculture 1995, Electronic Product, (September).

——— (1996), Food Security Situation (mimeo).

——— (1998), Regional Office for Asia and the Pacific, *Poverty Alleviation and Food Security in Asia; Lessons and Challenges* (Bangkok).

——— (2001), *The State of Food Insecurity in the World*, (Rome).

Gandhi, Vasant P. (1996), "Investment Behaviour in Indian Agriculture", *Indian Journal of Agricultural Economics,* Vol. 51, No. 4, (Oct-Dec).

Government of India, Central Water Commission, (1996), *Water and Related Statistics*, (New Delhi).

Gulati, Ashok and Sharma, Pradeep K. (1990), "Employment, Foreign Exchange and Environment: Implications for Cropping", *Economic and Political Weekly,* Vol. 25, No. 9.

Haggblade S., Hammer, J. and Hazell, P. (1991), "Modelling Agricultural Growth Multipliers", *American Journal of Agricultural Economics*, 73 (2).

Hayami, Yujiro (1988), "Community, Market and State", Elmhirst Memorial Lecture, in *Agriculture and Governments in an Interdependent World,* Dartmouth, Aldershot, (U.K).

Hazell, P.B. and Steven Haggblade (1990), Rural – Urban Growth Linkages in India, *Working Paper Series*, The World Bank, (May).

Huang, Jikun, Rozelle, Scott and Rosegrant, Mark W. (1997), "China's Food Economy to the Twenty-First Century: Supply, Demand and Trade", *Food, Agriculture, and the Environment*, Discussion Paper 19, IFPRI, (Washington, D.C., U.S.A.).

International Fund for Agricultural Development, (2001), *Rural Poverty Report 2001 - The Challenge of Ending Rural Poverty*, Oxford University Press, Oxford.

Jazairy, I., Alamgir, M. and Panuccio, T. (1992), *The State of the World Rural Poverty - An Enquiry into its Causes and Consequences*, published for International Fund for Agricultural Development, (New York University Press, New York).

Kahlon, A.S. and Tyagi, D.S. (1983), *Agricultural Price Policy in India,* (Allied Publishers, New Delhi).

Krishnaswami, K.S. (1995), "Agricultural Development Under the New Economic Regime", in Shoba Raghuram, Heiko Sievers and Vinod Vyasalu (ed.), *Structural Adjustment, Economy, Environment, Social Concerns.*

Kumar, Praduman and Mathur, V.C. (1997), "Agriculture in Future: Demand-Supply Perspective", in Bhupat M. Desai (ed.), *Agricultural Development Paradigm for the Ninth Plan Under New Economic Environment*, pp 142-166, (Oxford and IBH Publishing Co. Pvt. Ltd., New Delhi, Calcutta).

Lal, Deepak (1976), "Agricultural Growth, Real Wages and the Rural Poor in India," *Economic and Political Weekly*, Vol. XI No. 26, (June).

Lele, Uma (1967), *Working of Grain Markets in Selected States of India, 1955-56 to 1964-65.* Cornell University, Ithaca, (New York).

Mellor J.W. (ed.) (1995), *Agriculture on the Road to Industrialization*, Johns Hopkins University Press; (Baltimore).

Minhas, B.S. "Rural Poverty, Land Distribution and Development Strategy: Facts", *Poverty and Income Distribution in India*, op.cit.

Ministry of Agriculture and Irrigation (1976), Government of India: Report of the National Commission on Agriculture 1976, Part I, *Review and Progress*, (New Delhi).

MIMAP-India, (2001), Vol.2, issues 3 & 4, National Council of Applied Economic Research, (Delhi).

Myrdal, Gunnar (1972), *Asian Drama – An Enquiry into Poverty of Nations,* Random House, (New York).

National Sample Survey, various rounds.

Nayyar, Deepak and Sen, Abhijit (1994), "International Trade and Agricultural Sector in India", in G.S. Bhalla (ed.), *Economic Liberalization and Indian Agriculture,* Institute for Studies in Industrial Development, (New Delhi).

NSSO (1994), Sarvekshana, Vol. 27, No. 3, (Jan-March).

Osmani, Siddiq (1999), "The Entitlement Approach to Famine: An Assessment", in K. Basu, P. Patnaik and K. Suzumura (ed.), *Choice, Welfare, and Development.* A Festschrift in honour of Amartya Sen, (Oxford University Press, Delhi).

Pinstrup-Anderson, Rajul Pandya-Lorch and Rosegrant, Mark W. (1997), *The World Food Situation: Recent Developments, Emerging Issues and Long Term Prospects,* Food Policy Report, IFPRI, (Washington, D.C., USA.).

PRAG (1997), *Food Security in South Asia*, a report prepared by the Policy Research Action Group, Jaipur, (mimeo).

Ramesh Chand (2000), *Trade Liberalization, Agricultural Prices and Net Social Welfare,* ICAR/ACIAR Collaborative Project Report, National Center for Agricultural Economics and Policy Research, New Delhi (mimeo).

Radhakrishna, R. and Ravi, C. (1992), "Effects of Growth, Relative Price and Preferences on Food and Nutrition", *Indian Economic Review,* Vol. 27, Special No., pp. 303-323.

Rao, V.M. (1992), "Land Transfer in Rural Communities: Some Findings in Ryotwari Regions", *Economic and Political Weekly*, Vol. VII, No. 4, (Sept).

Reddy, V. Ratna (1991), "Under Utilization of Land in Andhra Pradesh: Extent and Determinants", *Indian Journal of Agricultural Economics*, Vol. XLVI, No. 4, (Oct-Dec).

Reddy, V. Ratna and Narayanan, K. Badri (1992), "Trade Experience of Indian Agriculture: Behaviour of Net Export Supply Functions For Dominant Commodities", *Indian Journal of Agricultural Economics,* Vol. 47, No. 1, (January-March).

Rosegrant, M.W. and Svendsen, M. (1993), "Asian Food Production in the 1990s: Irrigation Investment and Management Policy" *Food Policy 18, No. 2.*

Rosegrant, Mark W, and Hazell, Peter B.R. (2000), *Transforming the Rural Asian Economy: The Unfinished Revolution*, Asian Development Bank, (Manila).

Rosegrant M.W. and others, (2001), *Global Food Productions to 2020.* International Food Policy Research Institute, (Washington D.C.).

SAARC (1992), *Report of the Independent South Asian Commission on Poverty Alleviation*, (Kathmandu).

Sanyal, S.K. (1976), "A Review of the Conceptual Framework of Land Holdings Surveys", *Indian Journal of Agricultural Economics*, Vol. XXXI, No. 3, (Jul-Sept).

Satyasai, K.J.S. and Vishwanathan, K.U. (1996), "Commercialization and Diversification Indian Agriculture", *Economic and Political Weekly*, Vol. 31, No. 45 & 46, (Nov).

Saxena, N.C. (1997), "Agroforestry and Farm Forestry in India", in B.M. Desai (ed.), *Agricultural Development Paradigm for the Ninth Plan Under New Economic Environment.*

Scherr S.J. (1999), "Soil Degradation: A Threat to Developing Countries Food Security in 2020", *Food, Agriculture, and the Environment Discussion Paper*, International Food Policy Research Institute, (Washington D.C.).

Sharma, H.R. (1997), "Land Reforms: Status and Opportunities", in B.M. Desai (ed.), *Agricultural Development Paradigm for the Ninth Plan Under New Economic Environment.*

Sen, A.K. (1981), *Poverty and Famine: An Essay on Entitlement and Deprivation,* Clarendon Press, (Oxford).

Shimoji Ikon (1999), "Agricultural Reforms and Changes in Agricultural Land in Japan" in *Agricultural Land Tenure Systems in Asia and the Pacific*, Asian Productivity Organization, (Tokyo).

Singh, Karam (1997), "Efficiency of Inputs use in Indian Agriculture", in B.M. Desai (ed.), *Agricultural Development Paradigm for the Ninth Plan Under New Economic Environment.*

Srinivasan, T.N. (1998), "Foreign Trade Policies and India's Development", in Uma Kapila (ed.), *Indian Economy Since Independence*, pp. 563-597, (Academic Foundation, Delhi).

Suryanarayanan, M.H. (2000), "How Real is the Secular Decline in Rural Poverty", *Economic and Political Weekly* Vol. XXXV No. 25.

Thorat, Sukhadeo (1997), "Trends in Land Ownership, Tenancy and Land Reforms", in B.M. Desai (ed.), *Agricultural Development Paradigm for the Ninth Plan Under New Economic Environment.*

Tyagi, D.S. (1990), *Managing India Food Economy – Problems and Alternatives,* (Sage Publication, New Delhi).

UN.ACC. (1993), *Second Report on the World Nutrition Situation, Country Trends, Methods and Statistics*, Vol.II, (March).

United Nations Administrative Committee for Coordination: Sub-committee on Nutrition (ACC: SCN), (2000); *Fourth Report on World Nutrition Situation,* (Geneva).

UNDP (1995). *Human Development Report.*

——— (1996), *Human Development Report.*

——— (2001), *Human Development Report*, (New York).

Vyas, V.S. (1970), "Rural Labour Utilisation and Agricultural Development — The Case of India," *Artha Vikas.*

——— (1970), "Tenancy in a Dynamic Setting", *Economic and Political Weekly*, Vol. V, No. 256.

——— (1972), "Institutional Change, Agricultural Production and Rural Poverty – The Experience of Two Decades," *Commerce, 25 years of Independence – A Survey*, (August 19).

——— (1977), "Changes in Land Ownership Pattern – An Aspect of Structural Change in Indian Agriculture", Indian Institute of Management, Ahmedabad, (July) (mimeographed).

——— (1980a), "Some Aspects of Structural Changes in Indian Agriculture", Presidential Address at 38th Annual Conference of Indian Society of Agricultural Economics, *Indian Journal of Agricultural Economics*, Vol. 34, (Jan-Mar), Pp. 1-18.

——— (1980b), "Agriculture: The Next Decade", *Technological Forecasting and Social Change*, Vol. 17.

——— (1990), "Food Policies and Food Security in Asia, with Particular Reference to South Asia", in D.S. Tyagi and V.S. Vyas, (ed.), *Increasing Access to Food - The Asian Experiences*, (Sage Publications, New Delhi).

——— (1994), "Agricultural Price Policy: Need for Reformulation", in G.S. Bhalla (ed.), *Economic Liberalisation and Indian Agriculture*, ISID, (New Delhi).

——— (1994), "Agricultural Policies for the Nineties: Issues and Approaches", *Economic and Political Weekly*, Vol. 29, No. 26.

——— (1996), "Diversification of Agriculture and Food Security in Context of New Economics Policy: Concept Rationale and Approaches", *Indian Journal of Agricultural Economics*, Vol. 51, No. 4. (Oct-Dec).

——— (1996), "Agricultural Trade Policy in Asian Developing Countries", *Agricultural Trade Policy in Asia Pacific: A Study Meeting Report*, APO, (Tokyo).

——— and Kruse-Rodenacker, A. (1974), *Cooperative Processing of Agricultural Products*, Food and Agricultural Organization of the United Nations, (Rome).

Wilson, E.J. and Swami, K. (1998), *Integration of Agricultural Produce Markets in India*, Institute of Development Studies, (Jaipur) (mimeo).

World Bank, (1986), *Poverty and Hunger: Issues and Options for Food Security in Developing Countries*, World Bank Policy Study, (Washington D.C.)

——— (1993), *World Development Report - Investing in Health*, (Oxford University Press, New York).

——— (1996), *World Development Report*.

——— (2001), *World Development Indicators*, (Washington D.C.).

World Commission on Environment and Development, (1989), *Our Common Future*, (New York).

Name Index

Subject Index